Louis H. (Louis Henry) Gibson

**Convenient Houses, With Fifty Plans for the Housekeeper**

Architect and Housewife; a Journey Through the House

Louis H. (Louis Henry) Gibson

**Convenient Houses, With Fifty Plans for the Housekeeper**
*Architect and Housewife; a Journey Through the House*

ISBN/EAN: 9783744798709

Printed in Europe, USA, Canada, Australia, Japan

Cover: Foto ©Andreas Hilbeck / pixelio.de

More available books at **www.hansebooks.com**

# CONVENIENT HOUSES

WITH

## FIFTY PLANS FOR THE HOUSEKEEPER

ARCHITECT AND HOUSEWIFE — A JOURNEY THROUGH THE HOUSE — FIFTY CONVENIENT HOUSE PLANS — PRACTICAL HOUSE BUILDING FOR THE OWNER — BUSINESS POINTS IN BUILDING — HOW TO PAY FOR A HOME

BY

LOUIS H. GIBSON

ARCHITECT

---

NEW YORK:
THOMAS Y. CROWELL & CO.

Copyright, 1889,
By Louis H. Gibson.

C. J. PETERS & SON,
Typographers and Electrotypers,
145 High Street, Boston.

# PREFACE.

WHEN the reader is familiar with the writer's general purposes, it is easier to understand the details of his work. This book is intended to deal with houses in a housekeeping spirit. In doing this, the architect has in mind convenience, stability, and that ideal of housekeepers, beauty of surroundings.

In carrying out this idea, the relation of architecture to good and economical housekeeping is first considered. Following this division is "A Journey through the House." It begins at the porch, moves through the different rooms, and stops to consider the various details. This brings about not only a consideration of the general arrangement of a house, but such details as kitchens and pantries, plumbing, laundry, and heating.

These first two sections of the book — "The Architect and the Housewife," and "A Journey through the House" — are, in a measure, educational. After this, and in keeping with the general principles that have been set forth, plans of fifty convenient houses are illustrated and described. For the most part, they are houses that have been built.

The next section is devoted to practical house-building.

It is constructed by taking a complete specification for everything which may concern a dwelling-house, and ridding it, as far as possible, of all technicalities; thus putting in form all practical house-building questions for the benefit of the owner.

Following this is the consideration of business points in building, which sets forth methods of letting contracts with the view of securing the best results without waste of money.

The closing section is devoted to the getting of a home, — how to arrange the monthly-payment schemes, building-association plans, and other methods for getting a house on easy instalments.

LOUIS H. GIBSON, Architect.

Indianapolis, Ind., September, 1889.

# CONTENTS.

## *THE ARCHITECT AND THE HOUSEWIFE.*

### CHAPTER I.

THE HOUSEKEEPER AND THE ARCHITECT. — FLOOR-PLANS AS RELATED TO GOOD HOUSEKEEPING. — LABOR-SAVING DEVICES. — ECONOMY AND GOOD CONSTRUCTION. — COMPACT HOUSES NOT NECESSARILY CROWDED. — WOOD-WORK THAT IS READILY CLEANED . . . . 11–15

### CHAPTER II.

HOUSEKEEPING OPERATIONS. — THE WORK OF THE HOUSEKEEPER. — THE AVERAGE HOUSEWORK OF A WEEK. — THE ARCHITECT'S LESSON THEREFROM . . . . . . . . . . . . . . . 16–20

### CHAPTER III.

MODERN CONVENIENCES. — A LITTLE HISTORY. — PLANS THAT MAKE EXTRA WORK. — MODERN CONVENIENCES ENUMERATED . . . 21–25

### CHAPTER IV.

MODERN ARCHITECTS AND THE HOUSEKEEPER. — MISPLACED HOUSES. — OLD COLONIAL POVERTY IN MODERN COLONIAL HOUSES. — AFFECTATION IN DESIGN. — NATURAL DEVELOPMENT OF AMERICAN ARCHITECTURE. — AMERICAN ARCHITECTURE AND AMERICAN HOMES . . . . . . . . . . . . . . . . . . . . 26–28

## *A JOURNEY THROUGH THE HOUSE.*

### CHAPTER V.

JOURNEY THROUGH THE HOUSE. — PORCH. — VESTIBULE. — HALL. — LONG HALLS AND SQUARE HALLS. — THE HALL THAT IS A ROOM. — RECEPTION-HALL. — PARLOR. — SITTING-ROOM. — DINING-ROOM . . . . . . . . . . . . . . . . . . . . . 31–38

## CHAPTER VI.

KITCHENS. — THE KITCHEN A WORKSHOP. — WORK TO BE DONE IN A KITCHEN. — A PLAN. — FITTINGS. — DISH-WASHING CONVENIENCES. — SINK AND TABLES. — CHINA-CLOSET. — PANTRY. — COMBINATION PANTRY. — PANTRY FITTINGS. — WORK IN A PANTRY. — A DOUGH-BOARD. — FLOUR-BIN. — PANTRY STORES. — CUPBOARD. — REFRIGERATOR ARRANGEMENTS. — PANTRY UTENSILS. — A DRY-BOX. — SOAP-BOX. — VENTILATION OF KITCHEN. — GENERAL PRINCIPLES OF KITCHEN PLANNING . . . . . 39–50

## CHAPTER VII.

CELLAR. — FUEL DEPARTMENTS. — FURNACE CONVENIENCES. — COAL-BINS. — CEMENT FLOORS. — LIGHT IN THE CELLAR. — A CELLAR-CLOSET. — OUTSIDE CELLAR-DOOR . . . . . . . . . . . . 51–53

## CHAPTER VIII.

A LOW-COST LAUNDRY. — BLUE MONDAY. — BASEMENT LAUNDRY. — LOW-COST CONVENIENCES. — INEXPENSIVE LAUNDRY FITTINGS. — HOT AND COLD WATER ARRANGEMENTS. — A LABOR-SAVING LAUNDRY. — A PLACE TO DO FRUIT-CANNING . . . . . . . 54–58

## CHAPTER IX.

THE SECOND FLOOR. — STAIRWAYS. — THE COMBINATION STAIRWAY. — IDEAL NUMBER OF BEDROOMS. — LARGE CLOSETS AND PLENTY OF THEM. — A LINEN CLOSET. — PLACING OF GAS-FIXTURES. — SERVANT'S ROOM. — BATH-ROOM. — AN ATTIC. — ATTIC CLOSETS. — ATTIC ROOMS . . . . . . . . . . . . . . . . . . 59–63

## CHAPTER X.

PLUMBING. — IS PLUMBING ENTIRELY SAFE? — COMPLETENESS IN PLUMBING APPARATUS. — LABOR-SAVING PLUMBING APPARATUS. — SEWER CONNECTIONS. — SOIL PIPE. — A TRAP. — ACCIDENTS TO TRAPS. — FREQUENT USE OF PLUMBING APPARATUS DESIRABLE FOR SAFETY. — WATER-CLOSETS. — SIMPLICITY IN PLUMBING. — DRAIN CONNECTIONS. — TO KEEP PLUMBING APPARATUS FROM FREEZING. — CISTERN WATER SUPPLY. — GREASE SINK. — FLUSHING OF DRAIN. — BATH-TUB . . . . . . . . . . . . . 64–74

## CONTENTS.

### CHAPTER XI.

HEAT AND VENTILATION. — COMMON HEATING ARRANGEMENTS. — PRESENT METHODS GENERALLY UNSATISFACTORY. — IDEAL CONDITIONS. — PROPER AMOUNT OF MOISTURE RARELY ATTAINED. — A FURNACE DEFINED. — METHODS OF REACHING BEST RESULTS. — SUPPLY OF PROPER AMOUNT OF MOISTURE. — REMOVAL OF FOUL AIR. — SUPPLYING FRESH AIR WITH PROPER MOISTURE FROM STOVES. — STEAM AND HOT-WATER HEATING. — DIRECT AND INDIRECT RADIATION. — LOW-COST HEATING APPARATUS . 75–82

### CHAPTER XII.

HEATING DEVICES AS WE FIND THEM. — FURNACE ESTIMATES. — COMBINATION HOT AIR AND HOT WATER. — DISH-WARMING ARRANGEMENTS. — HOW TO GET A GOOD HEATING APPARATUS. 83–85

### CHAPTER XIII.

THE HOUSE AND ITS BEAUTY. — ARTISTIC SURROUNDINGS. — BEAUTY MORE A MATTER OF INTELLIGENCE THAN MONEY. — VESTIBULE DECORATIONS. — BEAUTY IN THE RECEPTION-HALL. — MANTELS AND GRATES. — FRET-WORK AND PORTIÈRES. — SPINDLE WORK. — SIMPLE FORMS OF GOOD DECORATION. — WOOD-CARVING. — DOOR AND WINDOW CASINGS. — A CONSERVATORY. — STAINED GLASS. — A CABINET ON THE MANTEL. — TINTED PLASTERING. — FRESCOING. — SAFETY IN THE SELECTION OF COLORS. — AN ATTRACTIVE SITTING-ROOM. — THE PARLOR. — A RECEPTION-ROOM. — PARLOR HISTORY. — THE IDEAL PARLOR. — THE LIBRARY. — A PLACE OF QUIET AND REST. — LIBRARY FURNISHINGS. — THE DINING-ROOM. — SOCIAL RELATIONS OF THE DINING-ROOM. — DINING-ROOM DECORATIONS. — CONSERVATORY AND DINING-ROOM. — A WOOD CEILING. — BEAUTY IN BEDROOMS. — QUIET AND LIGHT . . . . . . . . . . . . 86–100

### CHAPTER XIV.

EXTERNAL AND INTERNAL DESIGN. — AN OLD TOPIC BEFORE THE PEOPLE. — THE ARCHITECTURAL STUDENT'S DREAM. — A BEAUTIFUL HOME THE HOUSEKEEPER'S AMBITION. — IT COSTS NO MORE TO HAVE A HOUSE BEAUTIFUL THAN UGLY. — ARCHITECTURAL EDUCATION. — CHARLES EASTLAKE'S BOOK. — VULGAR ARCHITECTURAL REVIVALS. — THE GROWTH OF THE ARTISTIC IDEA. — BEAUTY A MATTER OF REFINEMENT . . . . . . 101–105

## PLANS OF FIFTY CONVENIENT HOUSES.

### CHAPTER XV.

EVOLUTION OF A HOUSE-PLAN. — RESPECTABLE DIMENSIONS FOR A MODERATE PRICE. — SIX PLANS. — COSTS FROM $1,500 TO $2,600 . . . . . . . . . . . . . . . . . . . . . 109–117

### CHAPTER XVI.

A SMALL POCKET-BOOK AND A LARGE IDEA. — AMBITION, DOLLARS, AND A GOOD HOUSE. — THE GROWTH OF THE HOUSEKEEPER'S IDEAS. — POINTS ABOUT THE HOUSE. — $2,900 . . . . . 118–125

### CHAPTER XVII.

"WE KNOW WHAT WE WANT." — A CONVENIENT PLAN. — MEETING THE WANTS OF PEOPLE WHO BUILD . . . . . . . . . . 126–130

### CHAPTER XVIII.

TWO GOOD ROOMS IN FRONT. — THE COMBINATION PANTRY. — TOO MUCH CELLAR A BURDEN. — $2,500 . . . . . . . . . 131–134

### CHAPTER XIX.

SITTING-ROOM AND PARLOR IN FRONT. — A CONNECTING VESTIBULE. — A CENTRAL COMBINATION STAIRWAY. — GOOD ROOMS IN THE ATTIC . . . . . . . . . . . . . . . . . . . . 135–138

### CHAPTER XX.

A COMPACT PLAN. — AN ISOLATED RECEPTION-ROOM. — COMBINATION STAIRWAY. — DESCRIPTION OF THE FLOOR-PLAN. — CELLAR ARRANGEMENT. — DINING-ROOM AND CONSERVATORY. — ANOTHER PLAN . . . . . . . . . . . . . . . . . . . . 139–144

### CHAPTER XXI.

WHAT CAN BE DONE FOR $1,600? — THE CLOSET IN THE HALL. — A SMALL, CONVENIENT KITCHEN. — CLOSETS IN THE BED-ROOMS . . . . . . . . . . . . . . . . . . . . 145–151

## CHAPTER XXII.

OUTGROWTHS OF ONE IDEA. — EVERYTHING COUNTS AS A ROOM. — ONE CHIMNEY. — CONVENIENCES OF A CONDENSED HOUSE. — COST FROM $1,600 TO $2,800 . . . . . . . . . . . . 152–156

## CHAPTER XXIII.

ONE-STORY PLANS. — DESCRIPTION OF FLOOR-PLANS. — BATH-ROOM NEXT TO KITCHEN FLUE. — KITCHEN, PORCH, AND PANTRY. — THE EXTERIOR. — ENLARGEMENTS ON THIS PLAN. — OTHER ONE-STORY HOUSES . . . . . . . . . . . . . . . . . . 157–163

## CHAPTER XXIV.

SIDE-HALL PLANS. — PLANS WITH BEDROOM ON FIRST FLOOR . . 164–170

## CHAPTER XXV.

MISCELLANEOUS COLLECTION. — SHORT DESCRIPTIONS OF ELEVEN HOUSE-PLANS. — VARYING COSTS. — SQUARE PLANS. — ONE-CHIMNEY PLANS. — REAR AND SIDE HALL . . . . . . . . 171–181

## CHAPTER XXVI.

EIGHT PLANS. — EACH SUITED TO FAMILY REQUIREMENTS. — DOUBLE HOUSES. — AN ELABORATE FLOOR-PLAN. — A SHINGLE HOUSE. — A BRICK HOUSE . . . . . . . . . . . . . . . . . 182–193

# *PRACTICAL HOUSE-BUILDING.*

## CHAPTER XXVII.

PRACTICAL POINTS. — WATER. — LOCATION OF HOUSE ON LOT. — DRAINING THE CELLAR. — MASON WORK. — FOUNDATIONS. — WALKS. — PIERS. — FLUES. — CISTERNS. — DAMP COURSE . . 197–200

## CHAPTER XXVIII.

BRICK FOUNDATIONS. — LAYING BRICK. — COLORED MORTARS. — COLORED BRICKS. — BRICK VENEERING. — HOT-AIR FLUES. — DETAILS OF BRICK CONSTRUCTION. — CHIMNEYS AND FLUES. — HOLLOW WALLS. — CELLAR. — ASH-PITS. — GRATES . . . 201–206

## CHAPTER XXIX.

STONE MASONRY. — CUT STONE. — TERRA COTTA. — PRIVY VAULTS. — CISTERNS. — FILTERS FOR CISTERNS. — BRICK PAVEMENTS. — CEMENT PAVEMENTS . . . . . . . . . . . . . . . 207–212

## CHAPTER XXX.

CARPENTER-WORK. — FRAMING. — SIZE OF TIMBERS. — HEIGHT OF STORIES. — JOIST. — STUD WALLS. — OUTSIDE SHEATHING. — BUILDING-PAPER. — ROOFS. — OUTSIDE FINISH. — OUTSIDE SHINGLE WALLS. — OUTSIDE CASINGS. — WINDOWS WITH BOX FRAMES. — HINGED OR PIVOTED WINDOWS. — OUTSIDE SHUTTERS. — PORCHES. — LATTICE PORCHES . . . . . . . . . . 213–221

## CHAPTER XXXI.

INSIDE WOOD-WORK. — FLOORS. — SOFT AND HARD WOOD FLOORS. — TABULATED STATEMENT OF INSIDE FINISH. — DIFFERENT KINDS OF WOOD. — DOORS AND FRAMES. — FLY SCREENS. — INSIDE CASINGS. — WAINSCOTING. — INSIDE SHUTTERS. — WOODWORK FOR PLUMBING. — KITCHEN SINK AND FITTINGS. — KITCHEN TABLES. — CELLAR-SINK FITTINGS. — WOOD-WORK FOR BATH-TUB. — WATER-CLOSETS. — WASH-STANDS. — TANK. — PICTURE MOULDING. — CLOSET FITTINGS. — BROOM-RACK. — CEDAR-CLOSET. — DRY-BOX. — CLOCK SHELF. — CHINA-ROOM FITTINGS. — PANTRY FITTINGS. — STAIRWAYS . . . . . . 222–235

## CHAPTER XXXII.

PLASTERING. — GRAY FINISH. — WHITE HARD FINISH. — BACK PLASTERING. — GAS-PIPING. — TIN WORK. — GUTTERS. — VALLEYS. — DOWN SPOUTS. — GALVANIZED IRON-WORK. — HOT-AIR PIPES. — THIMBLES. — PAINTING. — STAINING. — OIL FINISHING. — INTERIOR STAINING. — FLOOR FINISH. — GLAZING. — PLATEGLASS. — BEVELLED GLASS. — CATHEDRAL GLASS. — HARDWARE . . . . . . . . . . . . . . . . . . . . . 236–246

## CHAPTER XXXIII.

PRACTICAL PLUMBING. — WOOD-WORK FOR PLUMBER. — EXCAVATING FOR PLUMBER. — WATER DISTRIBUTION. — OUTSIDE FIXTURES. — HYDRANTS. — STREET-WASHERS. — SOFT-WATER SUPPLY. — HOT-WATER SUPPLY. — SOIL PIPE. — INSIDE FIXTURES. — KITCHEN SINK. — CELLAR SINK . . . . . . . . . . . . . . . 247–254

## CHAPTER XXXIV.

PLUMBING WORK CONTINUED. — BATH-TUBS. — BATH-SPRINKLERS. — FOOT-TUBS. — SAFES. — WATER-CLOSETS. — WASH-STANDS. — LAUNDRY FITTINGS. — SET TUBS. — OUTSIDE DRAINS. — GREASE SINKS. — NICKEL FITTINGS . . . . . . . . . . . . . 255–263

## CHAPTER XXXV.

COST OF A HOUSE. — SCHEDULES OF COSTS. — WHAT GOES INTO A HOUSE. — SCHEDULE "B." — COST DETAILS . . . . . . 264–269

## CHAPTER XXXVI.

VARYING BUILDING VALUES. — COST OF APPURTENANCES. — PRICES OF LABOR AND MATERIAL ON WHICH ESTIMATES ARE BASED. 270–274

# BUSINESS POINTS IN BUILDING.

## CHAPTER XXXVII.

LOW-COST HOUSES. — METHODS OF MAKING CONTRACTS. — ARCHITECTS' ESTIMATES. — BUILDING BY THE DAY. — THE SAFEST PLAN. — GUARDING AGAINST LIENS . . . . . . . . . . . . . 277–287

# HOW TO SECURE A HOME.

## CHAPTER XXXVIII.

MONTHLY PAYMENTS. — CALCULATIONS ON A LONG-TIME PLAN. — PURCHASE ON A RENTAL BASIS. — HOW IT MAY BE WORKED OUT . . . . . . . . . . . . . . . . . . . . . 291–294

## CHAPTER XXXIX.

BUILDING ASSOCIATIONS. — WHY DIVIDENDS ARE LARGE AND INTEREST LOW. — BUILDING ASSOCIATIONS AND SAVINGS BANKS. — ASSOCIATION SECURITIES. — BUILDING-ASSOCIATION METHODS. — DIFFERENT PLANS. — BORROWING FROM A BUILDING ASSOCIATION. — A BUILDING-ASSOCIATION REPORT . . . . . . . 295–311

## CHAPTER XL.

PURCHASE OF A LOT. — THE BEST THE CHEAPEST. — A GOOD LOT AS A BASIS OF SECURITY. — THE BASIS OF VALUE IS THE RENTAL . . . . . . . . . . . . . . . . . . . 312–316

# THE ARCHITECT AND THE HOUSEWIFE.

# CONVENIENT HOUSES.

## CHAPTER I.

THE HOUSEKEEPER AND THE ARCHITECT. — FLOOR-PLANS AS RELATED TO GOOD HOUSEKEEPING. — LABOR-SAVING DEVICES. — ECONOMY AND GOOD CONSTRUCTION. — COMPACT HOUSES NOT NECESSARILY CROWDED. — WOOD-WORK THAT IS READILY CLEANED.

THERE is a definite relation between the work of the housekeeper and that of the architect. This is the text of this book. It is a part of the business of the architect to do what he can to make housekeeping easy. He can do a great deal. He should understand the principles and practice of good housekeeping. This knowledge is something which cannot be derived from the architectural schools or offices; it must come from a home. The public press of the country has had a great deal to say about the artistic qualities of domestic architecture, a great deal to say about house decoration, and, altogether, has furnished much valuable matter. Little, however, has been said as to the relation of architecture to good housekeeping. The artistic element should not be neglected. There must also be considered the question of convenient arrangement, economy and ease, for the housekeeper.

Washing dishes is disagreeable work, but the architect can do his part toward making it easier. If we take a conglomerate mass of china, knives, forks, and spoons, pots, pans, and kettles, and bring them together on one small kitchen table, which has a dish-pan on one end and a wooden water-bucket at the back, with a scarcity of everything to facilitate the progress of the work, we have a condition quite different from that wherein there is a roomy sink with a table on each side of it, and plenty of hot and cold water above. An architect may plan a kitchen so that all of these conveniences are possible. He may plan it so they are impossible.

The floor-plan of a house has a definite relation to house-keeping requirements, which is not fully appreciated. The difference between a good floor-plan and a poor one may make the difference of three or four tons of coal in the heating of a house during the winter. It may influence the keeping of a servant, the wages to be paid, or may control the necessity for one or more than one. It makes more difference to a man who lives in a house that costs two thousand dollars or three thousand dollars, as to whether he burns seven or ten tons of coal in warming it, than it does to the man who lives in a ten-thousand-dollar or twelve-thousand-dollar house as to whether he burns fourteen or twenty tons. The cost of fuel is of more importance to a man of moderate means than to one of wealth. Then in the matter of service: it is difficult to keep a good servant in a bad kitchen, or in a badly planned house where there is a vast amount of sweeping and other work to be done every day Those who plan factories and mills arrange them with reference to the saving of labor. The idea in saving labor is to save money.

One can build a better house for a given sum of money at this time than ever before. The real reason for this is to be found outside the fact that material and labor are cheaper now than they have been in the past. It is because of the thought that is put into the planning and arranging of dwellings. It is the thought that saves the money. It adds external and internal attractiveness, convenience, labor-saving devices, and arrangements. Thought helps to make housekeeping easier.

Economical housekeeping can be most readily carried on in a compact house. To say that a house is compact does not necessarily imply that it is crowded, or that any of the conditions of comfort are neglected. If we avoid waste space, such as is frequently assigned to large halls and passages, we merely take away something that is not needed.

It frequently happens that a man and his wife go through life with the hope of building a better house " some day." They are economical; they live carefully; they live in a small house; they are crowded. At last, by dint of hard work and careful management, enough money is accumulated to build the new home. This is the great event which has been thought about for so many years.

The idea in building this house is invariably to get something as different from the old house as possible. It was square; the new building must be irregular. It had no front hall; the new house must have a large one. There were no grates in any of the rooms; in the new house there must be one in each. In the old building the rooms were very small; in the new house they must be very large. There was no porch before; now there must be one running across the front and along one side of the house. Altogether, the idea of the old house and that of the new are in direct opposition to each other. In one instance they were crowded; in the other they have plenty of room. There can be no doubt about the abundance of room.

The building is finished; they move into it. Almost the first person to leave it is the servant whom they had in the old house. She sees the amount of work which she will have to do. It was easy enough to sweep the old house, with its small, compact plan. Housekeeping was relatively a small matter; but with the habits of economy, which rendered the new home possible, they will not employ additional help. The work which is left over by the servant falls to the mistress. Strange as it may appear under such circumstances, it takes the mistress a long time to find the cause of the trouble. It is the house. It was planned with an entire disregard for the work which was to be done. It had not been thought of. The idea was merely to get something which was different from the disagreeable features of the old home. They thought that everything would be easier and pleasanter and more agreeable in every way. The only trouble with the old home was that they were too much crowded. In the new they are not, but have an impossible amount of work to do every day. The difference between what they wish to do and what is done, is represented by fretfulness in addition to the natural weariness at the end of the day.

What has this to do with architecture and economical housebuilding? Simply this. The house which is economically planned is economical as to money, carpets, sweeping, and strength. The architect may do a great deal for housekeepers by keeping this thought in mind.

To recur to the idea of economical house-building in a direct sense, it may be borne in mind that economy and good construction go hand in hand; that none of the conditions of permanency are sacrificed for the sake of cheapness. Of two houses which cost the same, one may be far more convenient and roomy by an avoidance of waste space and unnecessary material. Evidently one flue-stack will cost less than four. Therefore, if a house can be constructed which has only one flue-stack, it will cost less than one which has four; but the demands of the housekeeper, and those who live in the house, are that the one stack afford the conveniences of four. People do not like compromises in house-building, especially when they are building a home. The compromises come easier when one is planning property for rental. Evidently a house in which one-fifth of the floor space is given up to halls is more expensive than one which contains a smaller proportion of such space. According as one is able to diminish the amount of passage room, and yet meet all of the conditions of good and economical housekeeping, he can reduce the cost of the house as to its building, its furnishing, and the amount of labor required in caring for it. Thus economy in construction, and convenience and ease in general housekeeping movements, go hand in hand. Parallel illustrations might be carried forward, so as to include each detail of the house.

The architect may do a great deal for the housekeeper by making his mouldings and interior wood-work so that they will not catch dust, and can be readily cleaned. Some of our friends, who have studied the artistic qualities of house-building to the exclusion of all other considerations, will say that a regard for housekeeping requirements, in the matter of interior decorations and construction, is placing too great a limit upon their work. They will say that beauty and general artistic qualities are not always consonant with the means which will make easy housekeeping, — that they are limited by such considerations. This need not be so; it is simply a question of ingenuity and thoughtfulness. One may be careless of utility, and make very beautiful things. Another may be thoughtful and careful as to housekeeping requirements, and design something quite as beautiful and attractive as the former.

In the above statements will be found the guiding principles which affect all of the work of this book.

## CHAPTER II.

HOUSEKEEPING OPERATIONS. — THE WORK OF THE HOUSEKEEPER. — THE AVERAGE HOUSEWORK OF A WEEK. — THE ARCHITECT'S LESSON THEREFROM.

WITH the architect a house has been too often considered as something to be looked at. No one is disposed to criticise an architect for making houses, pretty and attractive. It is true, however, that many houses are nothing more than pretty; they are not convenient. They are not built with a regard to the requirements of housekeeping. A lady once said to the writer, that an architect would never live up to his opportunities until he had associated himself with a housekeeper, who would be strong enough, in her control over him, to see that the housekeeping conditions and conveniences were kept constantly in mind.

In order fully to reach the housekeeping idea, it will be convenient to consider in detail what is meant by housekeeping. Primarily, a house is a place in which to eat and sleep. The present requirements of comfort and luxury suggest that all should not eat and sleep in the same room. Originally this was the case. The primitive man needed only a hut or a cave, or the protection of a rude shed. Later on, he was satisfied with a hut with one or two rooms. If the weather was cold, the occupants would huddle around the fire, and eat and sleep without regard to other surroundings. A bath in cold weather was unnecessary. During the summer this was regarded more as a matter of recreation than of necessity. A neighboring stream served the purpose of more modern arrangements. Housekeeping operations under such conditions were light indeed.

There are many homes of this kind in America to-day. If we take the case of our Indians, we find that the squaws have time for much else than the absolute duties of camp-life and the care of children. There is much other labor which falls to their lot, house-work being regarded, as it is, insignificant. This is one extreme. There are various gradations which come with the instincts of a higher civilization. Education, and other conditions which go with it, increase housekeeping requirements, and thus far have not furnished to the majority compensating conditions in labor-saving devices. At the present time, the natural and affected requirements of housekeeping make the life of many a woman one of the extremest drudgery and hardship. Her condition is almost that of a slave; and this at a time when she is surrounded by many of the elements of a higher civilization. Her children and those around her frequently live under the shadow of her uncomfortable condition. The Indian's home, in the rest and peace which it affords, is often preferable. This condition is brought about by the increasing requirements upon the housekeeper, without the presence of other compensating conditions.

Assuming that an architect may do something to make the care of a house lighter, it remains to call attention to the modern requirements of a housekeeper, with a view of simplifying her work. Let us watch her work for a week; we will begin on Monday morning during the month of January, and assume that there is one servant in the house to help, — bearing in mind, at the same time, that it often happens that the work which is here outlined is done by the housekeeper herself, with possibly only the help of a wash-woman. First, the house is to be warmed, the kitchen fire to be kindled, the living-rooms to be swept and dusted, the washing to be started, the children to be dressed, breakfast to be cooked and put on the table, and, in many cases, all of this done before seven o'clock. The serving of breakfast is no small task to the housekeeper. The coffee is to be poured, food prepared for the children, and many other things done which no man can specify. As soon as breakfast is over the men are out of the house, but not usually before making more than one demand upon the time of the housekeeper. Then the dishes are to be washed, and the children made ready and started to school. Next, the grocery and butcher supplies must be cared for. Possibly they are ordered from the boy who calls at the door. In some instances a trip for this purpose is required. Next, the dining-room must be arranged, the dishes put in place, the chamber-work attended to, beds made, children's things put away, sweeping done, slops disposed of, fires looked after. Some time or in some way the clothes worn by the children on Sunday must be especially looked after, stitches taken, a little darn here and there, and then put away. During this time there may be the demands of one or more babies to be met. In this there is no compromise.

With the completion of other work dinner time is approaching, for, with the majority, this is a noon meal. The cooking must be done, and yet nothing else must be allowed to lag. The children in their confusion are home from school. Then dinner. Every one is in a hurry to get away. The children are sure they are going to be late. There is more work for them and the men, and then they are gone. Dinner dishes are washed, and the laundry work continues. The afternoon is little different from the morning; there is a little less rush and confusion, but a continuance of regular work. Before supper the evening supply of fuel must be provided. In the mean time the children are home from school with their demands. Now supper must be in mind. Where there are children in the house, this is one of the most trying times of the day. They are tired, hungry, and sleepy. Supper is over. The children go to bed at intervals during the evening. The men have a place by the fire. The housekeeper often feels it incumbent upon her to mend, darn, or sew, if no heavier work presents itself.

Tuesday morning calls for a repetition of the former day's work, with ironing substituted for washing. There is the carrying-out of ashes and the bringing-in of coal, and the same routine during the day. On the part of the housekeeper regular sewing-work is taken up as opportunity presents, and possibly calls are made or received. Wednesday, the same. Thursday, the servant, if one is kept, is out for the afternoon. Other regular work must progress. Compromises are not thought of. Friday is general sweeping-day, in which everything is thoroughly gone over. The housekeeper must find time to go down street one or more times during the week, for the purpose of doing necessary shopping. Saturday brings its scrubbing and cleaning. During the week must come the window-washing, cleaning of silver, baking, and many things besides.

Sunday is often the hardest day of all; the children require especial care. There is church in the morning, Sunday school in the afternoon, and, in many cases, church at night. In the mean while the children are on hand all the time. Where is the man who will say that his business life is as exacting or as harassing as the work which is here outlined?

In the pages which follow it is the intention to bear the housekeeper and her requirements in mind, and to suggest what is properly due her in the way of labor-saving devices, with a view to facilitate the manifold operations of housekeeping.

## CHAPTER III.

MODERN CONVENIENCES. — A LITTLE HISTORY. — PLANS THAT MAKE
EXTRA WORK. — MODERN CONVENIENCES ENUMERATED.

MOST of the conveniences of housekeeping are modern. It is only within the past few years that the demands of the housekeeper for helps or aids in making her work easier were thought worth considering. Even now we occasionally meet men who think that anything that was good enough for their mothers is good enough for their wives. We have in mind a farmer who, during fifteen years, purchased three large farms. He buried a wife for every farm. Their death was the result of more than slavish work. The disposition which leads in this direction often continues after the time when economy does not demand close living.

The man who moves west to a new country cannot pay for many of the modern conveniences. The demand for them is not great. Such a man usually builds a house of two or three rooms. The family cook and eat in the kitchen; they sit there between meals. The other rooms are for beds. There is not a great deal of house-work to be done in a house of this kind. The trouble comes when the pioneer becomes wealthier, and builds a large house " in town " or on the farm. Possibly his wife or daughters do the work as they did in the smaller house. If not, it is done by one servant. The work in this house is a great deal harder. There is a great deal more of it than there was in the two or three room house, which was built during their earlier life. In the former house, if they had coffee, it was poured from the pot in which it was made directly into the cups which were on the table. The meat was taken from the skillet in which it was cooked and put into the plates of those who ate it. If they had pancakes, the wife would sit with her back near the stove, where she could easily reach the griddle to grease it and turn the cakes while she was eating her meal. There was no formal dessert. The pie was eaten from the same plates as the rest of the food. There were no napkins; often, no table-cloth.

It did not take long to wash the dishes after a meal of this kind — there were not many of them. In from fifteen to twenty-five minutes after the meal was over, the wife could be seen sitting by the kitchen stove, sewing or knitting. The pans and the kettles were out of the way, and the kitchen was turned into a sitting-room. If the weather was cold, the door into the bed-room was open; the whole house was warm and comfortable. Wood was plenty and cheap.

This woman's troubles began when her husband, by dint of hard work and close economy, found himself in a position to gratify his pride in his accumulated wealth by building a new house. It was a big white house with green blinds. The stories were twelve or thirteen feet high; a large hall ran through the centre; the kitchen had nothing in it but doors and windows and a stove-hole; there was no sink, no conveniences of any kind. They now had a separate dining and sitting room, and an awful parlor with brussels carpet on it, which had red and green flowers all over it. The bedrooms were upstairs. They were all large; wood-work painted white. In the winter they were cold. The old habits of economy which made this house possible had so fixed themselves upon the occupants that they would not build a fire in the bedrooms. They said that they "didn't think it healthy to sleep in a warm room."

People go to see Mrs. Green in her new house. They go through and look at it, and say, " Oh, how nice." But they find a tired woman. She doesn't sit down to sew or knit in a few minutes after the meal is over, as she used to. She is at work all the time. The children must have clothes to fit the house. There is more sweeping and dusting to do; there are more dishes to wash; there is more of everything to do. Still, she came into the new house expecting to find things different and easier than they were before.

The modern conveniences are those arrangements and appliances which make it possible for people to live comfortably in a larger house, without seriously increasing the cares which they had in a smaller one. In the old house of two or three rooms the mother would bathe the children once a week in a tub by the kitchen fire. The tub would be dragged out the door, which was not very high above the ground, and the water emptied into the yard. In the new house it is different. The water is carried from the pump in the back yard, and from the kitchen stove, upstairs into one of the rooms. Then it has to be carried down again, emptied into the alley or the yard. The living habits are all changed without the compensating conveniences which naturally belong to them. It is probable that Mrs. Green keeps a "girl," but even then she has infinitely more work to do than ever belonged to the old home. She cannot understand it. She has a new house and a girl, and yet she is always tired.

Most of the houses in the newer cities and towns are, in a measure, similar to this. Nearly every one attempts to live up to the mark set by those who have all of the appliances of modern housekeeping. Coal and water have to be carried all over the house. Slops and ashes have to be carried downstairs and out of the building.

By attracting attention to the inconveniences of housekeeping, we may see and understand the full meaning of the term "modern conveniences." There is a natural call for dish-washing arrangements to take the place of the square table, with the dishpan, the tea-kettle, and the water-bucket. In its place, we have at one side of the kitchen, a sink, with cocks for hot and cold water immediately over it. The tables and drain-board are arranged to simplify the operations of dish-washing. The water, instead of being carried to the yard or alley, finds its way naturally into the drain through the sink. Modern laundry arrangements make it unnecessary to carry great tubs of water outside, or to delay wash-day on account of the weather, or to bring in the frozen clothes during the cold winter days. The bath-room, with the tub, the water-closet, and the wash-stand, is on the second floor. This saves a great deal of work. The water does not have to be carried upstairs nor the slops down. There is hot and cold water within easy reach of all the rooms. Often it happens that there are stationary wash-stands in the various bedrooms, though this is only usual in the most expensive houses.

The amount of work which a furnace saves is not readily estimated. It also saves money. Others of the modern conveniences are "places to put things;" large closets in the bedrooms, well supplied with drawers, shelves, and hooks; a general closet on the upper floor, which is accessible from all of the rooms, for bedding and other articles of common use; a ventilated closet in the bath-room, in which soiled linen may be put without contaminating the atmosphere. There should be a

closet or place on the second floor for brooms, dust-pans, and
dusters. Where there is no particular place for these articles,
the housekeeper or the servant has to use time in searching, or
in going up and down stairs. Anything which saves labor may
be regarded as a modern convenience.

## CHAPTER IV.

MODERN ARCHITECTS AND THE HOUSEKEEPER. — MISPLACED HOUSES.
— OLD COLONIAL POVERTY IN MODERN COLONIAL HOUSES. —
AFFECTATION IN DESIGN. — NATURAL DEVELOPMENT OF AMERICAN
ARCHITECTURE. — AMERICAN ARCHITECTURE AND AMERICAN HOMES.

NO one ever heard of the matter of house-planning being discussed in a convention of architects. Their reports will show that a great many subjects are handled, but none so near home as this. Sometimes there is an effort to discover that America has a style of architecture peculiar to itself. When such a thing becomes true, the effort to find it will not be necessary. An American architecture will have its growth in American necessities, and not through the blind copying of foreign styles and architecture. Nor to have an American style does it necessarily mean that we should ignore foreign precedent. It means that we should consider foreign architecture intelligently. Everything that is good should be adopted, no matter whence it comes. Those of us who see what is going on in the architectural world frequently notice English houses designed and built for those who live in the cold Northwest. In many of them the broad, English casement windows and general style of architecture, which is suited to the gloomy light and the mild temperature of Great Britain, is placed in the bright, cold climate of the Northwest. Nothing could be more out of place; it is an affectation, an exhibition of bad taste and poor sense. The cold Northwest, with its bright, clear atmosphere, presents its own architectural conditions. The work of blind copyists, those who have so strong a regard for precedent, is ridiculous. In one of the Eastern magazines there was an illustration showing what purported to be an old colonial cottage, situated possibly at Newport. The architect had copied the old colonial details, the old colonial forms, which were very nice, but he had also copied an idea which had its outgrowth in extreme poverty. He had placed a rain barrel at the side of the house, and had set it up on a rustic-looking bench or support, all of which was very ridiculous. This had been done in an old colonial house, and had its origin in old colonial poverty. Now, this architect, in his respect for that which was past, copied the faults, the inconveniences, and arrangements which belonged to those earlier times. A course of this kind, carried out to its fullest extent, would lead us to barbarism. In the same magazine was another house which was designed with great respect for precedent. In it was a front door which was divided about half-way up, so that the lower part might be shut and the upper part opened. Houses have been seen where something of this kind was reasonable, where it had its advantages. There are many places in this country where a door of this kind is almost a necessity; but it isn't on the seashore. If one has a house in the country, or in a small country town, where the horses and pigs, geese, chickens, and other animals, are allowed to roam about in the front yards, a door of this kind has its uses. In the summer time the upper part can be thrown back and the lower part closed, so that the most a horse can do in the way of getting into the house is to stick his head over the top rail and look in. In the country mills doors of this kind have a very proper and apt name; they are called pig-doors. They keep the pigs off the mill floor, and, at the same time, allow the light and air to come from above. But there is no necessity for a pig-door at Newport or Long Branch, or other seaside resort. Their use is a silly affectation. There is no beauty in them. There is no convenience which would lead to their use.

It is performances such as the above which retard the natural development of American architecture. American architecture will be simply carrying out, in an architectural way, the requirements of the American people in their buildings. From their homes the march of progress will be through the kitchens, pantries, and dining-rooms. It will unite with the parlor and sitting-room ideas, which have been more clearly worked out. The exterior will be formed in a natural way by the requirements of the interior, and by the variations of climate, and it will be decorated in a rational, artistic manner. We will not hamper the interior by the adoption of doors and windows which possibly belonged in a cathedral of the twelfth or thirteenth century, or the richer details of the later time, which had their special uses and forms as the development of the necessity and requirements of that particular period. The doors and windows of the nineteenth century should have their own special forms and positions. They should be decorated with a true regard for precedent so long as precedent does not influence the arrangements suited to modern times. The American style of architecture will not be developed through grand public buildings and enormous cathedrals, or expensive dwellings.

In this country every one is imbued with the idea of having a home of his own, and he desires to have it nice, convenient, and attractive. The average home is in a small, inexpensive house. The proper construction of these buildings, their arrangement with reference to their housekeeping requirements, their tasteful external designs considered in a rational way, will develop American architecture. It will be the expression of American wants in a natural, artistic spirit.

# A JOURNEY THROUGH THE HOUSE.

# CHAPTER V.

JOURNEY THROUGH THE HOUSE. — PORCH. — VESTIBULE. — HALL. — LONG HALLS AND SQUARE HALLS. — THE HALL THAT IS A ROOM. — RECEPTION HALL. — PARLOR. — SITTING-ROOM. — DINING-ROOM.

IN this section of the book we will make a journey through the house, stopping at various points of interest long enough to give general consideration to the details. From the principles herein derived, the plans subsequently given are constructed.

Every house should have a front porch. It should be wide, — if possible, eight feet, that one may sit at a distance from the railing and afford a space for others to pass behind. The porch is a protection to the front part of the house from the sun, wind, and, partially, from the cold. Nothing can be pleasanter than to sit on a shady porch during the warm part of the day or in the evening. It is an auxiliary to the vestibule.

The front door should be wide — three or three and a half feet. Double doors look very nice from the outside, but they are not as convenient or as easily handled as the single door. The door-bell should be at the right-hand side. The threshold should be elevated from three to six and a half inches above the porch floor.

### VESTIBULE.

In the plans that are given, various arrangements of vestibules are shown. In a few instances, direct entrances into the hall and reception-room are indicated, but such an entrance is not as desirable as where there is a vestibule. The arrangement of a vestibule for hat-rack, umbrella-stand, and other conveniences, changes the hall into an available room. Take, for instance, plan No. 16, page 153. At the right, as one enters, is a little closet; in it are hooks. At one side is an umbrella-stand; on the floor is a place for overshoes. Here one may arrange himself before going into the hall or reception-room. This is altogether better than having to pass across to one side of the hall or room, in order to find a place to deposit overshoes, wraps, umbrellas, etc. It saves work. If this vestibule have a hard-wood floor, and on it is placed a rug, one may stand there and divest himself of that which he would not carry into the house, and go into the room in good order, leaving the muddy overshoes, and the possible dampness of his umbrella and overcoat, behind him. This arrangement saves work; mud is not carried into the room. It is a very simple matter to care for the vestibule; the rug on the floor may be taken to the outside, and the deposit of mud and dust readily removed. It is well to have a small mirror at the side, or in the rack. The plan mentioned is merely suggestive, and does not apply to all houses. By looking through the plans given, various arrangements may be seen. In some of them there is no vestibule. Not all housekeepers want the same arrangement. Again, others do not care to pay for a vestibule. In other instances, the hall is too small to admit of one. As said before, a good vestibule changes the hall into a room. It makes a reception-hall tolerable, because it is not necessary to deposit there many things which should have another location. A vestibule does not properly serve its purpose where there is no room or arrangement for depositing wraps, etc. The closet part of the vestibule, shown in the cut, can, perhaps, be omitted, and hooks arranged around the wall sides. A curtain could be hung across the space occupied by the closet door: however, all these details are matters of taste and disposition. In the opening between the hall and vestibule may be placed tapestry curtains; these are sufficient storm protectors from the outside door, especially if the hall register is placed near it. No one who has not tried it, can realize the amount of protection from the weather that is afforded by a heavy curtain. It is not necessary or desirable that a door be placed in the opening from the vestibule to the hall.

### HALL.

This part of the house may be hall, reception-hall, or room. It is a hall or passage frequently, and not provided with a vestibule. It may be a hall from its shape; it may be a room for the same reason. It may be of no use as a room, if the stairway is improperly placed. The house arranged with a long, narrow hall, having the stairway at the side, is essentially wasteful of room. Such hall space is usually dark and gloomy as well as crowded. A hall eight feet wide and twenty feet long, contains one hundred and sixty square feet of floor-surface, though only a limited portion of it is available, on account of the shape of the space which remains after the stairway is placed. A hall twelve by thirteen feet contains one hundred and fifty-six square feet, but a great deal more available room. The space not occupied by the stairway is in better shape. A hall of this shape partakes of the nature of a room, and may be used as such. In the plan referred to a window-seat is shown. This window-seat may be used as a seat in warm weather, and, if the front is in the proper direction, as a conservatory in the winter. There are many such arrangements as this shown in the book.

The hall, in most of the plans, is a key to the whole arrangement. It has been a common, objectionable practice during the past few years to build houses of moderate cost, so that the hall is along one side with its entrance to the front, and the parlor next to it; back of the parlor is the sitting-room, and the hall opens into the dining-room; back of the dining-room is the kitchen, and so on to the extreme rear with summer-kitchen, pantry, etc. This makes a long house with only one room in front on the first floor, and one chamber and alcove facing the street on the second. Thus the hall serves only as a passage-way. The living-room has no front view. To obviate this, the halls in the plans, that are considered with most favor, are arranged to be used as rooms, and the vestibules are built so that such a thing is possible. If the hall is to be used as a vestibule, the hat-rack and other arrangements for hanging wraps, and the umbrella-stand, etc., are placed as near the front as possible. Where this is not done there must necessarily be a track from the front to the back, as a mark of travel.

The stairway may start at one side, and should lead towards the centre of the house. The nearer it can be started to the rear of the hall, the better; this gives more room in front. Sometimes the stairway is started immediately in the rear of the reception-hall, or from an alcove space at one side; these are good arrangements, depending, of course, upon other conditions. Upon one side, or in the rear, should be placed a grate. Nothing can be pleasanter when coming in from a disagreeable outside than an open-grate fire; this needs no argument. Under the stairway, or in some convenient nook, it is well to have a lavatory. The hall should be arranged as a centre from which to pass to the parlor, living-room, and dining-room. It is important to consider in this connection that the hall, and the stair-

## A JOURNEY THROUGH THE HOUSE. 35

way in it, should be placed so that the stair-landing above is in the centre of the house. Thus we have in the centre of the building only a small hall as a starting-point ; hence less waste room. When the stairway lands near the front wall on the second floor, a passage must be provided to the rear of the house. Where the landing is in the centre, we have only to pass into rooms without extra steps through long halls. For example, see plan No. 1, page 110.

Not every one cares to use the front hall as a reception-room. There is certainly no objection to naming and using it otherwise.

### RECEPTION-HALL, PARLOR, AND SITTING-ROOM.

During recent years there is more of a disposition to live all over the house; one reason for this is the improved heating arrangements. The terms sitting-room, parlor, reception-room, mean less in a distinctive sense, and are used largely for the purpose of classification. We will consider the parlor and the sitting-room in the same connection. The parlor has lost the awful stiffness of times past. It is now a reception-room.

In a house where there is a reception-hall in front, and the sitting-room to one side, both having a distinct front view, as is shown in many of the plans, a lady may occupy the front room and have her children and work around her, if desirable. A caller may be received in the reception-room ; these, however, are matters of individual preference. The vestibule may be planned so that it will have an entrance to both reception-room and sitting-room.

In some instances the arrangement of sitting-room and reception-hall are reversed. The hall is the sitting-room, and the other room the parlor. If doors are used between hall and sitting-room, they should be sliding; the effect is better, and the separation of the rooms as complete as necessary. Such doors should always be hung from the top. The sitting-room should certainly be as good a room as any in the house; as well located. There should be a closet on the first floor, and, if possible, it should communicate with this room; if not that, with the dining-room or reception-hall next to it. Certainly the sitting-room should always be provided with a grate.

A window-seat in the hall, parlor, reception, or other room, is really a great addition in more ways than one. It is not only attractive, but it adds to the availability of a room. Where there is space for three or four people to sit, in case of necessity, it is like seating that number of people outside of the room. They are comfortable, and the room has that much added to its seating capacity. A bay window arranged in this way is pleasant indeed.

Wall space is of great importance in these rooms. In planning a house, the piano, pictures, lounges, book-shelves, bookcases, bric-à-brac, etc., should be in mind. In a house of moderate size, it is, ordinarily, not necessary that the reception-hall, parlor, or sitting-room should be wider than thirteen and a half feet, and from fifteen to eighteen feet in length. However, this is not wide enough for those who entertain largely. A room thirteen and a half feet, with much furniture in it, is not wide enough for dancing.

A house arranged with a reception-hall, parlor, sitting-room, dining-room, etc., is used when it is desired to entertain a great deal; but for those who are living economically, whose means are limited, one of these rooms may be omitted. In many of the modern houses the number of rooms on the first floor has been decreased and their size increased. Oftentimes there is a reception-hall, a small library, and a dining-room only, as belonging to the living part of the house on the first floor. An arrangement of this kind belongs more particularly to a house which is occupied during only a part of the year; say as summer cottages in the North, and winter houses in the South. Modern ways of living make a larger number of rooms less desirable.

When it is possible, it is pleasant to have a little room off from the library as a study, or for a doctor as a reception-room or office. Where one does work at home, it is advantageous to have a private room that insures isolation, be it never so small. Often the library, so called in an ordinary sense, is not a library at all. There may be a few books in it, but it is used as a sitting-room or passage, and has no distinct necessity or use.

Additional rooms require more work than the same amount of floor space in a less number of rooms. The addition of rooms multiplies corners, windows, doors, etc., and adds more cost and labor, than does mere additional space. The availability of a room is not always dependent upon its size. A good deal depends upon the arrangement of wall space. A room may be large and still have no room for the furniture that is to go into it. It may be small and still have room enough.

### DINING-ROOM.

A good width for a dining-room is thirteen feet. Where one can afford it, it should be from fifteen to twenty feet in length; larger than this is a luxury. Its location, for the most part, is back of the sitting-room or hall. A grate in the dining-room is not altogether desirable; it is always at somebody's back. Again, a grate does not heat a room uniformly. It is very common to provide sliding-doors to connect the dining-room with other parts of the house, even with the parlor, but they are not the best kind to use. Sound and the odors of the food are more readily communicated through sliding-doors than others. For that reason they should not be used. A large, single door, three and a half feet wide, is preferable, though it does not always give the desired opening. Generally speaking, it is easier to provide wall space when planning a dining-room than in any of the other rooms in the house. A large number of windows is not necessary, and one of them can be placed high, and thus afford space for a sideboard. This sideboard should be placed at the end of the room nearest the entrance to the kitchen and china-closet, where such is used. The sideboard has various uses, according to the plans of the housekeeper. In some cases it is merely a place to display dainty china and other table furniture. Below are places for linen and table cutlery. In other cases, the sideboard is used as a buffet; as a place from which to serve the food. Sometimes this is carried to the extremest degree, and includes the carving, and the serving of that which goes with the meats.

It was very common in times past to use a slide connecting kitchen and dining-room. A passage is much better. The slide is worse than a door in communicating sounds and odors. In some of the plans in this book, doors are shown opening directly into the kitchen. This is done under protest; the owner of the house would have it so. The sideboard may be built as a part of the house. This is well enough when the question of cost is not important.

From the dining-room we will pass to the kitchen.

## CHAPTER VI.

KITCHENS. — THE KITCHEN A WORKSHOP. — WORK TO BE DONE IN A KITCHEN. — A PLAN. — FITTINGS. — DISH-WASHING CONVENIENCES. — SINK AND TABLES. — CHINA-CLOSET. — PANTRY. — COMBINATION PANTRY. — PANTRY FITTINGS. — WORK IN A PANTRY. — A DOUGH-BOARD. — FLOUR-BIN. — PANTRY STORES. — CUPBOARD. — REFRIGERATOR ARRANGEMENTS. — PANTRY UTENSILS. — A DRY-BOX. — SOAP-BOX. — VENTILATION OF KITCHEN. — GENERAL PRINCIPLES OF KITCHEN PLANNING.

THE kitchen existed in its state of greatest cleanliness and order a good many years ago in New England, where it was largely used as a sitting and dining room. As people became more prosperous, they moved out of the kitchen; they had a separate sitting-room. It was then that the kitchen began to decline. After this it was often literally as well as figuratively separated from the living part of the house.

The public has not suffered through lack of information on cookery and general housekeeping topics. Little has been said, however, about the house itself, with regard to its arrangements for facilitating the manifold operations of housekeeping. The subject is a broad one, and may be treated with some respect to detail. As the heart of the house, the kitchen may be given serious consideration.

In the modern house the kitchen is merely the place where the food is prepared for the table. The controlling idea and its arrangements should be to afford facilities for doing the work with as little labor as possible.

The kitchen is the workshop of the house. It should be arranged and planned according to the same general principles as any other workshop. A manufacturer arranges his foundry, his mill, or his printing-house, with reference to the saving of labor, for the purpose of saving money. When we save labor in a kitchen, we save the energy of the housekeeper, and, possibly, money.

An article on this subject was probably never written that did not pretend to describe the "model kitchen." It is safe to say that no such kitchen was regarded as "model" by all readers. A model kitchen is something which is out of reason. No two housekeepers have the same requirements. Housekeeping practice varies greatly. Again, the kitchen that can be built to one floor-plan cannot be built to another. In describing a kitchen, it is in mind to set forth certain general principles for the benefit of those interested.

There is little difference between the requirements of a kitchen for a house of moderate cost and an expensive house. Work of the same general character is done in every kitchen. The conveniences are more a matter of thought than of money. Elaborate details add much to the cost, but little to the convenience. There is little or no difference between the cost of a well-planned kitchen and one which is poorly planned.

To state the case broadly, a kitchen should be arranged solely with reference to the work which is to be done in it: the cooking, dish-washing, the care of the kitchen itself, and possibly the laundry work. This latter work should be removed from the kitchen — in any event, the washing should be done elsewhere — when it is at all possible. The steam and odor from the washing, which not only fill the kitchen but permeate the house, are enough to render whatever food there is in the kitchen unfit for use. It is altogether possible to arrange in the cellar of any house that is being built, and in many that are already built, at a trifling cost, a laundry in which the washing and ironing may be comfortably done. Of course this does not contemplate set tubs; but set tubs are not found in houses where the washing and ironing are done in the kitchen, and it is possible

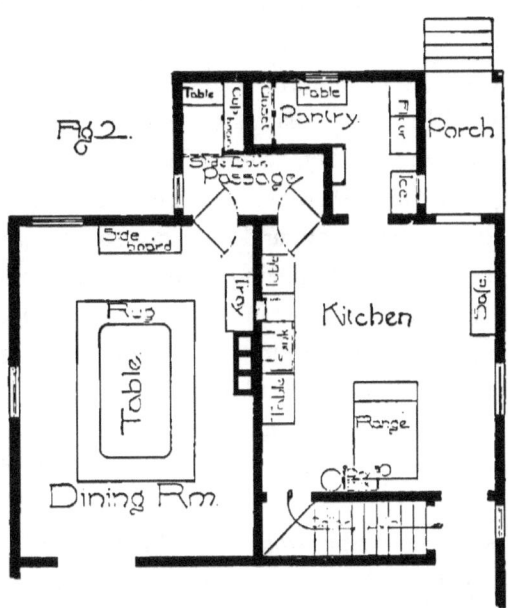

to do this work both well and easily without their use. There is little or no objection to doing the ironing in a well-ventilated kitchen. It is clean work, and while doing it the servant may attend to any cooking which is necessary, and see that the other work of the house moves forward.

The kitchen the plan of which is here given (Fig. 2) has been in use for three years under the varying conditions of one or two servants, and at times none at all. These are the conditions under which most housekeepers operate. There have been no emergencies in which the kitchen and pantries have not proven themselves ample, and none in which the housekeeper thought that they were too large and complicated. It is as necessary in houses where the means for maintenance is simply moderate, that a kitchen should not be too large as that it should afford ample facilities for accomplishing any work which may be done.

The kitchen itself is thirteen and one-half by fourteen and one-half feet. In it are placed the range, tables, sink, drain-board, etc., and the kitchen safe. The room has been found large enough for the work which is to be done there, and not so large that the tables, range, and safe are so far apart that time and strength are wasted moving from one to another. The kitchen has one large window in it, which is three feet from the floor. This permits the placing of a table, ironing-board, or chair under it, and thus gives additional wall space. There are two windows in the pantry, and a draught is secured through them, the kitchen window, and the transom over the door. The door is glazed.

The most disagreeable work of a kitchen, and that which takes much time, is the dish-washing. It is possible to make this work lighter and pleasanter than is usual. The necessary conditions are plenty of water, hot and cold, a place where the dishes will drain themselves, an abundance of table room for them both before and after washing. In the kitchen given the sink is placed next the kitchen flue. This gives a place for the pipe duct next the warm bricks, which prevent freezing even in severe cold weather. During the three years in which this kitchen has been in use they have never frozen, even when the temperature was twenty degrees below zero. The exact construction of this kitchen pipe-duct and other kitchen wood-work is given elsewhere. The range, which is usually next the flue, is, in this instance, placed at some distance from it. There is no reason why this should not be done, as it has been in many instances, with no disagreeable results.

The sink is not enclosed, but stands upon legs. Enclosed sinks are places which cannot be kept clean even with the

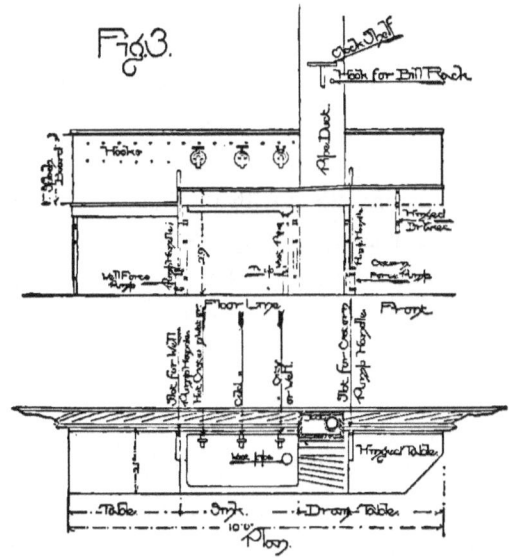

utmost vigilance. The brushes, scrub-rags, and buckets, which are usually kept there, are in this kitchen provided a place elsewhere.

At the left of the sink is a table; at the right, a drain-board, which is inclined toward the sink, and provided with grooves. At the right of this is a swing-table on the same level. The soiled dishes are placed on the table at the left, washed in the sink, which is provided with cocks for hot and cold water, drained on the drain-board, and, when wiped, placed on the table at the right. A glance at the plan will show that they are then beside the door which leads to the china-closet, and may be quickly placed where they belong.

It may be well to say a few words about the china-closet. The shelves are placed in a passage which leads from the kitchen to the dining-room, and are separated from the passage by doors. This passage is lighted by a window, and has two doors leading into it — one from the dining-room, and one from the kitchen (Fig. 2). These doors are swung on double swinging hinges, so that they may be opened by merely pushing against them, and will then swing back noiselessly into a closed position. One may pass through doors of this kind with a tray full* of dishes without touching them with the hand. This arrangement dispenses with the necessity for a slide, and also does away with the noises and odors from the kitchen, which so readily find their way to the rest of the house where a slide is used. However, if a slide is really desired, it can be placed over either the table at the left of the sink or over the swing-table at the right, and be convenient from both kitchen and dining-room.

The china-pantry could be readily enlarged into a butler's pantry, by extending it across the end of the dining-room, and placing the end window of this room on one side, thus bringing two windows on the same wall. There is a movable shelf under one of the permanent shelves in this china-closet, which can be drawn out in order to place a tray of dishes on it while they are being put away, and which can be pushed out of the way when not in use. This shelf is also of service as a place upon which to arrange the different dishes needed for the several courses of a meal, and in this way facilitates the table service.

In Fig. 4, the combination idea is carried out in pantry and china-closet. The pantry-cupboard projects into the room in a way to form a partition between the pantry and china-closet, and, at the same time, admits of a passage between the kitchen and dining-room with a separation of two doors.

Fig. 5 indicates an approved form of construction of china-closet and pantry, such as may be used in most of the pantries and china-rooms which are in this book.

The work which takes the most time is the preparation of food,

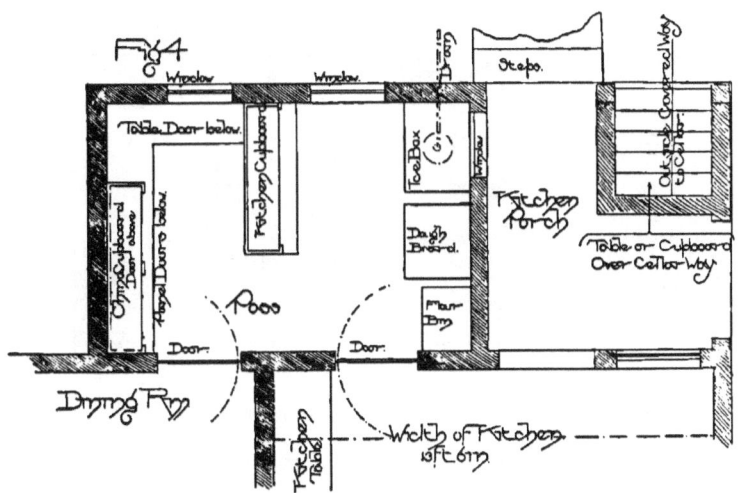

and every well-planned kitchen has its arrangements for lightening this burden. The first consideration is the location of the utensils, and the table and sink where the meats and vegetables are prepared. All should be near enough to the range so that there are no unnecessary steps to be taken. The number that are taken where the sink is in one corner of the kitchen, the table in another, and the range removed from both, is innumerable. In this kitchen the table proper and the sink are together, and they are but a step from the range.

There is a small swing-table attached to the wall at one side of the range. This provides a place for utensils, such as spoons, and forks, and dishes, such as those holding pancake batter, which are in constant use during cooking, and which cannot be held in the hand while the cooking is in progress. This alone saves many steps. The drain-board is a good place for draining vegetables, and to place utensils which are used in the preparation of food. Above the sink are hooks, etc., upon which to keep small utensils. In localities where there is much dust

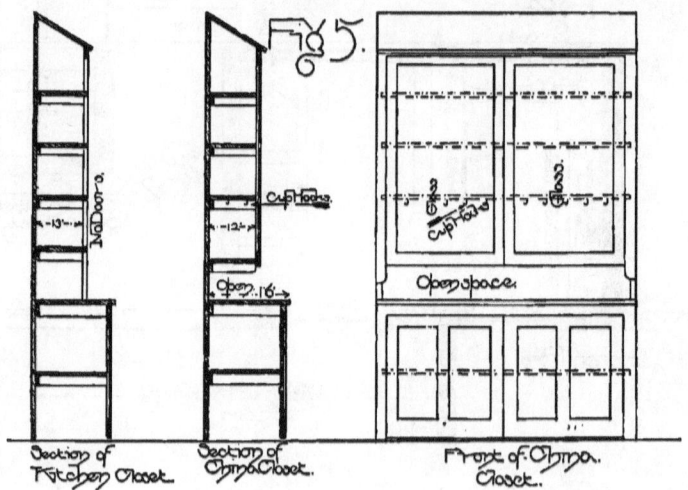

coming in from the outside thése utensils must be kept elsewhere, behind closed doors.

For the preparation of bread, cake, pastries, etc., the pantry is provided. In it are places for everything which can be used for such preparation. One can go out of the heat and noise of the kitchen into a little room which holds everything that can possibly be needed, and there prepare those articles of food which take the most time and careful attention. In Fig. 2 are two windows; under one is the dough-board. This is a table fastened to the wall at a convenient height for moulding and general work of this character. On one end is a piece of marble, twelve inches wide by sixteen long, which is used for moulding purposes. The advantages of such a piece of marble are numerous. It is as easily cleaned as a dish and requires no scouring, and, as dough does not readily stick to it, moulding can be done without the trouble which comes from the use of a board. This piece of marble is not fastened to the dough-board, as is sometimes done. Where it is set into the board there will always be creases in which dough will lodge, and it can only be cleaned with the greatest trouble. Where it is free, it can be raised from the board occasionally, and everything thoroughly cleaned.

At the right of the board is the flour-bin, which contains places for various kinds of flour and meal. Next to it is the refrigerator. Over the refrigerator is a window which opens on the porch, and through which the ice may be placed without the iceman going through the kitchen with his wet feet and dripping load.

At the left of the dough-board are shelves for keeping stores. The lower shelves are enclosed by doors and provided with a lock, so that extra stores may be placed there for safe keeping, where this is found desirable. The upper shelves are exposed. On them are kept sugar, tea, coffee, baking-powder, and kindred stores, which are in every-day use, and can be reached easier if there are no doors to be opened and closed. They should be kept in air-tight cans, which prevent their exposure to dust, insects, and air. Back of the door opening into the kitchen are hooks for the utensils which more properly belong in the pantry than the kitchen.

Many housekeepers prefer to keep the refrigerator in the cellar, on account of the waste in the ice. This waste, to the mind of the writer, is a small matter. The time spent by either housekeeper or servant in going into the cellar could much better be occupied in doing something else which would save more than does keeping the refrigerator below. Then, again, when it is kept in the pantry it can readily be provided with a zinc drain to the outside, which saves some little labor. In the cellar such a drain would only be possible where sand could be reached. A refrigerator should never, under any circumstances, be drained into the sewer, as is sometimes done.

The utensils which properly belong to the kitchen are kept in an old-fashioned kitchen safe, rather than in a closet opening out from the kitchen. A safe is more readily cleaned than a closet, and the perforated metal doors render the upper part of it an excellent place for storing cold food, which it is not desirable to keep in the refrigerator. Then if, as may happen in any kitchen which is left to the care of servants, vermin should take possession, the safe can be moved from the room, and trouble from this source avoided.

The entrance to the cellar is near the table, as marked. At the head of the cellar are placed brooms, mops, and dust-pans, and above these, well away from the head when going below, is a shelf upon which two buckets can be placed.

Back of the range is a small wooden box, thirty inches long by twenty-two inches wide and twelve inches deep, which is provided with a door and shelves. These shelves, as well as the top and bottom, have holes bored through them in order to allow the passage of hot air. In this box scrubbing-rags and brushes dry at once, and never have a bad odor. The box is of the same wood as the other kitchen finish, and looks as if it were a part of it.

A soap-box, with construction similar to the above, may be

provided. It should have a tin-pipe connection with flue or other ventilating apparatus. It will dry the soap and render its use less wasteful.

The ventilation of the kitchen is an important matter. The ideal kitchen has no rooms over it, and has ventilators in the ceiling. But this is not possible in most houses, and a substitute must be provided. An inverted sheet-iron hopper placed over the range, with an opening into either the flue or the outside of the house, will carry out the odors from cooking. An opening into the pipe-duct which holds the plumbing pipes will keep them from freezing in cold weather at the same time that it helps ventilate.

An important consideration in a kitchen is to build it so that it will not readily accumulate dirt, and can be easily cleaned. A large amount of time is spent in every well-kept house in cleaning the kitchen. The floor should be of oak, maple, or other hard wood, oiled, waxed, or finished with regular floor-finishing. The casings and doors are, of course, kept in better condition, with less labor, when of hard wood. Where this is not attainable, poplar, or other similar wood, finished with a varnish which will stand warm water, will prove a very good substitute. The tables should be either of oak, which requires little scrubbing, or poplar, which is so easily scrubbed that it is always white enough to delight the heart of the most particular housekeeper. A kitchen finished in this way is much less care than when the floor is of soft wood, and the finish a soft wood painted.

All kitchens in this book are planned according to the principles here set forth. They do not pretend to be exactly like this one, but the same general principle runs through all.

There are very good reasons why wainscoting should not be used in a kitchen, and no compensating advantages. The bead-joints and extra wood-work thereof make labor in the impossible task of keeping it clean. The less wood-work there is in a kitchen, the better. There are various kind of water-proof proprietary plaster finishes which may be used in finishing the walls and ceiling of a kitchen. Where they are not used, a white skim coat should be put on and painted after about a year's use.

## CHAPTER VII.

CELLAR. — FUEL DEPARTMENTS. — FURNACE CONVENIENCES. — COAL-BINS. — CEMENT FLOORS. — LIGHT IN THE CELLAR. — A CELLAR-CLOSET. — OUTSIDE CELLAR-DOOR.

THE cellar was originally a hole in the ground. In the modern house, that is arranged to please the housekeeper, it is well lighted; provided with a smooth cement floor that is easily cleaned; is not open as one room, but has apartments — one for a laundry, another for fuel and furnace, and still others for fruits and general stores. In the matter of fuel there is no reason why the entire winter supply should not be in the basement. It is certainly a great deal worse to go outside of the house in winter time from a hot, steaming kitchen, than it is to go into the basement for the fuel. However, there is some objection to storing wood in the cellar, for the reason that it brings bugs, ants, and vermin into the house.

Coal-bins should be constructed with hopper bottoms, — with bottom and sides slanting from level of outside grade-line to cellar floor, — where the location will admit of it. When there is not a cellar under all of the house, it is generally possible to arrange the coal-bin under the part without cellar, and slanting down to the part so used. This is illustrated in plan No. 11, Chapter XX. There the coal is put through the windows into the bins, and slides down to the opening in cellar. For each shovelful of coal taken away from the lower opening, another will take its place. This is particularly true with crushed coke, or anthracite coal, or nut and egg sizes of other fuel. The lump sizes require a larger opening than the usual twenty-inch-square opening for the coal mentioned. These bins should be lined on the bottom preferably with bricks laid in cement. If this is not used, two-inch oak boards will do. Partitions of the same material should be used to separate the various bins. With an arrangement of this kind a large amount of storage capacity can be provided. Under some circumstances this plan cannot be adopted. In such a case the ordinary bins may be used.

As houses are now planned, the first tier of joists are placed from twenty to twenty-four inches above the grade-line. Where it is not possible to secure that height for cellar-windows, areas may be built of brick or stone, and additional light provided. Light is the enemy of disorder and uncleanliness; where there is exposure there will be less disorder.

It is not necessary to have the cellar under the whole house, for reasons as mentioned, and on account of the cost. It is sometimes important that savings of all kinds be made. The furnace may be set in a pit with its face directed to the cellar. It is best that the opening from the hoppered coal-bins, above described, be close to the furnace. If it can be opened at the side, so that one can stand in the pit and throw coal in the fire-box, it is better than any other arrangement.

The ordinary cellar is seven feet in the clear, and, for this reason, it is nearly always necessary to pit the furnace. This is done by digging an extra depth, and lining the area and opening with brick.

Near enough to the furnace to be warm, should be a closet for canned fruit, made of flooring-boards, if not of more substantial material, and provided with a door and lock. It should be shelved with board about seven inches apart. Other winter stores, like potatoes, cabbage, etc., should be kept in a dark cellar with an earth floor. It is the opinion of farmers and others that vegetables keep best when lying next the ground. The cellar-involving arrangements here outlined may be seen in plan No. 11. The outside door, which leads into the cellar, should bolt on the inside, and the upper cellar door on the outside. There should be doors provided to separate the different rooms. Where cost is an item, they may be made of two thicknesses of flooring. Cellar-windows should be hung on hinges, and provided with bolt fastenings; catches are not secure.

## CHAPTER VIII.

A LOW-COST LAUNDRY. — BLUE MONDAY. — BASEMENT LAUNDRY. — LOW-COST CONVENIENCES. — INEXPENSIVE LAUNDRY FITTINGS. — HOT AND COLD WATER ARRANGEMENTS. — A LABOR-SAVING LAUNDRY. — A PLACE TO DO FRUIT-CANNING.

THE term "Blue Monday" probably originated on account of its being general wash-day, and a day in which everybody about the house undertook to do an impossible amount of work with limited resources.

Most of the washings in this country are done in the kitchen. The wash-boiler is on the stove, and the servant or mistress of the house, or both, attempt to wash and do their cooking without seriously disturbing the routine of meals. There is a fussiness about everything pertaining to that day, which creates an atmosphere of blueness which is proverbial. The steamy, crowded kitchen, the almost inevitable wetness or slipperiness, the great physical exertion required, the carrying of water, the lifting of tubs, are all uncomfortable, and the work is done at a great disadvantage. In an expensive house, where there is plenty of money, Monday is not so blue. Immunity is purchased. Possibly the clothes are sent from the house to be washed in somebody else's kitchen; maybe to be worn by some one else before they are returned, and often to be injured or destroyed by the strong washing-mixtures and soaps, which are made to save rubbing. This kind of immunity is expensive. It is too expensive for the large majority of people. It is annoying to all alike.

Laundry work will sometime be done at a cost which will admit of people of moderate means having this work done at a public laundry. At present, the general laundry work of an ordinary household cannot be done in this way, on account of the expense.

The general public laundry, where arrangements are made to do the entire family washing at a low cost, is a complete solution of the Blue-Monday problem; but until the laundry is an accomplished fact, such work will be done at home, and a family laundry must be considered in house-building. It would be a very easy matter to arrange a laundry which would meet all the desired conditions, if we were to operate independent of cost, but the large majority of people are not independent in this way. If it were not a matter of cost, we would have an independent room for the laundry work, with porcelain tubs, and hot and cold water running into all of them; we could have a steam-drier, and many other things, which it is useless to mention here. It is the laundry of the moderate-cost house which interests the largest number of people.

We must have a place to do laundry work which is a compromise between the foggy kitchen and the laundry with porcelain tubs.

As houses are now built, the first floor is usually from two and a half to three feet above the grade. This affords abundant opportunity of getting a well-lighted basement. If the basement is dark, put more windows in it, and whitewash the walls and ceilings. Cement the floor. Put in a slop sink, and give it a trapped connection with the vault or sewer. Provide a pump over this sink to connect with the cistern. If the city water is soft, this will be used and no pump will be required. Then a laundry stove is to be provided. Thus we have everything ready for use without much labor, and certainly at a very low cost.

The basement should be light under any circumstances. The floor should be cemented, the joists should be whitewashed, so that the only additions necessary to make the laundry work easy are a laundry stove, a place to throw waste water, and a supply of hot and cold water. If one does not care to heat the water in the ordinary boiler, there is a very simple device for heating water which may be placed in any laundry. An open tank, which will hold two or three barrels of water, can be placed over the stove and next to the joist. From it a connection can be made with the laundry stove by means of lead and iron pipe. This pipe should start from the bottom of the tank and connect with an iron pipe which enters the stove, and passes around the inside of the fire-pot, then to the outside and connects with another lead pipe, which empties into the tank again on a level above the first opening. Thus the cold water would come from the bottom of the tank, through the stove where it would be heated, thence upward and into the tank. This would give a hot-water circulating connection, and in this way provide hot water for use in the laundry. This arrangement would require a low-cost force-pump to force the water to the tank. There are many kinds of these pumps, which are substantial and can be secured at a low cost. The pipe from the stove could be supplied with a compression cock from which the water could be drawn into the tubs. The better way would be to have an independent tank connection. Lead pipe was mentioned as being the pipe to use in making the connection with the iron pipe in the laundry stove. Galvanized iron pipe would answer every purpose and cost a little less. Where set tubs are not used, the water could be readily distributed by means of a hose pipe. If the above arrangement is too expensive, the stove only can be used for heating water.

Set tubs might be used instead of the ordinary wooden ones which were contemplated, and would save a good deal of labor, but the cost is something which all cannot afford. The arrangement described here can be reached by nearly every one of moderate means. It provides a place to throw slop water, and brings hot and cold water close at hand. It isolates the washing from the cooking, and the smell of washing from the whole house. It is very different from the conditions in most houses, where the water has to be carried from the backyard into the house, lifted to the stove, poured into the tubs, and afterward carried out, a bucket at a time, and emptied over the back fence, if the tub is not dragged out and emptied into the yard.

It is well in building a new house to have an outside cellarway to facilitate the use of the laundry below. In such a case the clothes can be carried into the yard without being taken through the kitchen. There will be times when the weather will not permit taking the clothes outdoors. In very cold weather it should never be done. It is murderous for a woman to have to carry clothes from a hot, steamy laundry or kitchen at eighty degrees to the cold, dry air of the outside. There is no woman so strong that she can stand this. All the clothes can be readily dried in the basement. Here is presented another argument in favor of the laundry below. The washing can always be done at the appointed time in spite of the weather. When one goes into a large attic he is apt to say, " What a splendid place to dry clothes." People who dry clothes in the attic usually do the washing in the kitchen.

A basement laundry is a cool place in summer and a warm one in winter. There is no better place for ironing in warm weather, for even with a fire the basement is always cool. Nor can there be a better place for canning fruit. The conveniences of plenty of water, a fire, and yet a cool place for doing this extremely laborious work, will be readily appreciated.

# CHAPTER IX.

THE SECOND FLOOR. — STAIRWAYS. — THE COMBINATION STAIRWAY. — IDEAL NUMBER OF BEDROOMS. — LARGE CLOSETS AND PLENTY OF THEM. — A LINEN-CLOSET. — PLACING OF GAS-FIXTURES. — SERVANT'S ROOM. — BATH-ROOM. — AN ATTIC. — ATTIC CLOSETS. — ATTIC ROOMS.

IN many houses a combination stairway is used. By this is meant one in which the front and rear stairways run together in a common landing. In this case, there should be doors separating the rear from the front stairway, one at the beginning, and one at the end of the rear part. The combination stairway is a compromise. Oftentimes, however, one can secure other things which are desirable by its use. There are other compromises more objectionable than the combination stairway.

A stairway of this kind is not used as the most desirable thing, but as the least objectionable of other compromises; for instance, if one can secure, for a given cost, an additional room or two by using a combination stairway, the room is frequently preferable. No one can doubt but that a front stairway, entirely separated from the one in the rear, is the best thing to have; however, it is easy to understand that a combination stairway may be used for reasons above stated. In some of the plans a stairway is shown, starting from a stair-hall in the rear of reception-hall or room. Under such circumstances, a combination is not necessary. One can come from the kitchen and go upstairs without being observed from the other parts of the house. Again, combinations are sometimes used so that they apply to the servant's room as a continuous stairway, and as a combination to the other parts of the house. This is true of several plans given.

It is almost superfluous to say that a stairway should be easy, still it is known that not all are so. The one in the front part of the building should always be made without winders; that in the rear, the same way if possible. Landings are preferable, and make a staircase beautiful. Stairways may be considered from a hygienic standpoint. This, however, is not necessary in this connection. Where there is only one stairway, it is not uncommon to have it start from the dining-room, and, if one stops to think about it, this is not a bad arrangement. The dining-room is centrally located, and the stairway may be used by the servants when this room is not otherwise in use. Certainly it is less objectionable than placing it in a hall through which all have to pass, or where it is necessary to pass through other rooms to reach the second floor from the rear. A combination stairway, or one that starts up from the dining-room, is less objectionable in a house where there is a bath-room on the second floor than it would otherwise be. Where the bath-room is so placed, it is not necessary that the slops be carried down or the water carried up stairs; and, in other respects, it is less necessary to use the stairway in a disagreeable way.

The rear stairway should be connected with the front part of house by means of a hall on the second floor. It is generally found desirable to have a girl's room near the rear stairway, and to cut off that part of the house from the front by means of a door. There should be means of lighting, artificial and otherwise, at the beginning and landings of all stairways.

In a young and growing family, five is the ideal number of rooms for the second floor. This number may be increased or decreased according to the size and development of the family.

Where there are five rooms it affords, first, a family room in front, built over the parlor or sitting-room; next to that is a room in front for the very young children, and afterwards for the girls; then the room in the rear of the family room may be for the boys; the fourth room for guests, and the fifth for the servant. The guest-room view is to the side and the rear. There are cases where one must accommodate a large number of people with a smaller number of rooms, and, again, a larger number of rooms is thought indispensable. In connection with the size of bedrooms, we may say what was said before,—that their availability does not depend entirely upon their size. A room may be large and still not contain a place for a bed or other furniture. It may be moderately small and yet have space for all.

The more we think about the arrangement of houses, the larger appear the number of indispensables. It used to be thought unnecessary to have a closet in every bedroom; one was certainly enough in the family room. Now it is almost a necessity that there be two closets in the family room—one for the lady, and a smaller one for the gentleman. There should certainly be one closet in every bedroom, and, in addition to that, one which opens from the hall, to be used for bed-linen and general bedroom supplies. A suitable place for brooms and dust-pans is the attic stairway when a special closet is not provided.

In lighting bedrooms there should be at least one window for each outside exposure. Where the size will admit, there should be two windows placed so that the dressing-case can be set between them, either in the corner or otherwise. Most bedrooms are lighted artificially by bracket lights instead of the centre light. There should be one bracket on each side of the dressing-case; if not, a pendent light immediately over it. Centre connections for gas-fixture are usually provided, but in practice many houses are not supplied with the fixture.

Grates on the second floor make work: carrying of fuel and ashes is always disagreeable in the extremest degree. The placing of ash-pits in the cellar may make it unnecessary to carry the ashes, but still grates make work. At the same time it is very pleasant to have a grate in the bedroom; they are the best means of ventilation known.

The servant's room is not usually very large, seldom large enough. It should be provided with a closet, the same as other rooms. The window in that room should be set high enough from the floor so as to admit of the placing of a trunk under it, without interfering with the light or in other ways appearing uncomfortable.

The bath-room and general plumbing work are considered in detail in the following chapter. It is sufficient to say that there should be as little wood-work as possible in the bath-room. Water-proof plastering should be used, and when this becomes soiled it can be washed and painted.

There is nothing a housekeeper appreciates more than a good attic and an easy stairway leading to it. Often attics are not plastered; they should always be floored at the same time the house is built. Where it is not possible to make divisions by plastering, and other substantial material, light wooden partitions will serve the purpose of providing means of classifying that which is stored in the attic, and prevent it from being in a continual state of disorder. The rooms may be fitted with shelves, closets, etc.

Where it is possible so to do, the attic room should be plastered. It makes the rooms below appreciably cooler in summer.

In most of the plans herein illustrated, the roof is high enough to provide space for good rooms, with ceilings as high and as square as those of the rooms below. It is cheaper to provide rooms in this way than to spread over more ground; and there is certainly no valid objection to their use by the boys of the family.

# CHAPTER X.

PLUMBING. — IS PLUMBING ENTIRELY SAFE? — COMPLETENESS IN PLUMBING APPARATUS. — LABOR-SAVING PLUMBING APPARATUS. — SEWER CONNECTIONS. — SOIL PIPE. — A TRAP. — ACCIDENTS TO TRAPS. — FREQUENT USE OF PLUMBING APPARATUS DESIRABLE FOR SAFETY. — WATER-CLOSETS. — SIMPLICITY IN PLUMBING. — DRAIN CONNECTIONS. — TO KEEP PLUMBING APPARATUS FROM FREEZING. — CISTERN WATER SUPPLY. — GREASE SINK. — FLUSHING OF DRAIN. — BATH-TUB.

IN considering the plumbing apparatus of a house, the question is often asked, "Are these things safe? Do they not endanger the health of the occupants of the house?" The answer is, The plumbing apparatus may be entirely safe. That it is not always so, we all know. We hear of many cases of typhoid fever, diphtheria, scarlet fever, and other diseases, which are traceable to, or aggravated by, defective plumbing. In some sections of the country so much trouble has been caused by poor plumbing, that the people, as a class, have come to be suspicious of all. The reason for this is the effort to cheapen the work. Suffering from bad work has led to safety. In larger cities this work is under the control of the city government. It may be said that it is possible so to arrange the fixtures and apparatus appertaining to plumbing that it is entirely safe. The question naturally follows, "How is this done?"

It may be said that good work is not a great deal more expensive than poor work. Again, good work is not always a question of money. It is one of knowledge or inclination on the part of the plumber.

One in moderate circumstances, who builds a house to cost from twenty-five hundred to four thousand dollars, should have well water or city water, and hot and cold cistern water in the sink in the kitchen. There should be at least a slop-hopper in the laundry. In the bath-room a water-closet, a tub, and generally a wash-stand. This latter feature is not absolutely necessary, as will be explained later. In the attic there should be a tank to hold the cistern water, which is connected with the fixtures using soft water below. A force-pump, or water-motor, may be located in the kitchen or basement to lift the water to tank. In more elaborate houses a completer plumbing apparatus may be used. There may be an especial sink in the china-closet. There may be wash-stands in the various chambers, and one on the first floor.

There may be, also, an additional water-closet on the first floor, or in the cellar, located where it is accessible to the members of the family. There are many ways of expending money in plumbing fixtures; but, with those first mentioned, one may be entirely comfortable, and derive all of the housekeeping benefits which may be expected from such conveniences. Unless the house be large, an increase in the number of fixtures would increase the amount of work done in keeping them clean, rather than save labor.

In the matter of safety, another question, which sometimes arises, is as to the danger from the plumbing apparatus where there is no sewer connection, or where it has to be made with a vault. The protection against sewer-gas is not from the sewer itself or the vault. It is entirely through protective apparatus in the house, and the manner of the connection with the vault or sewer.

One may consider the conditions of safety in plumbing apparatus under two general heads. First, as to the workmanship; second, as to design or plan of the apparatus. Nothing need be said as to the workmanship, excepting that the execution of the design, or the benefits to be derived from it, may be entirely lost by defective workmanship. If the work is not properly executed, the design need not be considered. The result will be bad irrespective of the plan.

In considering the design of the apparatus, we will take into account the arrangement of the connections and fixtures. By the latter expression is meant the tub, the water-closet, the wash-bowl, and the sink, pump, etc. The connections which have to do with the safety of the apparatus are the traps and the waste pipes, or pipes which connect with the vault or sewer.

The main waste pipe inside the house is called the soil pipe. The smaller waste pipes from the fixtures connect with it. The soil pipe is of cast-iron, and usually four inches in diameter on the inside. It connects, full size, with the water-closet. Most other wastes are of lead, and are usually an inch and a half in diameter. In the soil and waste pipes there will naturally be the odors from the vaults and sewer, or from the foul matter which is in or passing through the pipes. Therefore, there must be means in each waste pipe, which connects a fixture with the main soil pipe, of preventing the passage of gas or air from it into the house. This is done by means of what is called a trap. The "S" trap is the commonest form; this name is given it from its shape, and illustrates its construction. If we take a letter S and turn it sideways we will get the form of such a trap. The right side or end would continue directly down toward the drain or soil pipe, and the left side would continue upward and connect with the fixture (see Fig. 6). The water from the fixture comes down and is forced upward through the bend by the pressure of water above, and from thence runs into the soil pipe or drain. Thus it will be seen that there is always a seal of water in the trap. There is always water in the trap as indicated by the depth of the bend of the S. There are hundreds of different forms of traps, but they are all constructed on the same principle; the idea being that the gas or air from the pipe would have to pass through the water in order to get into the house. The water in the trap is called the seal; it seals the passage of air as stated.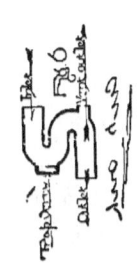

There are many conditions under which a trap may fail to do its full duty. It may be foul in itself, or it may be rendered foul by the bad air in the drain. The trap may be siphoned by a heavy flow of water through the main drain, or it may be siphoned by a string or a rag which may readily find its way into the trap, and hang over the bend so that all of the water will run out. Again, the water in the trap may evaporate. All these dangers may be guarded against. In the first place, there should be means which allow fresh air to pass through all that portion of the main drain or soil pipe which is in or close to the house. The means of accomplishing this are various.

The soil pipe is ventilated by continuing up through and well above the roof with a full opening at the top. The smaller drains should be ventilated in the same way when far removed from main soil pipe or other connection. The traps should be ventilated by 1½-inch or two-inch connections with the outer air, as shown by cut.

Frequent use of plumbing fixtures contributes to safety. It causes a large volume of water to pass through the pipes. The flushing of the pipes and drains in this way makes them cleaner and thus safer. It is frequently said by those who have plumbing fixtures in their houses that they use them as little as possible, because they are afraid of them. Nothing worse could be done. The water in the traps evaporates or becomes foul, and thus the gas has a free entrance to the house. A water-closet helps greatly to cleanse the soil pipe and outside drain. It discharges a large volume of water into it suddenly, in a way to keep it clean. It is not a bad plan to use the closet at least once a day, solely for the purpose of flushing the drain. In houses where there are a number of wash-stands distributed through the various chambers and halls there is danger from neglect in using them. The water seal in the traps may evaporate, and thus give direct sewer-air connection with the house. Particularly is this so in the guest's room. A wash-stand is a more dangerous fixture for this reason than any other in the house.

The water-closet problem has received a great deal of attention. A few years ago they were quite complicated, there being levers and pipes, pans, springs and weights, to a degree of complexity which caused a great deal of trouble. There has since been a return to first principles and great simplicity. The water-closet of to-day is nothing more or less than a large bowl connected by means of an "S" trap four inches in diameter with the soil pipe, and provided with means of flushing with large volumes of water. Such a closet is known as the "washout closet." In other closets there is an intermediate plunger-valve separating

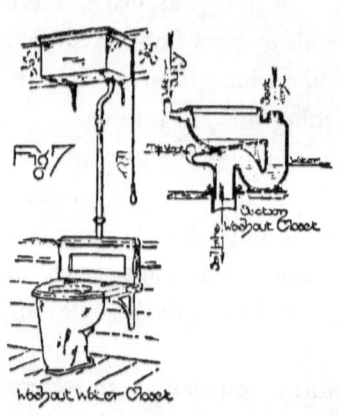

## A JOURNEY THROUGH THE HOUSE. 69

the hopper from the trap. The plunger-valve is defined by its name. It is a large stopper which plunges into and closes up the opening to the trap by means of its own weight when released. That which makes one closet different from another has to do more with means of flushing than anything else. By flushing is meant the pouring into and distribution of water in the hopper. The most popular closets, those which have given the most satisfaction, are "washout" closets, made entirely of white earthenware, not alone the bowl, but the trap and connecting neck. Closets are best flushed from an independent tank, which is placed about seven feet above the closet and connects with it by means of $1\frac{1}{4}$-inch pipe. The height gives it a strong flush of water, which cleanses it thoroughly.

In the past it has been usual to conceal the earthenware or iron body of the closet. It is best to leave it entirely open around the sides, that the entire apparatus may be exposed. Sometimes it is necessary to support the flap and seat by legs, though the modern closets are arranged so that all of the woodwork may be secured to the upper part of the hopper or the wall. There should be the solid flap covering to the wooden seat with the opening in it, both of which should be hinged, so as to allow them to be thrown back. It is convenient to use the water-closet as a slop hopper. In order to do this the seat should be hinged, so that it may be thrown back out of the way.

One frequently hears it said by those who exercise their authority over household matters that they do not allow anything to be put into the water-closet except that which is naturally intended for it; meaning that they do not allow the slop water to be put into it. There is no reason in this. The closet that cannot be used for this purpose cannot, with safety, be allowed in the house. The use of the water-closet as a slop sink is not only legitimate but desirable. It flushes the drain.

There is a movement toward simplicity in general plumbing apparatus. At the time the water-closets were in the complicated state mentioned, everything pertaining to plumbing was in the same general condition. It was thought necessary to fill a house with a wilderness of pipes and traps to have it safe or satisfactory. The very complexity of the arrangement made it not only unsafe but expensive to maintain.

We have all heard a great deal about the expense of maintaining a plumbing plant, if it may be so called. There is no reason why there should be constant repairs and expense. It is pleasant to know that additional expense is not necessary to secure immunity from trouble. The idea of simplicity in arrangement, general excellence in the fixtures, material, and labor, which go to form the completed work, has to be borne in mind. The arrangement of the plumbing apparatus has to be planned with the same care and thoughtfulness as the other parts of the house.

It should be remembered that if the pipes are placed in a position where the temperature is liable to fall below thirty-two degrees the water in the pipes will freeze. Thus it is suggested that all pipes should be on an inside wall, — if possible, next to the kitchen flue, — and that there be here arranged an especial pipe duct of wood to ventilate the kitchen, and, at the same time, keep the pipes from freezing by means of the warm air which will pass through it. This duct should be covered on the face with a wide board, which can be readily removed by taking out a few screws. Thus the pipes may be exposed at any time desirable.

If the hot-water boiler in the kitchen is surrounded by an

enclosure which has an opening in the bottom, and which connects from above with the pipe duct previously described, there will be a current of warm air passing upward through the pipe duct as long as there is warm water in the boiler. The water in the boiler will be warm long after everything else is cold. This will insure safety from freezing when other helps fail.

The cistern water is supplied to the bath-room, and to the hot-water reservoir, by means of a tank placed in the attic, or at least above the highest fixture. It sometimes happens that the supply pipe from the tank above the attic floor freezes. All this may be prevented by enclosing the tank, and the pipe which connects with it, with a large box or canvas covering which is six or eight inches larger than the tank. This confines the warm air from the duct mentioned, so that as long as there is heat it will always be in this enclosure.

The outside drain, which connects with the vault or sewer, is, in some instances, trapped previous to its entrance to the sewer or vault. In such cases, this trap should have a connection with the outer air, and on the side of the trap towards the house. Sometimes this outer-air connection is made into the water spout from the roof; but this is not proper, for the reason that the sewer gas, or the gas from the vault, is almost certain to destroy the spout. Again, this spout may come out near a dormer, or may pass near a window, and in either case may contaminate the air in the house. It is better that this ventilating connection should be in the yard, at some distance from the house, or, better yet, that there should be a long iron pipe extending well above the ground. It should be understood that this vent has no direct connection with the sewer, but merely with the soil pipe and drain back of the trap; with that part of it which is nearest to, and in, the house.

Sometimes it is necessary to run the down spouts into the sewer connection; in such a case one should be certain that the down-spout openings are not near the dormers, and that they have no connection whatever with the cistern. It is common to have a switch or cut-off in the down spout, so that the latter may be connected either with the cistern or sewer. This is very bad practice. While it is connected with the sewer or with the drain pipe, the down spout is contaminated with all the foulness of the air of the drain. On its being connected with the cistern, the water is poisoned.

Immunity from sewer gas in the house is largely dependent upon the flushing and ventilation of the drain and the soil pipe. In the case of a drain which is trapped as described, there is an air connection through the vent before the trap; then the soil pipe which is in the house should continue upward through the roof. Thus there is a fresh air inlet through the drain, and upward through the soil pipe of the house. Such a connection prevents the possibility of siphoning the traps, as it gives an outward air connection. The water passing through the drain or soil pipe can draw its supply of air from the upward soil vent, rather than through the traps which contain water. When there is no upward vent of the soil or drain, the water in the traps which connect therewith will be drawn out by the passage of water through the drain where fixtures are used.

There are those who maintain that there should be no trap in the yard or adjacent to the house, but that there should be a straight run from the soil pipe to the sewer or vault, and upward through the roof and above the house. It is good practice to use the trap as described for sewer connections, but not for open vault connections.

A grease sink is frequently placed in the drain to intercept the passage of grease into the vault. It is so placed and connected that only the water from the kitchen sink, or other fixtures where the water contains grease, may enter it. It is made of brick, and is usually of six or eight barrels capacity. A four-inch pipe connects it with the kitchen waste, and if the grease sink is placed adjacent to the main drain, there can be a similar connection between it and the main drain. It should be a siphon connection, so that the sink will become nearly full before it discharges. When it discharges through the siphon the water will go out with a rush and leave the grease in the sink. This makes an intermittent discharge into the main drain, which flushes or cleanses it thoroughly and is much better than a constant small flow of water. This grease sink must be cleaned from time to time. Small cast-iron grease sinks are sometimes placed under kitchen sinks in very large dwellings or hotels.

Nothing particular need be said in regard to wash-stands more than has been said, excepting, possibly, that the drain should be trapped, ventilated, and connected with the soil pipe; also that there should be a lead safe or safety pan on the floor under the wash-stand when they are enclosed; it is preferable that they should remain unenclosed. It has been common to connect this safe with the soil pipe. It is only intended that it should be useful in cases of accidental overflow; but, notwithstanding the fact that there be a trap in the safe waste or drain, it would be empty most of the time, because of the evaporation of the water. It is proper to make direct connection with the cellar or kitchen sink.

The bath-tub should have the same-sized drain connection as the wash-stand; that is, one and one-half inch in diameter, trapped. The overflows from both the wash-stand

and tub should be flushed with hot water quite frequently, to avoid the soap smells which are so common to bath-rooms. It often happens that those who have bath-rooms in their houses imagine that they smell sewer gas, when it is nothing more or less than the smell of rancid soap.

# CHAPTER XI.

HEAT AND VENTILATION. — COMMON HEATING ARRANGEMENTS. — PRESENT METHODS GENERALLY UNSATISFACTORY. — IDEAL CONDITIONS. — PROPER AMOUNT OF MOISTURE RARELY ATTAINED. — A FURNACE DEFINED. — METHODS OF REACHING BEST RESULTS. — SUPPLY OF PROPER AMOUNT OF MOISTURE. — REMOVAL OF FOUL AIR. — SUPPLYING FRESH AIR WITH PROPER MOISTURE FROM STOVES. — STEAM AND HOT WATER HEATING. — DIRECT AND INDIRECT RADIATION. — LOW-COST HEATING APPARATUS.

IT is only within a short time that the heating and ventilation of buildings of any kind have been in any measure satisfactory. This applies only to the largest buildings; the heating and ventilating of smaller structures are still in an unsatisfactory condition. Most dwelling-houses are heated with stoves, which, as now arranged, are not successful. The same air is heated over and over again. Fresh air in the proper quantities or from the proper source is not supplied to the interior of the building. Grates are very well in their way in that they take large quantities of air from the room. Thus far they ventilate. The supply of air is necessarily irregular, unless special means are provided.

Furnaces are used for heating a very large number of houses. While they are satisfactory in some respects, they are deficient in others. The same thing may be said of steam, hot-water, or other heating apparatus.

As the statement has been made that heating systems in general, as applied to dwelling-houses, are unsatisfactory, it may be well to state the fault, and what is to be desired. It is not the purpose to consider this question chemically, or from a highly scientific standpoint; there is no occasion for it. It is well to bear in mind that we are considering the heating and ventilating of a house during cold weather, and not its ventilation during the summer, when natural means are to be relied upon. Then it may be asked, What is to be done? Primarily the air should be at the proper temperature at all times; it should be in its pure state, as found on the outside of the building, and not contaminated with any of the gases of combustion. It should be supplied with its proper equivalent of moisture, at the temperature at which we find it in the room. As it becomes impure from natural causes, there should be some means of effecting its withdrawal.

These are the ideal conditions. How far do they exist in practice? The temperature is ordinarily high enough. The air of the room is apt to be contaminated by the gases of combustion, and vitiated by breathing and otherwise. Rarely indeed does it contain its proper equivalent of moisture; it is dry and parched. Now that we know the conditions in their ideal state and as they exist in fact, we will consider in detail what may be done to bring about more satisfactory results. If the heating apparatus be a furnace, it should be constructed of steel or wrought-iron plate, the joints thoroughly riveted and calked; or, if of other material, it should certainly be gas-tight. Every precaution should be taken to prevent the passage of the air of combustion from the furnace to the warm-air chambers and from thence to the rooms above. The furnace is nothing more or less than a large stove with various radiating arrangements, surrounded by an iron or brick enclosure, with a supply of fresh air from the outside, and with connecting tin pipes to the rooms above. It is important that the inner parts, the fire-pot, the radiating surface, etc., be thoroughly well built and gas-tight, to prevent the heated air from becoming contaminated by the gases of combustion. The supply of outer air should be ample. It should be so arranged that it can never be entirely cut off. The furnace should be of sufficient capacity so that means of reducing the outer air supply should not be necessary. However, if such arrangements are made, they should be limited.

The proper equivalent of moisture should be given to the air at the temperature at which it reaches the room. It may be said that there is a water-pan connected with every furnace, that will do everything necessary in supplying moisture. This is a mistake. So far as I know, the furnace or other heating apparatus for dwellings has not been constructed which is provided with a proper evaporating apparatus. The pan is set in the side of the furnace, with an opening to the outside into which water may be poured. It is small, and has very little evaporating surface on the inside. Oftentimes the joints at the outside are so poorly made that the cold air from the cellar may be drawn in over the water in the pan, and in that way prevent its proper evaporation. Winter air heated to a summer temperature is dry and parched, whereas natural summer air contains the proper amount of moisture. The outer air during the winter time has its proper equivalent of moisture for the winter temperature, which is a much smaller amount than would belong to it at a higher temperature. Therefore when we take winter air into the furnace or other heating apparatus, raise it to a summer temperature, and carry it into a room, we have a very dry air, which seeks its equivalent of moisture from the occupants of the room, from the furniture, carpets, walls, ceiling, and everything in it. The air will not take additional moisture unless that moisture be supplied after it has reached a higher temperature.  For instance, if a spray or a series of wet blankets be arranged in the cold-air duct, before the air gets to the furnace, the air will not take the moisture from that spray or from the damp blankets.  The moisture must be supplied after the air is heated.  Where the water-pan is set on the side of the furnace, and where there is a supply of air through the pan from the cellar, as there frequently is, evaporation is naturally retarded by the cold air, as indicated.  Again, if this pan be never so well protected, it is small, the proper amount of evaporating surface is not presented.  An evaporating pan or other device should be placed above the fire-pot and should occupy a large proportion of the area of the heating chamber.  The supply of water should not be dependent upon some one's attention.  It should be constant by means of a ball-cock or otherwise.  It should run into or drip into a shallow pan, or should be supplied to sheets of felt or blanket so that the air will come in contact with the moist surfaces, at the temperature at which it is to go into the room.  Thus it has the proper amount of moisture which belongs to it at that temperature.  In this way we have winter air from the outside going into the room at a summer temperature and with a summer equivalent of moisture; that is, we have summer air in the winter time.  People sometimes undertake to get around this by putting water-pans in the registers, but they are rarely ample.  They are neglected, or they interfere with the supply of warm air, and are abandoned.

Where a furnace is already in a house, or where it is not possible to make elaborate arrangements for providing the air with moisture, there is a very simple makeshift which is quite effective.  It consists in suspending in the registers in the floor small water receptacles — a quart bucket answers every purpose — in which is placed a broad strip of linen.  This cloth should go to the bottom of the receptacle and be long enough to hang over and below it for several inches. When the bucket is filled with water this piece of cloth acts as a siphon, and carries the water, a drop at a time, into the furnace-pipe, where it is converted into steam. A piece of old table-linen is the best material to use, for the reason that it carries the water fast enough, that the heat from the furnace does not dry it out before it can drop into the pipe; otherwise the cloth becomes dry at the end, and the siphonage ceases. For the same reason it should be broad, — about twelve inches. Where a moderate heat is carried through the furnace-pipe, three quarts of water may be evaporated in this way in twenty-four hours from each bucket. A bucket of the size mentioned does not in any way interfere with the passage of heat.

The next point for consideration is the means of getting the foul, contaminated air to the outside. One way is through the use of grates. Another is by means of ducts in the wall, opening near the floor, which draw the foul air from the room to the outside. These should consist of heated flues, with connecting registers in the ceiling and floor, which may be open when necessary. Under any circumstances, the grate is best. Sometimes the flue may be heated by a supply of warm air from the furnace, or by a steam-pipe in case steam is used for heating the house. In natural-gas regions, the supply of additional heat in a flue from a furnace or by a jet would be a small matter.

We have mentioned heating by stoves, grates, and furnaces. The same principles which apply to the furnishing of fresh air to a furnace may be applied to a stove. The fact is, they never have been. A stove should be made, and will be made some day, that is surrounded on the outside by a second jacket, the space between being connected with the outer air by means of a tin tube to the under side of the stove. The supply of cold air could be so arranged as to be shut off when there was no heat in the stove. The warm air would pass out at the top of the jacket. On top of the stove could be placed an evaporating pan, and the supply of moisture come therefrom. In connection with the stove-pipe, which should be jacketed, a second ventilating flue, starting from the floor and having an opening both above and below, could be arranged, and in that way the supply of fresh air and withdrawal of impure air could be accomplished.

Next we may speak of steam and hot-water heating. So far as a change of air and the ventilation of the room are concerned, heating by direct radiation, that is, by radiators placed in the room, is no better than stove heating. It may be that the air is not so severely parched by the extreme heat, also the escape of steam may contribute somewhat to the moisture of the air; but the escape of steam is not agreeable, and is not allowed to exist to any great extent; — its odor is not always pleasant. Certainly the addition of moisture to the air by this means would be a mere makeshift and unsatisfactory.

Hot-water coils act the same as steam radiators in that they heat the same air over and over again, and are no better than stoves, so far as the provision for fresh air, at proper temperature and humidity, is concerned.

A steam or hot-water apparatus, with indirect radiation, is superior to furnace heat as ordinarily provided. The means of supplying moisture to an indirect steam apparatus, as ordinarily constructed, are not convenient. There is a radiator for each hot-air connection above, that is, a radiator for each register, with a distinct and direct supply of outer air thereto. Sometimes there are two registers connecting with a single radiator. But under any circumstances the radiators are somewhat separated, having steam or water connection with the boiler at the proper point. Steam apparatus for public buildings has been constructed where the radiators have been bunched, that is, put into a single chamber, the air passing through the chamber containing the radiators, where it is heated to the proper temperature, and the moisture afterwards supplied before it enters the room. Where this arrangement is used, there must be conductors, tin or otherwise, from the chamber to the register, as in the case of a furnace. Again, it will be found that the supply of air will not be uniform through all of the openings; for instance, the register that is farthest removed from the warm-air chamber may fail to act. In this event, auxiliary radiators may be placed under that register, and the operation of the heating apparatus greatly facilitated thereby. This plan is superior to a furnace, and can be applied to hot-water or steam apparatus in dwellings. The reason that it is superior to a furnace is that the supply of heat is more uniform. It does not require the constant firing or attention that is necessary in the case of a hot-air furnace. It may be known that the temperature does not change with the pressure of steam or in the same proportion.

There are inexpensive automatic arrangements in connection with furnaces and steam apparatus, which control the dampers and keep the steam pressure measurably uniform, as long as there is fuel of sufficient quantity in the fire-pot. The hot-water apparatus is more uniform in its operation than steam, and for that reason more satisfactory.

A furnace plant is the most inexpensive apparatus that may be used for general heating ; the steam apparatus is next higher as to first cost, though no more expensive in amount of fuel used. The hot-water apparatus costs more than steam, and is somewhat more economical in the cost of maintenance. It is probable that a house of moderate size can be warmed all over at a less cost, as far as fuel is concerned, by a furnace or a steam or hot-water heating apparatus than by stoves and grates. However, grates are generally used in addition to these for the purpose of comfort and appearance, and for ventilating. Under such circumstances, they consume very little fuel.

## CHAPTER XII.

HEATING DEVICES AS WE FIND THEM. — FURNACE ESTIMATES. — COMBINATION HOT AIR AND HOT WATER. — DISH-WARMING ARRANGEMENTS. — HOW TO GET A GOOD HEATING APPARATUS.

FOR the present, people who build must take things as they find them, and use heating and ventilating apparatus as regularly manufactured. Experiments are uncertain. The theory of the proper heating and ventilating of a house as set forth in previous chapter is correct. The fulfilment of the ideas in dwelling-house heating remains to be practically worked out. It is not the business of the architect, or the housewife, or the owner of the house, to work out these mechanical details. It will be done in time by competent mechanical experts.

In the estimates subsequently given, the furnace is the only means considered for general heating. However, this does not indicate a prejudice in favor of that particular method. The furnace is considered and figured upon as the ordinary method of heating houses of moderate cost. It is the least expensive plant to be used for general heating. Indirect radiation from hot water or steam is to be preferred to a furnace. A combination of a hot-air furnace with hot water, or steam, is used with fair success. In this case, a hot-water coil is placed in an ordinary furnace, which connects with hot-water radiators in a conservatory or other room for the purpose of contributing a uniform degree of heat to that room. The water supply is a tank, located well above the level of the radiators, and connecting through an inlet pipe with the coil in the furnace. The proper means of supplying this tank with water is through a ball-cock or float-cock, the float of which opens the valve when the water gets low in the tank. Thus the supply is as constant as the source. A hot-water radiator of this kind may be used in connection with a device for warming dishes or keeping food warm. The heat is gentle, uniform, and constant. This is a general advantage of all hot-water heating.

Aside from the automatic arrangements for controlling the steam or water pressure in the heating apparatus, and thus measurably controlling the temperature in the building, other more positive automatic arrangements are provided which undertake to maintain any fixed temperature. These are proprietary devices, patented and advertised.

Complaints are made of the general inefficiency of everything under the sun: hence, furnaces and other heating apparatus come in for their share. An architect is sometimes asked how he would heat a certain building. He answers, "Hot water, steam, or furnace." — "Oh, I wouldn't have steam. My uncle had a steam plant in his house, and they nearly froze to death all last winter; and they burned over a ton of coal a week." The same things are said, and truly, of every kind of heating apparatus made, when we consider them in general classes. General complaints of a similar nature are made of everything. In regard to the steam plant or hot-water apparatus, or anything else of which this thing may have been said, one may first acknowledge its truthfulness, and then consider what it all means. Something is at fault. It may be that the whole design of the apparatus is faulty. The design may be right, and the construction bad. Everything else may be right, but the apparatus too small; or there may be some little defect which has to do with the placing of the apparatus in the house. Sometimes, when everything is in good form, the apparatus does not receive proper attention: hence trouble.

It may be asked how one is to get a good heating apparatus for a dwelling-house. The first thing to be determined is, the particular kind to be used: whether hot-water, steam, or hot-air furnace. There are many manufacturers of the various apparatus, who are regularly in the business. To these may be submitted plans of the building, and a request for estimates and suggestions. It is the experience of an architect that one who is putting money regularly in the manufacture or production of anything will not waste his energies for a great length of time on a bad thing, if he knows it. The evidence that an establishment has been putting up good furnaces or other heating apparatus is long-continued business success. If the owner of a house writes to an old-established, wealthy concern, and sends his plans, he is as certain to get a reliable proposition as he can be of anything. A local agent of an establishment of this kind may misrepresent, unintentionally or otherwise. The surest way is to go to headquarters. The local agent does not always know exactly what should be done. A competent architect can settle all these matters for an owner. However, if an architect says there are only one or two furnaces or heating apparatus which are all right, he is either ignorant or dishonest. There are many different kinds which will give fair satisfaction.

The idea in this chapter is to take things as we find them, and suggest what may be done. The theories outlined in the previous chapter may be correct, but they do not amount to anything to a man who is building to-day. The only purpose of this chapter is to suggest to those who are building that they go to a first-class house, pay a fair price, and get the best possible apparatus regularly in the market.

# CHAPTER XIII.

THE HOUSE AND ITS BEAUTY. — ARTISTIC SURROUNDINGS. — BEAUTY MORE A MATTER OF INTELLIGENCE THAN MONEY. — VESTIBULE DECORATIONS. — BEAUTY IN THE RECEPTION-HALL. — MANTELS AND GRATES. — FRET-WORK AND PORTIÈRES. — SPINDLE WORK. — SIMPLE FORMS OF GOOD DECORATION. — WOOD-CARVING. — DOOR AND WINDOW CASINGS. — A CONSERVATORY. — STAINED GLASS. — A CABINET ON THE MANTEL. — TINTED PLASTERING. — FRESCOING. — SAFETY IN THE SELECTION OF COLORS. — AN ATTRACTIVE SITTING-ROOM. — THE PARLOR. — A RECEPTION-ROOM. — PARLOR HISTORY. — THE IDEAL PARLOR. — THE LIBRARY. — A PLACE OF QUIET AND REST. — LIBRARY FURNISHINGS. — THE DINING-ROOM. — SOCIAL RELATIONS OF THE DINING-ROOM. — DINING-ROOM DECORATIONS. — CONSERVATORY AND DINING-ROOM. — A WOOD CEILING. — BEAUTY IN BEDROOMS. — QUIET AND LIGHT.

THE journey through the house is hardly complete until we abandon the material view, and consider it from the standpoint of beauty. As is said in another connection, the architect does not do his full duty in making a house a model of convenience and utility. The housekeeper always looks toward a beautiful home, something that will be recognized for its beauty and elegance. A house that is beautiful and attractive gives pleasure to all who see it, as well as to the occupants. A beautiful, artistic house is a source of education to the occupants. A porch with clumsy columns, rude mouldings, heavy ceiling, coarse details of all kinds, cannot but affect one's living. One that is fine in detail, generous in size, decorated in artistic spirit, must of necessity not alone contribute to the comfort of those who live in the house, but serve to lift them from that which is common and ordinary. People may be surrounded by that which is beautiful and artistic, and for a time fail to realize its true excellence, or they may be surrounded with that which is homely and crude without knowing the full measure of its ugliness. The time must come, however, when the truth will be realized to a certain extent. If it is in the direction of the appreciation of what is beautiful, it must necessarily bring about a higher state of mind. No man can walk across a front porch, time after time, and take hold of a beautiful door, without being affected by it. For this reason the vestibule, the front door, and all that belongs to it, should be designed in a thoughtful spirit, with the idea that it is the first of all things that will impress those who enter the house. There may not be much money to put into this door, but what there is may as well bring something beautiful as something ugly. The same money that will make an ugly detail will make a beautiful, artistic one. If the glass of this door must be inexpensive, let it be the ordinary cathedral glass. Instead of being brilliant in color, select a soft, mild tint, — a light amber or a straw color. If there are divisions in the door so that a number of sheets may be used, two tints at most are all that are necessary. It is best that they should be quiet in tone. If money is more abundant, and an elaborate stained-glass design may be had, put the work in the hands of an artist, one who is well known, and the result cannot but be satisfactory. As to the door itself, nothing can be nicer than natural wood, properly finished. The detail of the design should be refined; there should be an avoidance of all that is clumsy and heavy. The spirit of the interior may be stamped upon this door. Where one cannot encompass the expense of an artistically designed glass for the door or vestibule opening, a very pretty effect may be secured by the use of a plain sheet of plate-glass; or, if desired, a slight additional expense will give glass with bevelled edges. Sometimes this bevelled glass is in small squares, with leaded joints. This gives a very simple and rich effect from either side.

As one opens this door and steps into the vestibule, there may come to his sight a beautiful mantel and grate-fire in the reception-hall beyond. This is particularly beautiful when shown through the folds of a tapestry curtain which separates the vestibule from the reception-hall. Sometimes this vestibule is arranged so that there is a small window at one side of it. Nothing can be nicer than to have this filled with glass, of the same general design as that of the door. The hooks for wraps should be of polished brass, secured to a natural-wood strip. An umbrella-stand of the same material is attractive. The floor is best of hard wood, all but covered with a heavy rug. This is a pleasant place to stop a moment, with a more beautiful view beyond.

A reception-hall is, from an architectural standpoint, the easiest room in the house to handle; that is, it can easily be made to look well. This is because of its connection with the vestibule, the stairway, the grate, often a window-seat, the large openings into the other rooms, and the portières which go with them. All these things combine well to make a pretty room. Stairways, as now designed, are much more beautiful than those made a few years ago. Then it was a habit to start at one end of the hall and continue to the second floor in a single run, with winders only at the upper end, to change the direction of the movement. Now it is common to have at least two landings in each run; oftentimes there will be only two or three steps, then a landing, from which steps lead to another near the top. At the beginning of the stairway there are the newel posts, and at each landing a corner post. This arrangement frequently admits of the placing of a seat along one side the outer part of the lower landing. If not that, possibly one along the side of the stairway, below the run of steps which starts from the lower landing. The space between the railing and the steps is usually occupied by turned balusters, though there are many forms of filling and decorating this space. Sometimes it is of turned spindle-work, scroll-work, fret-work, and squares or panels, arranged in different forms.

It is not unusual to have stained-glass windows at each landing. These windows are not necessarily large, and are usually hung on hinges. Sometimes a small bay-window projection is made from one or both of these landings. In them may be placed seats, and in this way add beauty and convenience to the room. It is quite usual to cover the reception-hall with rugs rather than carpets. The hard-wood floor idea probably had its origin in the reception-hall. If it ever takes its departure it will be first from this room. If a hard-wood floor is not largely covered with rugs it requires a great deal of labor.

The mantel in the reception-hall should be of wood. It is pleasant to have the larger part of the entire setting made of tile. These tiles are now made in most beautiful designs and colorings. Beautiful figured designs may be had, if not for the entire facing, for certain parts. It is not uncommon that only a narrow margin of wood-work borders the sides of a mantel of this kind. The shelf and cabinet above may be as ornamental as desired. No treatment of wood-work can add to the beauty of a large surface of tile facing. In some instances, no shelf is provided; simply a bevelled facing, with a margin of wood-work, not over an inch wide, to cover the joint where the tiling comes in contact with the plaster. The hearth should be large. The grate border is best of brass.

The walls of the reception-hall may have a gray plaster finish, or be tinted or papered, as desired. The picture moulding may come pretty well down from the ceiling; certainly not higher than the tops of the doors. The part below may be tinted in one color, and the upper, in another. The picture moulding should always be of the same kind of wood as the finish, and not gilded or treated in any other highly artificial manner.

The openings into other rooms, even where sliding or hinged doors are used, are frequently filled a short distance from their top with what is popularly called fret-work. It may be fret-work, pure and simple, or spindle-work, or simply scroll-work. It is a very pleasing form of ornamentation. The curtains come below. In one of the plans furnished, the entire vestibule is made up of turned work, which, with a curtain, is the only separation from the main hall. Sometimes arches are decorated in the same manner, and the space between the circle and frame is filled with these ornamental forms. A very simple way of making screens is by the use of thin quartered oak-strips, woven into basket patterns of ornamental form.

Only one general design of door and window casings is shown in this book. There is no limit to the ornamental forms which may be used in decorating casings of any kind. During recent years, many ladies have used their energy and ability in the direction of wood-carving, and, under competent instruction, have done good work. For the most part, the patterns are in low relief. The designs are frequently conventionalized, foliated patterns. In the smaller communities it is hardly possible to get good carving through ordinary channels, for the reason that there is not a sufficient amount of this kind of work to be done to justify a high grade of talent in occupying so unprofitable a field. It is unfortunately true, however, that very few workmen who can carve at all, but have an idea that they do this kind of work exceedingly well. No matter how crude their efforts may be, there is no lack of self-appreciation. They profess to be able to do that of which they are entirely ignorant. It is best to be content with the simple mechanical forms of interior wood-decoration, unless there are those of known and recognized ability, who are capable of executing the more artistic patterns.

Door and window casings are made much narrower and less complex than was the custom several years ago.

The sitting-room of the lower floor is more clearly defined by the term "living-room." It is a room with much more wall space than the reception-hall. It usually contains a grate and mantel; has a large window to the front, and one on the side. It is very nice if one of these windows can be arranged in the form of a bay, with or without a window-seat. In the latter case, it may serve the purpose of a conservatory in the winter and a window-seat in summer. The use of large quantities of stained glass in a sitting-room is objectionable. It is very well to have a certain amount of it in the upper sash of some of the windows. If the colors are mild, the effect upon the atmosphere of the room is pleasant indeed — the light coming through the soft amber or straw tints adds a mellowness and richness to the light of the room, which is opposed to the colder effects of light which comes through white glass. The mantel of the sitting-room may contain a large number of compartments in the form of small shelves, brackets, or cabinets, in which may be placed bric-à-brac of various forms. A little cabinet on each side of a mantel, with a high door, is a very pretty feature. A mirror between these cabinets gives a pleasing effect. This mantel, like the one in the reception-room, should be of wood with tile hearth and facings.

If this room is plastered in a gray finish, the walls may be tinted in fresco colors, and, if desired, certain parts of it ornamented by stencilling or otherwise. Unless this ornamental work is done by an artist of recognized ability, it should be of the simplest character. One or two simple lines, or a series of short dashes, is much better than scrawling figures drawn by an untrained hand. The ordinary fresco done by the foreign artist is the ugliest, most ungraceful work possible. In the larger cities, there are usually a few artists who do very beautiful work, but the ordinary, cheap, conventional fresco stuff is barbarous. Plain tinted walls are preferable to such glaring monstrosities. There is not much risk, if one is careful in the selection of colors; the part above the picture moulding may be tinted differently from that below. There are very few people but feel themselves competent to select colors for the interior or exterior of a house. The fact is, there are very few who can do it with any assurance of success. It is well for those who have no special training in this line to pursue a safe plan in the selection of tints for the walls and ceilings. This may be done by choosing different shades of the same color for use in the room. Say one begins with a terra-cotta body for the part below the picture mould. That above the moulding may be a lighter terra-cotta with a tendency to a buff. Then the ceiling may be lighter still, or, to be entirely safe under almost any circumstances, a gray with a leaning towards the color of the wall. Other colors may be selected in the same way. Very light, vivid blues have frequently been selected for ceilings, presumably because of the supposed resemblance to the sky. It is certainly an illogical but by no means uncommon thought. Soft, undecided grays are much pleasanter to those of quiet tastes. There may be variations in it according to the character of the wall decorations and surroundings. If one without special knowledge wishes something more ambitious, he should consult some one of acknowledged ability in this particular line. One cannot afford to try experiments. Extremely beautiful wall decorations are to be had in wall-paperings, and, while rather expensive, are entirely satisfactory if carefully selected.

Very little more may be said about the sitting-room, excepting to call to mind that a great deal depends upon the fittings and furnishings of the room, which, however, should not be glaring or rich. The quality of everything may be of the finest and best, yet this room should essentially be quieter in tone than the reception-hall or parlor, or even dining-room, which are not in constant use. Anything which is rich and in any way approaches the gorgeous is wearisome, and directly opposed to the idea of a sitting-room.

The parlor may be merely a reception-room, — a room where a lady may receive her callers in the afternoon, or the more formal calls of ladies and gentlemen in the evening, or it may be one room in addition to the others in the lower part of the house. It may be the room which adds capacity to the lower floor during times of general entertaining. In some cases, particularly where the parlor is merely used as a reception-room, it need not be large. In such a case it is merely a place separated from the sitting-room, and in which to go for the purpose of receiving friends in a room somewhat removed from the slight confusion which may legitimately belong to a sitting-room. The parlor is made distinctive in its appearance from the sitting-room by its furnishings. It is not usual to have any great difference in the design of the woodwork in the different rooms of the lower floor. Generally speaking, the doors are of the same design, and likewise the casings, base, etc. The parlor belongs particularly to the society life of the occupants of the house. It is not generally a family room. It is removed from the ordinary home life except in so far as the general social conditions draw all together. The parlor, in its connection with the living-rooms of the house, and the house itself, is entirely legitimate. There is a good deal of sneering at the old parlor idea. This feeling has its origin in the memory of the parlors of a few years ago, — those which contained the one Brussels carpet, covered with red and green flowers, furnished with black hair-cloth furniture, chairs arranged around the wall in military style, a sofa — stiff of back and commanding an attitude — in a most conspicuous position ; walls covered with coarse-figured, gilt paper, and rendered more offensive by cheap, family portraits in oil, and elaborately framed chromos.

The parlor of to-day is still a formal room ; it does not greatly differ from the older one in idea; it is the execution of the idea which has changed. There is a greater refinement in all the details ; there is an artistic spirit which pervades everything. There is harmony of color, quietness in tone. The pictures are of a different character. The furniture is graceful and comfortable. It is rarely separated from the other part of the house. The doors leading into it are nearly always open. Oftentimes there are only portières of tapestry or lace to separate this room from the others which lead to it. It is a room which is made necessary by the social life of the time.

The ideal parlor is a long room, — a large room. It is long

in proportion to its width. Sometimes there is an archway near the middle, which suggests the division of the room into two parts. There is a mirror at the end, and, lending dignity to the room, there is the hall or library at one side. By its size, its arrangement, its dignity, it is inspiring to a congenial company. This is the ideal parlor, and the one of which the vulgarly furnished parlor of a few years ago was a corruption. The ideal parlor is shown in its completest original form in some of the old mansions of the East and South. Some of the old Virginia and Maryland houses carry out this idea in the completest way. In Natchez, Miss., are houses built long before the war, and designed by the French architects, which contain parlors of splendid proportions and most artistic details. These were designed in the purest classic architecture. The ceilings were high, the paintings rich. All this is somewhat removed from the common idea of a parlor as carried out at this time. However, it is a pleasant thing to look back upon, or, when the opportunity and means are at hand, a proper thing to enjoy in the reality.

The library, as now understood, is, in the ordinary house, a room for books, papers, and magazines, in which the members of the family may gather, who have use for that which it contains. It should be a room which may be isolated from the other parts of the house; a room in which one may study or read or write, and have the quiet which belongs to such occupations. A room which may be used as a passage from one part of the house to another cannot be dignified by the name of library. In such a room there must be quiet. There are very few homes to which such a room would not be a material and practical addition. There are times when nearly every one desires the quiet and freedom from interruption which a room of this kind affords.

It need not be a large room, but should contain all of the paraphernalia of work: a desk, conveniently arranged, book-shelves which are readily accessible, possibly portfolios arranged along the walls, drawers with proper compartments, cases for circulars and catalogues, and other "places for things." The nicest thing about book-cases is the books. Ornamental glass doors and rich trappings add nothing to the beauty of the library. People who make large use of books do not care to have them protected by glass cases. The other furnishings and fittings of a library should be quiet in tone, the chairs easy but not rich, the carpet of a neutral color, the wall decorations preferably without figured outlines, the pictures small and quiet. Sliding doors between the library and any other room of the house are not to be considered. Close-fitting doors on hinges are proper. They exclude the sound. Sliding doors permit the ready passage of sound, for the reason that they are more or less open at top, bottom, middle, and sides. A low ceiling in a library adds to the quiet and restful effect. One may have a low ceiling in a library, even if they are higher in other rooms, by studding down from above, — that is, putting in a false ceiling. The expense is light indeed, and by such means additional protection from the sounds above may be afforded.

The dining-room, in many houses, is the room in which the entire family is gathered, perhaps for the only time during the day. In this sense it is an assembly room. There is in this busy country a growing respect for the social value of the dining-room. In the family meetings at the table, there may be an interchange of experiences that does not occur at other times, for the reason that there is no opportunity for it. After the meals the members of the family go to their various occupations, and probably do not come together until another meal.

These facts may be considered in the planning of a dining-room.

We have thought of this room before in its mechanical sense; we have looked at it through housekeeping eyes. We have now to consider its artistic and social features. We look at it as one of the family rooms. It has its shape or proportion suggested to it from the table. It is oblong. The light coming into it should be ample, but subdued in tone. It is pleasant, as one enters a dining-room, to come into full view of a sideboard which is decorated with that which belongs to this room in a utilitarian way — its china, cut glass, and beautiful linen, than which nothing can be more attractive.

It is a pleasant thing to have a conservatory attached to one side or at a corner of the dining-room. The odor of flowers or plants may not be agreeable constantly in a sitting-room. The periodical occupation of the dining-room makes this pleasant rather than otherwise. Most of the plans which are shown will admit of the placing of a conservatory in connection with the dining-room in the manner indicated.

The old English dining-room was large in its general proportions, and heavy and rich as to its details; it was so large and impressive that there was an offshoot which took form in a breakfast-room. In our homes at this time we have the compromise. Our habits of living do not demand the breakfast-room: all come to breakfast together, and the requirement is the same as for other meals.

Where one wishes to have a wood ceiling panelled or with decorated beams, the dining-room, or the hall connecting with it, may be chosen as the proper place to be treated in this way. Where expense is not a great object, it is agreeable to have a large part of the walls finished in wood. A wood finish

one-half to two-thirds the height of the wall, and a ceiling of
wood above, with the intervening space finished in rough, tinted
plaster, gives a very pleasing effect. Projecting from the top
of the wood wall-finish may be a little shelf extending, say, five
inches beyond the wall. It may have a simple moulded edge.
In the top may be cut grooves; on the under edge may be
arranged, at regular intervals, cup hooks, which may be used in
part for suspending china, or, upon certain occasions, as a means
of securing floral decorations — say, a little train of ivy or smilax.
On the upper part of the shelf are placed pieces of china.
This shelf may be placed in any dining-room; if not around the
entire room, between two windows, or between the chimney
breast and the adjacent wall. Six feet from the floor is a good
height. If it is not overloaded, or if the idea is not generally
overworked, the effect will be very satisfactory.

The coloring of a dining-room may be a little heavier and
richer than that of the other rooms. A very pretty feature
which may be introduced in a room of this kind is a china-closet,
which opens into the dining-room as well as into the china-room
adjoining. The dining-room side of the china-closet should be
glazed with clear glass above its lower section, and the china-
room or back side of the china-closet should be glazed with cathedral glass of a semi-transparent character. There are doors on
hinges on each side. The drawers in the lower part, if provided,
open from both sides. If doors are used they should be
arranged in the same way, so that the lower shelves may be
approached from both dining-room and china-room. The glass
door on the dining-room side should not come down to the
shelf at the top of the lower section, but should be arranged to
leave an open space, as is indicated in the chapter on kitchens
and pantries. However, the doors on the china-room side of

this closet should come down, so as to cut off communication between dining-room and china-room at will. This space between the upper and lower section of the china-closet gives space in which to set a tray, and, by opening a door on the back, it acts as a slide between the china-room and dining-room. This arrangement is not only very beautiful, but very useful. See china-closet plan Fig. 5, page 46.

The conservatory mentioned does not need to be in conventional conservatory form, which usually has cheap glazing and often common wood-work, but may be a bay-window with more than an ordinary amount of glass, preferably plate.

The chambers and bedrooms, in their ideal form of arrangement, have an abundance of light and sun, ample means for ventilation, and a greater air of restfulness and airiness than the rooms below. The carpets are in lighter tints, the walls more nearly white, the windows not so heavily draped, the pictures and frames of a lighter character, the chairs not so heavy as those of the other rooms. From a chamber it is sometimes desirable to have a bay window projecting from side or front. It adds to the availability of the other floor space, affords additional light and ventilation. Nothing can be nicer than a grate fire in a bedroom. It should be surrounded with a wood mantel, with tile facing and hearth. Above the mantel it is useful to have a short plate-glass mirror. A dressing-case takes its proper place on the side wall between two windows, or in a corner with a window in each wall adjacent to it. Bedrooms are, for the most part, lighted with brackets rather than central lights. When attainable, a small dressing-room adds to the attractiveness of a chamber.

In some houses there may be an alcove, a bay window, a window-seat, a conservatory, or something of this kind, from every principal room. These are features which add to the beauty and attractiveness of the house. While all of these things are not possible in every home, some one or two of them may be attainable. In mentioning the various details which go to make the beauty of a house, it is in mind that all these features can be taken into account in but a very small proportion of all the houses that are built, yet some one or more of them may be used in every house, and thereby add to its attractiveness.

## CHAPTER XIV.

EXTERNAL AND INTERNAL DESIGN. — AN OLD TOPIC BEFORE THE PEOPLE. — THE ARCHITECTURAL STUDENT'S DREAM. — A BEAUTIFUL HOME THE HOUSEKEEPER'S AMBITION. — IT COSTS NO MORE TO HAVE A HOUSE BEAUTIFUL THAN UGLY. — ARCHITECTURAL EDUCATION. — CHARLES EASTLAKE'S BOOK. — VULGAR ARCHITECTURAL REVIVALS. — THE GROWTH OF THE ARTISTIC IDEA. — BEAUTY A MATTER OF REFINEMENT.

IT often happens when one gives especial attention to a particular branch of a subject his neglect in other lines is measured by the depth of his attention to the particular branch. Matters which have to do with the utilitarian features of house-building are considered in this work much more fully in the text, than has the appearance of the buildings. It is desired that this fact will not lead any one to believe that matters relating to the appearance of the exterior have been neglected. Domestic architecture is an old topic before the people. It is old in what has been said in regard to the appearance of the buildings. The subject, as a science to the architect, is new when considered from the standpoint of convenience. The architectural student's dream is not of kitchens, pantries, closets, convenient and economical arrangements of floor space, but is principally of large public buildings, libraries, court-houses, and cathedrals. When he descends to dwelling-houses, it is of something unique, or odd, — something that is pretty or rich. When it relates to details, it is hallways that are peculiar in their beauty, parlors and sitting-rooms that are full of odd conceits. There has been a tendency toward strange things during recent years. Matters of this kind have fed the fancy of many architects. The housekeeper has been neglected.

Nothing attracts more attention than a beautiful house. It is a pleasure to every one. It is as important to have a house beautiful as it is that it should be convenient. The same education and thoughtfulness that will enable an architect to design a convenient house will make it beautiful. No one can be conscientious in the consideration of the comfort of the housekeeper and neglect the smallest detail leading to the beauty of the house. The housekeeper lives in the hope of having a beautiful home. It has been the purpose, in writing this book, to bear all this in mind, and to add the element of convenience to what has been said and done by others toward making beautiful houses.

It costs no more to have a house beautiful than to have it ugly. Beauty, like convenience, is largely a matter of thoughtfulness and education. The only excuse for ugliness in house-building is ignorance. The student of architecture has had a great deal done for him. And, in considering that which has to do with appearance, he has only to accept the advantages of the best architectural schools and offices. Without these he cannot expect to succeed. To be a designer of beautiful houses, one must have had the same special training and advantages that are necessary for success in other lines of professional work. A physician must know the history of his profession, aside from the more formal knowledge which leads him through his practice. It is the same way with the student of architecture. The successful designer of a small cottage will do better from having a knowledge of the history of early architecture. Such a knowledge is indispensable, in order to reach the best results. One who has made a study of Greek architecture is much better equipped to design a beautiful low-cost cottage, of four or five rooms, than one who has not availed himself of these advantages. He will make a better house for the same money. He will do better work with simpler means. To take another illustration : We may suppose that an architect has a porch to design, and that the owner of the house does not have a great deal of money to put in it. There are four turned columns, a cornice, with a rafter finish, and underneath, a space in which may be inserted a small band of inexpensive scroll-work. A knowledge of the earlier architecture comes to his assistance in a wonderful way. For the turning on the columns the architect may select that from a column of the early English Gothic architecture of the fourteenth century. These are simple profiles, which can be turned at no greater cost, if the drawing is furnished, than some crude, modern invention of the turner or an uneducated designer. For the jig or scroll saw work, he can arrange figures from some of the earlier ornamental forms of the same period, and by drawing them full size the scroll-sawyer can reproduce a beautiful design, which has a history, with no more labor than he would give some corrupted design which has filtered through the minds of careless housebuilders. For his rafter feet, this designer will have no difficulty in recalling some simple form which has had a refined development. This same line of procedure can be followed in all details of house-building, and not add one dollar to the cost of the structure. At the same time it brings about most beautiful results, — the results of successful experience.

It may be said again that it takes no more money to make a beautiful detail — one which has been the development of experience and refinement — than it does something which is clumsy and coarse. It requires, however, a knowledge of what has been done, — a knowledge of the history of design. It requires the faculty of using intelligently the results of the past, not merely as they originally existed, but in their adaptation to the wants and conditions of the present.

Several years ago Mr. Charles Eastlake wrote a book entitled "Hints on Household Taste." The book accomplished a great deal, by merely leading people to think. To this day there are a great many architectural features which, in the builder's parlance, go under the name of "Eastlake" designs. There are so-called Eastlake doors, Eastlake frames, etc. In truth, Mr. Eastlake had little to say about architecture in a distinctive sense, and many evil things have been perpetrated in his name. The best thing that Mr. Eastlake did was to teach people that the furniture and other things which they had around them could be beautiful and not expensive. That it was not necessary to have a chair or a piece of wood-work loaded down with something called ornament, in order to be beautiful. After this people lost confidence in the furniture manufacturer, and did not depend solely on the price of his wares as a measure of their elegance or attractiveness. This was the sole work of Charles Eastlake, with the masses of the people. He was a missionary in his way. A man of no particular knowledge in regard to architecture or design, yet one who was the means of doing a great deal for architecture. He taught people to look for beauty in simple things.

After a time came a certain something in domestic architecture which was designated as the "Queen-Anne" style. We all know what it is, yet it is difficult to describe. The veritable Queen-Anne architecture meant something; the "Queen-Anne" architecture of a few years ago meant anything — particularly something that was pointed, erratic, and unusual. It, however, did a good work. It enabled the architects to get out of the old beaten paths. A great many beautiful houses were built, which, by the public, were said to be in this style. The name "Queen Anne" was the vehicle for the passage from an old conservatism, which had to do only with the commonplace, to something which was fresh and attractive. In this way a great many beautiful houses were built during this so-called Queen-Anne revival.

More recently there has been a movement toward the revival of the old colonial architecture — a style that was developed by a class of educated builders among the earlier settlers of this country. Their knowledge was particularly of classic architecture of the period of the Italian renaissance. A great many strange and unusual things are being perpetrated in the name of old colonial architecture at this time. At the same time, a great deal that is beautiful and refined is being built in this style. In the work of the very recent period which has to do with this architecture, one may find a great deal of encouragement. It shows a decided re-action from the extravagant crudeness of the so-called Queen-Anne architecture, and in the end we will reach something that is rational and beautiful.

Thus it is to be seen that, in whatever lines architecture is moving, we shall find good work; that it is not so much the style that it is named, as the resources of the designer: resources which have to do with his education, and his disposition to select that which is fine and beautiful — the sense which leads him to discriminate.

FIGURE B.

# PLANS OF FIFTY CONVENIENT HOUSES.

## CHAPTER XV.

EVOLUTION OF A HOUSE-PLAN. — RESPECTABLE DIMENSIONS FOR A MODERATE PRICE. — SIX PLANS. — COSTS, FROM $1,500 TO $2,600.

THE number of times that a house has been built indicates the popularity of the plan. Plan No. 1, in one form or another, has been used oftener than any other in the book. Plans Nos. 1, 2, and 3 are more frequently selected by people who do not keep a servant. This arrangement makes a compact and low-cost house. There is a porch over which the small front bedroom extends on the second story. In Plan No. 1 the hall is seven and one-half by ten feet. There is a corner grate for the living-room and the parlor. A stove might be used in the dining-room in a way to moderate the temperature of the entire lower floor.

There is one very large window opening into the dining-room. It is a very pleasing thing to have the upper sash of the dining-room glazed with simple colors of cathedral glass. This glass gives a very pleasant tone to the light of the room, and, at the same time, excludes the hot rays of the sun in summer. It is possible to dispense with outside shutters when cathedral glass is used in the upper sashes. A metal rod running across the window on the inside, on a level with the horizontal dividing-rail of the window, may be made to carry curtains which will exclude the view from the outside. Thus, in the glass, and by the aid of the curtains, we have much that might be expected from the shutters.

There is a china-pantry between the kitchen and dining-room. It is lighted by a small window at one side. It serves as a passageway between these two rooms, and thus keeps the odor of the cooking from the front part of the house. The pastry pantry is immediately back of the china-pantry, and is entered

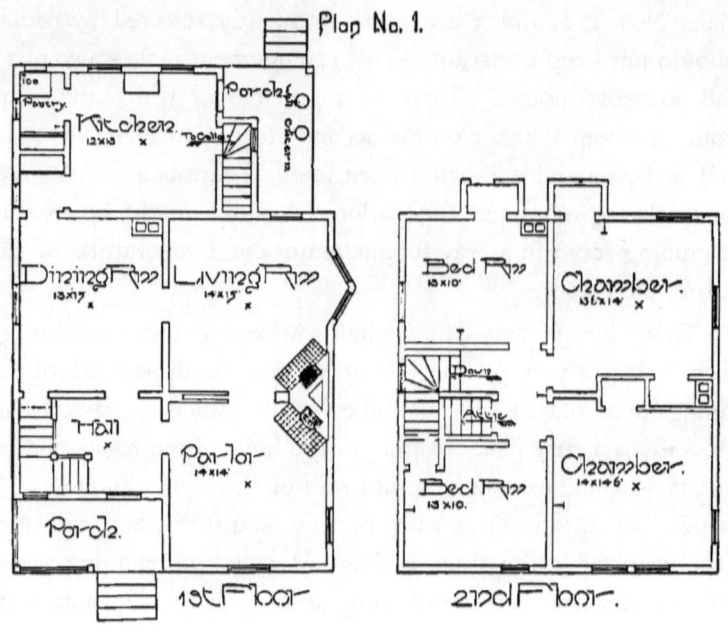

from the kitchen. It is also provided with a small window. In the kitchen is a sink with a swinging table at one side, and room for a portable table on the other. At one side of the sink may be the cistern-pump, and on the other side the well-pump. It should be placed back against the wall, and with handles that are well out of the way when not in use.

It is entirely unnecessary to place the pumps in the yards of low-cost houses, as is so common. If a driven well is used, it could be driven so as to be next to the kitchen sink. If it is a dug well, it may be placed on the outside, and connected through lead pipes with the sink on the inside. The cistern may be connected in the same way. The entrance to the cellar stairs is conveniently placed in one corner of the kitchen. The cellar

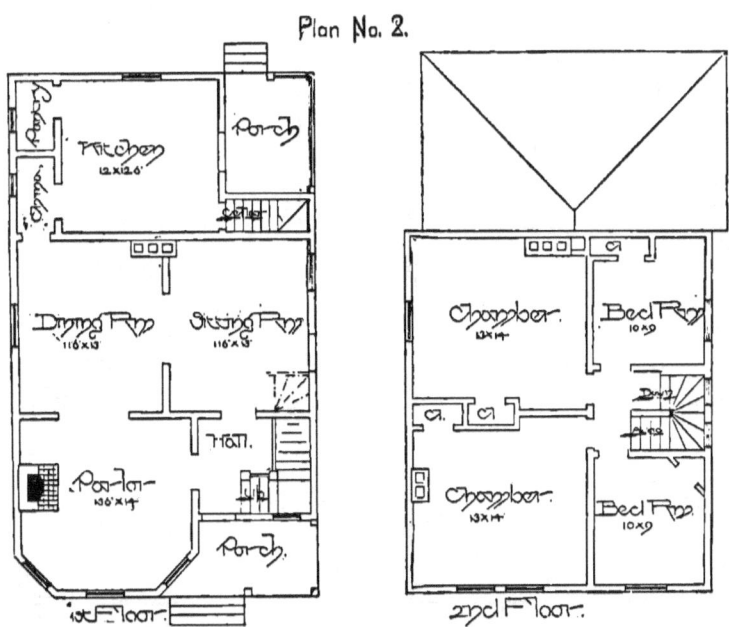

Plan No. 2.

itself is under the sitting-room. The side-porch is large enough to be used as a summer kitchen.

It is to be noticed that there is no waste room in the upstairs hall. There is merely wall space enough to admit of doors leading into the various rooms. There is a small window which lights this hall; the window may be reached for cleaning from the stairway. This plan illustrates as clearly as possible the advantage of having the main stairway land in the middle of the house. There is no better way to economical use of space. From the second-floor hall there is a stairway leading to the attic. This passage is lighted in the same way as the second-floor hall.

It may be said that the bedrooms of this house are not large. The house is not large. The problem involved a low-cost,

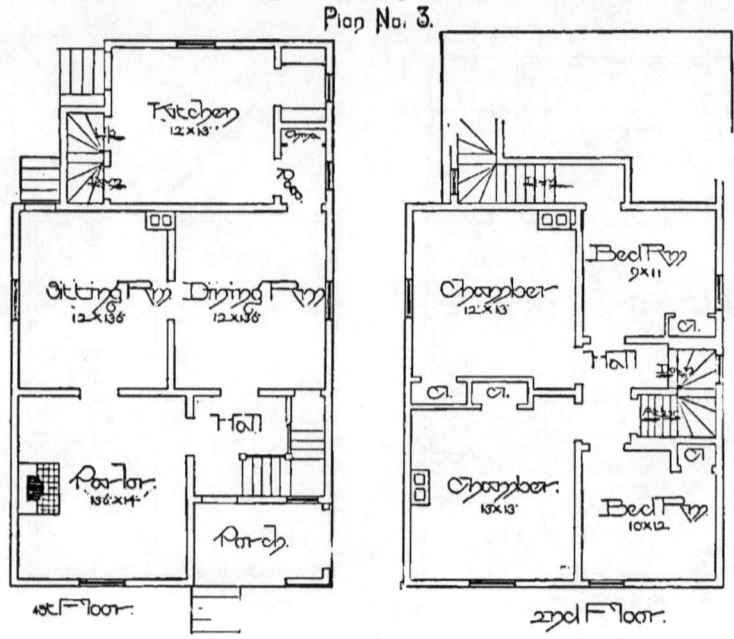

roomy house. We get a large number of rooms within a small enclosure, and, necessarily, some of them are small. It is to be borne in mind, however, that the value of a room is not dependent upon its size. A room may be of respectable dimensions, but yet not have the necessary wall space for the furniture. Such a room would not be as satisfactory as a smaller one, had care been taken to provide this space. In each bedroom there should be space for a bed, a wash-stand, and a dressing-case. The latter should be near a window. It will be found that there is room for such furniture in each of the bedrooms shown on this plan. All are provided with ample closets. In one of these houses which was built, there was a door between the bedroom in front and the chamber. In another case, there was a door connecting the two larger rooms. All these things are matters of personal preference, or special family requirements, depend-

Plan No. 4.

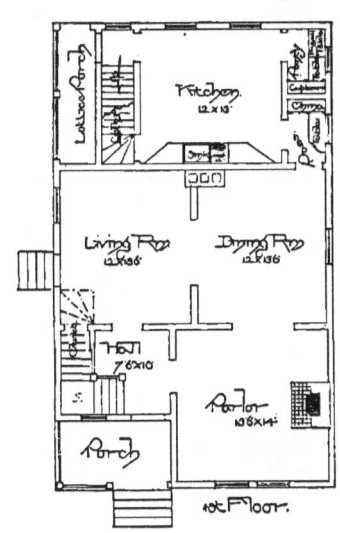 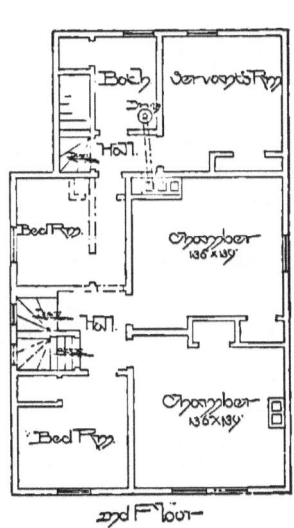

ing upon the age and number of the children, and other family conditions.

Plan No. 2 is similar to No. 1, excepting that there are a few changes in detail. The rooms are smaller; the hall is relatively shorter; it illustrates the process of contraction. No. 3 is similar to No. 2, excepting that it has a front as well as a rear stairway, and the position of the dining-room is changed.

No. 4 is a development of the same class of plans. There are the front and the rear stairways, also a bath-room over the kitchen, and a servant's room. The dotted lines running through the little bedroom on the second floor indicate the position of a hall, which may be constructed connecting the

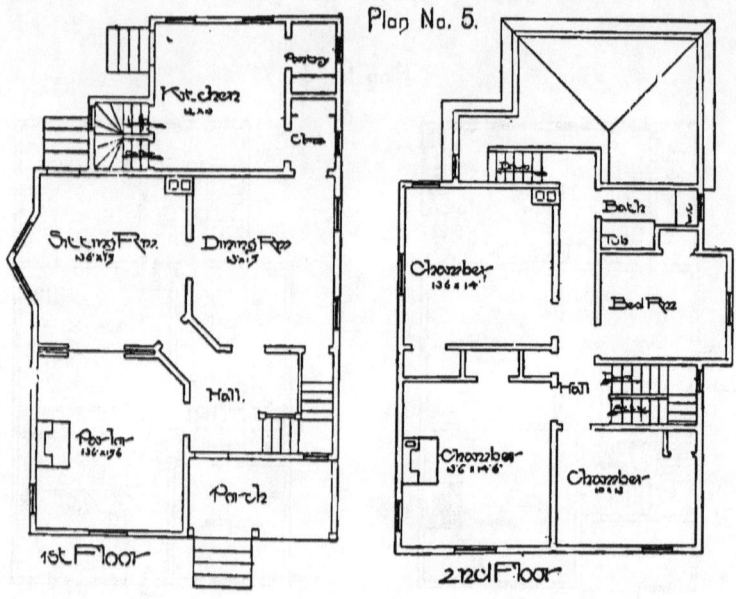

front and rear part of this house. As will be noticed, this is a nine-room house in a very economical form.

Plan No. 5 is a further development and improvement of the same idea. The objection that one may raise to any of the plans just described is, that one has to pass through the parlor, or the room in the rear of the hall, to reach the room back of the parlor. Plan No. 5 solves this problem. From the hall we can go into the living-room, the dining-room or parlor, without passing through another room. The second floor is an improvement

Figure 10.

over No. 4, in that the little bedroom in the rear is enlarged by allowing it to project over the room below the width of the hall. In the rear of this comes the bath-room.

As to cost. The building, without appurtenances, on the basis outlined in schedule " B," would cost as follows: —

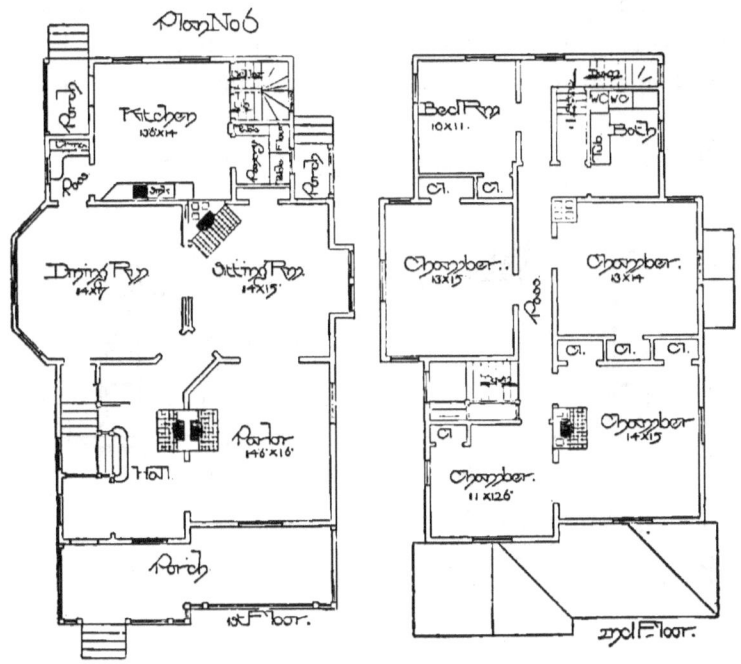

Plan No. 1, $1,700; No. 2, $1,550; No. 3, $1,550; No. 4, $1,800; No. 5, $1,900. Figures 8 and 9 are elevations suited to these plans.

Plan No. 6 had its origin in Plan No. 1, and was developed through the successive stages indicated in the description of plans from 1 to 5 inclusive. The position of the grate-stack has been changed, so that it acts for the reception-hall on one side, and the parlor on the other. The reception-hall, instead of receding, projects. In one corner thereof is arranged a vestibule, partitioned from the rest of the rooms by ornamental fret-work backed with curtains. This will make a very beautiful feature. It changes this hall into a room. From here we may pass to the parlor, sitting-room, and dining-room. In the rear of the sitting-room is a porch; at one side, a projecting window-seat. The sitting-room closet is cut off from the pantry. The dining-room is connected with the sitting-room by sliding-

doors. A convenient china-closet connects the dining-room and kitchen. On one side of the china-room are arranged drawers. Under the china-closet proper are shelves enclosed by panelled doors; the china-shelves above being protected by glass doors, according to the general ideas previously expressed when considering the china-closet in particular. The kitchen is the same as others, which are described elsewhere in a more detailed way. There is a laundry in the basement, and an outside cellar-way connecting with the back yard. The inside cellar-way is shown. The next door is that which leads to the second floor. There are five bedrooms on this floor. The elevation of this house is shown in Fig. No. 11. The building, without appurtenances, according to schedule " B," costs $2,600.

Elevations Nos. 1 and 2 indicate a simple form of exterior, which may go with either of these plans excepting No. 3.

The photographic view, Fig. No. 10, shows an exterior of No. 1, as built at one time.

## CHAPTER XVI.

A SMALL POCKET-BOOK AND A LARGE IDEA. — AMBITION, DOLLARS, AND A GOOD HOUSE. — THE GROWTH OF THE HOUSEKEEPER'S IDEAS. — POINTS ABOUT THE HOUSE. — $2,900.

IT is frequently said of those who would build, that their ideas are larger than their pocket-books. It is certainly not discreditable to any one that his ideas should be larger than his immediate resources. Such a condition causes the enlargement of the individual and his pocket-book at the same time. The man who says that he wants two thousand dollars' worth of house does not get as much for his money as he who in effect says, "I want three thousand dollars' worth of house for two thousand dollars." The latter is an ambitious man; the former has only a little ambition. He merely wants a house. Fortunately, however, there are few such people. It is more likely to happen that a man and his wife, who have worked hard for several years, get enough money together to build a home, and it is possible that this home has been talked about for several years previous to their building. In fact, they have been educating themselves in house-building. They have acquainted themselves with all of the modern conveniences. They have studied porches, vestibules, and stairways; they know how many rooms they want on the first floor and the bedrooms that they will have above. At first this house presents itself in a very crude form; but in the course of time the plan shows itself more clearly to them. They begin to place the furniture in the imaginary rooms, and as they do this their ideas enlarge. They add at first inches, and then feet, to the size of the various rooms. At first their ideas of a kitchen were quite moderate; in time a sink begins to assume certain vague outlines, then it takes definite form on one side of the room; then a pump is placed beside it; afterward the wife says, " How nice it would be if we could have a hot-water faucet over the sink." At first they shake their heads and say that it would cost too much; but in the course of a few evenings' talk on this and kindred subjects, they come to the conclusion that if the hot-water arrangements do not cost too much, they will have them; and that as things are so much cheaper than they used to be, they certainly ought to get all of these for about what they originally expected to pay for the house. Their ideas have been of slow growth, but continuous, and in the aggregate the growth has been great. During all the winter months, previous to the time when they would build in the spring, many sketches are made, of the floor-plans of the house that is to be. Finally the net result is handed to a builder or an architect, — more frequently the former, as most small houses are built without professional service. The figures from the builder come in, and are very much higher than was expected. It is quite a shock, for certainly there is nothing there that they can well do without. Everything has been thought of so much. Nothing that their plan contains appears to them to be less than a matter of necessity. Other builders are asked to figure with results little more satisfactory. In the end there must be a compromise; the builder and the owner both yield, and, as a result, a very satisfactory house is built. There are little things which they would have different, but, in the main, the house is satisfactory.

This is the universal experience, and the effect upon the

domestic architecture of this country has been very pronounced. We can now get a better house for a given sum of money than ever before. Better not only as to general construction, but as well on account of external appearance, and the convenience of its internal arrangements. One may get more of what are regarded as the little conveniences, which mean so much to the housekeeper. This is not altogether the result of lower prices of the material and labor which go to make a house, but is as well on account of the skill which has been developed in planning and arranging buildings, with reference to economy in space, and cost of general construction. The planning of houses has undergone a revolution within a few years past; and instead of having the long, narrow halls at the side and in the middle of a house, and the long halls and narrow passages through the upper floor, all of which was ugly and inconvenient, we now have the same area thrown in large square rooms, so as to be available.

It may be known that chimney stacks are quite expensive. For this reason an effort has been made to group them, so that they may be made to answer for a number of rooms; and the success with which efforts in this direction have been attended has been wonderful indeed. The modern floor plan is altogether different from that of the past; it is more convenient and less expensive to build; and, as said before, this is largely the result of efforts of the owner, who has ideas larger than his pocket-book, and the architect or builder, who exercises his ingenuity to bring the ideas and the money together.

Plan No. 7 is of an eight-room house, and is fairly representative of the ideas expressed. The general form, it will be seen, is square. It is a two-story house with a reception-hall, parlor, dining-room, kitchen, china-closet, pantry, and stair-hall on the first floor; there are three chambers, the servant's bedroom, the bath-room, and a communicating hall on the second floor. The first floor is ten feet six inches high, and the second, nine feet six inches. From the second floor there is a stairway going to the attic, which is large and roomy, and which may have various uses. The cellar is seven feet high, and is well lighted by having the joist set well up from the grade line. There may be

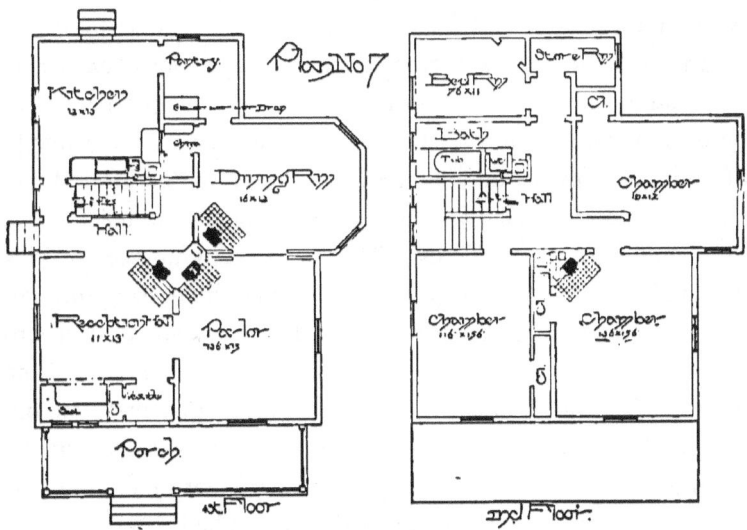

a laundry here, and, separated from it by a door, we may have a coal-cellar and a furnace-room. As we approach the house, there is, first, a broad porch about eight feet in width, and fourteen feet in length. At a slight additional expense, say fifty dollars to sixty dollars, this porch might be extended across the entire front. Before reaching the front door, there is a small vestibule, — arranged with or without storm-doors, as may be thought desirable. It is the impression of the writer that storm-doors are seldom used. The distinctive feature of this house is the hall, which is large enough — thirteen feet six inches by fifteen feet — to be used as a sitting-room. In the front part of this hall, and at the right as we enter, are a window-seat and a broad window in front and immediately above it; this is slightly separated from the main room by the small pilasters or casings on each side. Immediately in front of the doorway, there are a grate and mantel set in one corner of the room. There are large doorways, five feet wide, leading into the stair-hall immediately back of this room, and into the parlor at the left as we enter. In this case there are merely door openings, portières or curtains taking the place of ordinary doors. Sliding-doors might be used in addition to the curtains, and thus have the advantage of both curtains and doors. From this room the outlines of the stair-hall and the stairway are visible or not, according to the arrangement of the portières. There is a side entrance into this hall, and from it one may go into the kitchen by passing through two doors. It is a good principle in planning a house always to have two doors between the kitchen and any other part of the house. One door could as well be used in this instance, but a second one is added to make the isolation more complete. In the plan here given, it may be noticed that there are cellar stairs passing under the main stairway in the hall.

The dining-room may be entered either from the front parlor or from the stair-hall. In each case doors are used. It is always desirable to have a dining-room so arranged that it may be closed from the other parts of the house. There is a grate in each of the two principal rooms, the hall, the parlor, and the dining-room, and all communicate with a single stack. This is much more economical than having three distinct stacks, which are so frequently used for accomplishing the same result. The only other chimney stack is in the kitchen. The two answer every purpose. The outside corners of the dining-room are cut off at an angle of forty-five degrees, so that the end of the dining-room presents the form of a large bay window. In the middle space at this end may be placed the sideboard, in which event a window will be placed over it, — that is, well toward the ceiling. The dining-room communicates with the kitchen through a large pantry, eight feet square, or through a slide in the back of the china-closet. In the kitchen there are broad windows on the two sides, and a door leading into the back yard.

In following the stairway to the second floor, it will be noticed that there is a broad landing something more than half-way up, and that there is a large window, slightly above it, which lights the hall below, and partially lights the one above. The advantages of having a stairway which lands approximately in the centre of the house, as does this one, is that no room is lost by having long halls which have to lead from the front to the rear of the house. All we need have is a short hall in the centre of the building, which will communicate with the rooms around it. Another convenience of this arrangement is that all of the front of the house is utilized for chambers. Where the stairway lands in the front of a house, there must either be a long hall, which is a waste of room, or one must pass through one or more chambers to get to others. In this plan the rooms are arranged around the hall, there being three large ones over the three principal rooms below. In each of these chambers there is abundant space for the usual bedroom furniture, — viz., a bed, dresser, wash-stand, and chairs. In these rooms there are closets, and at the end of the hall there is a store closet for bedding, etc. The servant's room, as shown, is over the kitchen, as is also the bath-room.

It may be noticed that the fixtures in the bath-room — that

is, the bath-tub and closet — are directly over the sink below, so that the pipes may have the most direct and the shortest runs possible, which is not only economical, but also safer from flooding in case of accident. The tank in the attic, which contains the soft or cistern water, is directly over the tub, and the laundry sink in the cellar is directly under the kitchen sink.

Thus, from cellar to attic, all the plumbing fixtures are in line, and all pipes exactly vertical, excepting where it is desirable to take a short branch to connect the fixtures. Having the bath-room slightly separated, as it is, from the main hall, it is safer, from a sanitary point of view, than if it opened directly into the main hall. There is a closet for soiled linen next to the bath-room, which is accessible either from it or from the short hall leading to it. The stairs to the attic lead out of the hall, as shown. The attic is floored, but is otherwise unfinished. If found desirable, one or more rooms could be finished here, which would be quite as large and pleasant as any of the other rooms in the house. This house can be finished complete, including fences, sheds, walks, gas fixtures, plumbing, mantels, and furnace, for $2,900.

Fig. No. 12 is an elevation.

# CHAPTER XVII.

"WE KNOW WHAT WE WANT." — A CONVENIENT PLAN. — MEETING THE WANTS OF PEOPLE WHO BUILD.

FLOOR plans develop from the varying necessities of those who build. There is no reason why the same arrangement should suit any large number of people. A floor plan, if carefully and thoughtfully made, will meet the requirements of the individuals whose wants are particularly considered. While there are certain general principles, which affect the value of a floor plan for good or evil, the detailed requirements are almost as varied as the tastes and dispositions of the occupants.

A lady and gentleman come into an architect's office, and explain that they are intending to build, and want to look at something with a view of selecting a plan. The architect has a great many plans which he might show them, but he knows well enough that none of them will be selected. He says : —

"I shall be glad to show you anything I have, but not with the expectation of finding something that will please you. By doing so, I shall probably find out what you do not want, and in that negative way meet your requirements."

"I think I know what we want," says the lady, "but I do not know just how to arrange it. The stairways bother me, and there are things which I do not get to suit me."

"Well, tell me what you want, and then we will make a sketch; and from that, corrections; and, in the end, we shall probably have something satisfactory, though not wholly so at once."

"Before we go any farther," says the gentleman, "I want to say that we have only twenty-five hundred dollars to put into a house."

"Yes, that is all we can afford," says the lady; "but I can tell you what we want."

The architect reaches for a note-book and a piece of paper.

"We want a reception-hall, with a grate and stairway in it. There must be a small vestibule, with a place for overshoes, hats, and overcoats. Somewhere near the reception-hall, or in it, I want a closet where I can put my own wraps, and those of the children, and other things which I do not care to keep upstairs, and yet wish to have out of the way. It does not need to be a large closet, but must not be unusually small. We want a parlor and dining-room, which connect with the reception-hall. The parlor will be used as a sitting-room not a little, but not in the ordinary way, for the reason that I stay upstairs with the children most of the time. I do my sewing there. If I should use the parlor regularly as the sitting-room, I could receive my callers in the reception-hall. It would be nice if we could have some kind of a window-seat in that room. We want a grate in the sitting-room, but not necessarily one in the dining-room. I want a back stairway, but it must not go up directly from the kitchen. The kitchen and pantry I want you to make as convenient as possible in a house of this cost."

"How would a combination stairway do?"

"Oh, I don't want that at all. It would be bringing the two together. I want the rear stairway in the rear of the house, and entirely separate from the one in front. It should land near the girl's room on the second floor, so that it can be cut off from the rest of the house. We must have plenty of closet-room upstairs."

"How many children have you?"

"Two: a baby and a little boy about six years old."

"Then you must have at least four bedrooms," was suggested. "For the present, the baby can sleep in your room, and the boy in a room next to and connecting with it. There must also be a guest's room and a servant's room."

"Yes, that will have to do for the present; but don't forget the bath-room, and be sure to have plenty of closets. There is one thing I had almost forgotten. There must be some arrangement so that the servant can get from the kitchen to the front door without going through the dining-room; but we don't want the smells of the kitchen to get into the front part of the house."

After two or three sketches had been made, the result, as here illustrated, was reached. The architect has it in mind that the space at the right of the entrance door in the vestibule would serve as a place for overcoats and other winter equipments. He suggests that a portière be placed between the vestibule and the opening leading into the reception-hall. This will prevent draughts of cold air from making their way into the front room when the door is opened. It will also lend a certain amount of privacy. The porch is placed in front, as a matter of course. In the recess of the hall which is made by the vestibule a window-seat is placed. In the rear of the reception-hall is the closet required. As a means of getting from the kitchen to the reception-hall without passing through the dining-room, two doors are arranged leading to a passage under the stairs. This will prevent the passage of kitchen odors over the house. The parlor and dining-room are arranged as shown. Between the window and the door leading to the china-closet is space for the sideboard. The pantry is separated from the china-closet by the cupboard of the former. It has doors above and shelves below. The ice-chest is placed in the pantry. It is readily accessible from both china-closet and kitchen.

The passageway to the second floor is from this room, and, considering the limited means and large general requirements,

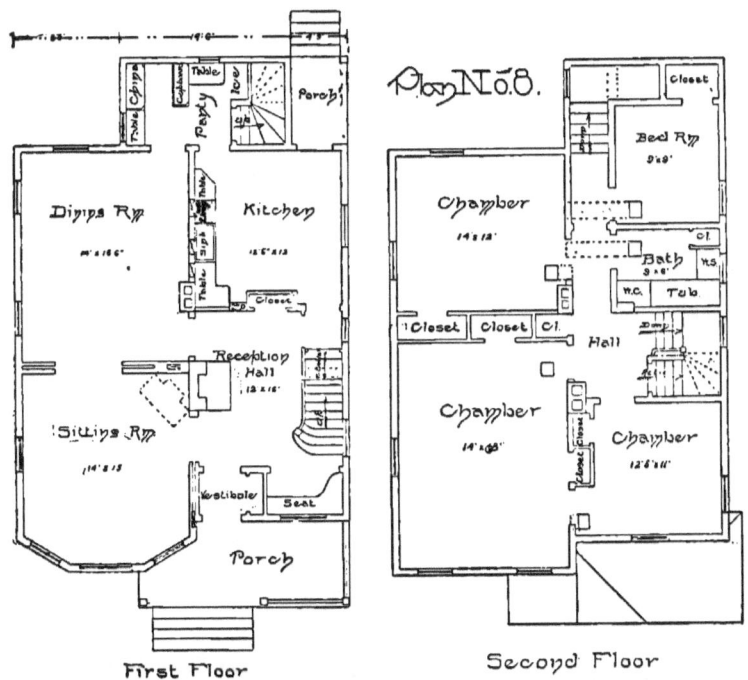

this arrangement will no doubt be satisfactory. The stairway is accessible from both dining-room and kitchen. As there is a bath-room and water-closet above, there is no necessity for carrying slops downstairs and through the kitchen. The kitchen has the usual fittings. The passage to the cellar is under the front stairway. As will be remembered, there is a door shutting this passage from the reception-hall. Upstairs there is a closet in each room, two opening into the hall — one for bed linen, and one for dust-pans, brushes, etc. There is also a closet in the bath-room. The attic stairway is shown. An inspection of Plan No. 8 will show how all of the requirements were met.

Cost, as per schedule " B," $2,200.

## CHAPTER XVIII.

TWO GOOD ROOMS IN FRONT. — THE COMBINATION PANTRY. — TOO MUCH CELLAR A BURDEN. — $2,500.

IN Plan No. 9, the reception-room contains the front stairway. This stairway lands near the front of the house on the second floor, for which reason we are enabled to have in the front part of the house the two rooms which are most used on each floor. We have the two chambers above, and the reception-room and the sitting-room below. If we had a long, narrow stair hall constructed in the usual way, we should have the sitting-room towards the rear, and only a little alcove bedroom over the hall in front.

The dining-room, which is a large room, is connected with the front part of the house by sliding-doors. It has a grate in one corner of it. On general principles, a grate has no business in the dining-room. It is nearly always at some one's back, and makes him uncomfortable at meal time. Being in the corner of the room, it is farther from any one than it would be if located on a side wall: hence it may be allowed. There is a porch in the rear of the dining-room, and between the door leading to it and the door to the china-closet there is a space for a sideboard. There are two windows at the end of this dining-room. The door which passes into the pantry should be on double spring-hinges, so that it will swing both ways. One can push against it and open from either side, and when it is released it will take its natural position.

The pantry is a large one. Pantries, in general, may be regarded as a kitchen annex — a store-room and preparing-room. This pantry is on the combination plan. It connects with the china-closet by means of a slide. Aside from this china-closet, which projects into it, there is a cupboard with double doors at one end, a flour-bin at the side, a pastry table next to it, and a

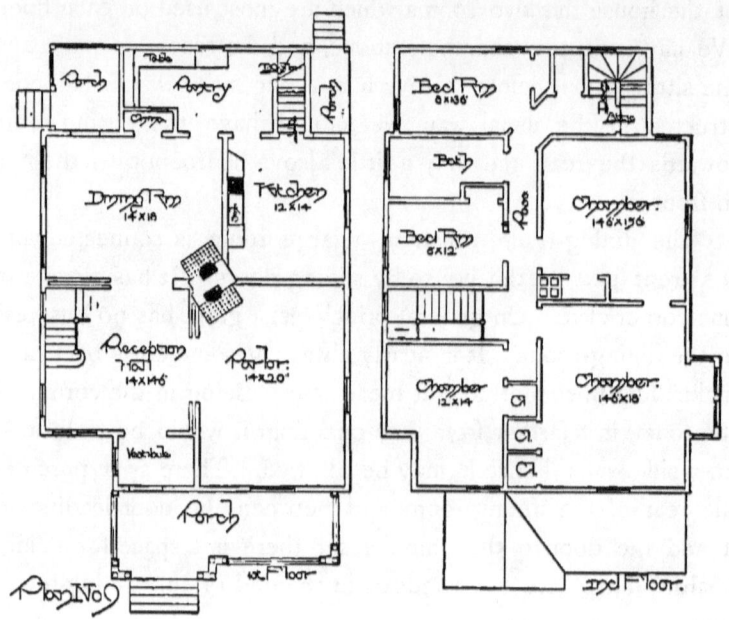

refrigerator by the window. One reason for placing this refrigerator near the window is, that a flight of steps and a platform might be arranged on the outside, so that the iceman could put in the ice without going through the kitchen. We go down cellar from this pantry.

There is a cellar under about half of this house — the kitchen and the dining-room. It should have a cemented floor, and numerous windows for lighting it. The part under the kitchen could be used for a laundry, that under the dining-room for coal storage and furnace. There could be an excavation under a part of the sitting-room for vegetable storage. "Why not put a cellar under the whole house? It would cost but little more," has been asked many times. It is the little things, the smaller economies, in a building of this kind which makes

Fig. 13.
C

the difference between an expensive house and a house of moderate cost. Every foot of cellar space beyond what is needed for actual use is a burden to the housekeeper. The arrangement has more to do with the number of apartments than with the amount of space. We have a laundry-room, a place for furnace and fuel, and a room for vegetables, which is about all that can be used. From the cellar we can go up the stairway and into the kitchen, from the kitchen to the second floor, and from the second floor to the attic.

It is a large attic, a place for large rooms if one should need them. Under any circumstances this attic should be floored. There could be no better place for general storage, and at times for drying clothes.

It seldom happens that two houses from exactly the same plan are built. While this plan has pleased many people, there are others who would not be attracted by it; who would not care to build this house as their home. The universal floor plan has never been made, and never will be. There are general principles running through all plans which are valuable, and if rightly understood will contribute to the improvement of the homes of the people.

Fig. 13 is an elevation.

Cost, without appurtenances, $2,500, as per schedule " B."

## CHAPTER XIX.

SITTING-ROOM AND PARLOR IN FRONT. — A CONNECTING VESTIBULE. — A CENTRAL COMBINATION STAIRWAY. — GOOD ROOMS IN THE ATTIC.

WHEN we say that the sitting-room should be in the front part of the house, it does not necessarily imply that the parlor should be disturbed. As shown in Plan No. 10, they may both be in front. The vestibule, which is large enough for a hat-rack, and for the occupants of the house to stand while putting on their overshoes and wraps, is in front of both parlor and reception-room, but yet in a way so as not to disturb the view to the street from either of these rooms. We cannot have all of the rooms in front. The kitchen we do not want there. The dining-room is convenient if placed immediately in the rear of the sitting-room. Thus we have two rooms in front and two in the rear. This is practically a square house. The old habit has been to place the stairway along one side of the parlor in the hall which served as a passageway from the front to the rooms immediately in the rear. This distribution of halls is what has thrown the sitting-room back of the parlor. In the plan here given the change has been made so that the hall has relatively the same position that did the sitting-room in the past, though it is by no means as large. It is essentially a stair-hall, and incidentally a passage. As placed, we may enter it from the parlor, sitting-room, dining-room, or kitchen. Its position is central. There are two doors between this stair-hall and the kitchen. The central position of the stairway has other advantages than those just stated. It makes long halls on the second floor entirely unnecessary. As will be seen by looking at the floor plan, it gives two good bedrooms in front.

The dining-room is immediately in the rear of the sitting-room. There may be sliding doors connecting these two rooms. One door, three and a half feet wide, usually makes a suffi-

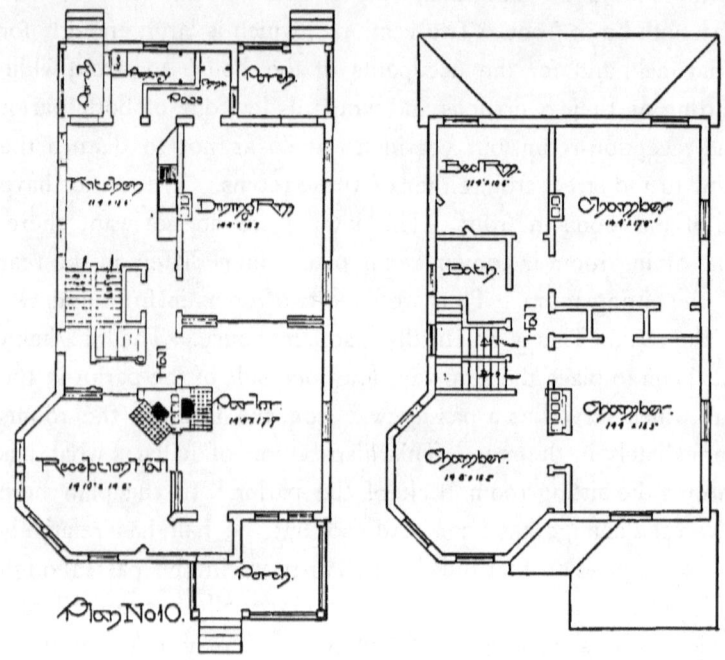

ciently large opening for the dining-room connection. There are sliding doors between the parlor and sitting-room, and dining-room and sitting-room, as shown. The kitchen has the advantage of a certain amount of isolation from the rest of the house, for the reason that there are two doors between it and any other room. The pantries are arranged with reference to their most convenient use. In the kitchen-pantry there are places for a refrigerator, flour bin, bread-board, and cupboard. The dining-room pantry is a china-closet, with glass doors above and closed doors below. The doors connecting the dining-room pantry or passage should be hung on double-spring hinges.

In the plan of this house it is shown how we may go from the kitchen to the same landing that is used for the main stairway, and thus avoid the necessity for a distinctively back hall and back stairway. However, if it is so desired, it is easy to place a stairway in the rear, and thus have them entirely independent. In that event a room may be placed over the pantry, and be used by the servant. This part of the house could be cut off from the front rooms and the bath-room on the second floor by a door. But to take the house as it is, we have a combination stairway, there being two doors separating the kitchen approach from the common landing in the main stair-hall.

On the second floor there is a hall about fourteen feet long from which we pass to two bedrooms in front, two in the rear, the bath-room and the store-closet. Each room is independent. They may be connected one with the other as family necessities suggest. The store-closet is accessible from the hall, as such a closet should be. This makes it available from any of the rooms. The bath-room is directly over the kitchen.

In each bedroom there is a place for a bed, a dressing-case, and a wash-stand, which is not always the case in bedrooms. If there is a place for these things, if the dressing-case bears its proper relation to the sources of light, if it is so placed that the light from the window or from the gas shines in the face of the user, if the wash-stand is conveniently disposed, and there is room at the side of it for a slop-jar, if there is a large closet, then the architect has done his full duty in the arrangement of the bedroom.  The room that is called the family room should be especially well cared for in the matter of closets.

A hundred dollars would lath and plaster the entire attic of this house, and provide a room in the front part which could be used by the boys or the servant. There is no objection to this except in the necessity for climbing an extra pair of stairs. The mere mention of a bedroom in the attic is distasteful to many people. It arouses memories of hot, dusty, and uncomfortable places in which they have passed the night. All this depends on the attic. The roof in this house is pitched at an angle of forty-five degrees. The house at the narrowest point is 29 feet wide. This would make the attic at the highest point 14½ feet. We can stud down from this and have a nine-foot story and at the same time a large room, one which would have none of the disadvantages of a half-story room, and which would have all the advantages of a well-ventilated, comfortable bedroom, for summer or winter. The plastering of the attic suggests neatness. Having it well lighted by dormers exposes all disorder. Cost, as per schedule " B," $2,600.

## CHAPTER XX.

A COMPACT PLAN. — AN ISOLATED RECEPTION-ROOM. — COMBINATION STAIRWAY. — DESCRIPTION OF THE FLOOR PLAN. — CELLAR ARRANGEMENT. — DINING-ROOM AND CONSERVATORY. — ANOTHER PLAN.

THE floor plans in No. 11 are of a house of small area, 30 × 34½ feet, for the body of the structure. There is a porch in front, a circular bay window at one side, and a pantry and china-closet projecting at the rear. In the house there are eight available rooms besides the bath-room and the attic. In the attic, rooms quite as liberal as any in the house could be constructed at a small expense.

On the first floor, as we enter, there is the reception or sitting hall, which is so common in the more modern arrangements of dwellings. This reception hall or room has a certain amount of isolation from the passage which leads from the vestibule to the stairway and the rear portion of the house. It may be separated therefrom by curtains or portières. It would be entirely possible to separate the two by means of sliding doors, in which event the opening from the room into the passage would have to be a little narrower than shown in the drawings. This room could be used as the office of a physician, or of a gentleman who did more or less business at home. By making the front vestibule about six inches deeper, a separate entrance to this room could be provided. In this event, a door from the room into the passage leading to the living part of the house would be a necessity. The circular bay end of this room would present an attractive feature. The windows in this part of the room could be placed about four feet from the floor, in which event book-shelves could be arranged below them. The window in front goes to within seventeen inches of the floor. Under the stairway, and leading from this room, may be placed a very liberal closet, in which there should be a small window.

Leading from the passage is the stairway, and two closets. The little passage in which one closet is placed is separated from the hall by a door. There is another door opening from this passage into the kitchen. Thus there are two doors between the kitchen and the front part of the house. This arrangement has in mind the isolation of the kitchen from the other rooms in a way to prevent the passage of the usual kitchen odors.

The stairways in this house are of the class known as combination stairways; while they are convenient and easy of construction, there is a certain amount of complication in their arrangement which makes them difficult of description so as to be understood by those not accustomed to examining floor plans. There is the stairway from the front hall to the floor above, and one from the kitchen to the landing of the front stairway. The landing of the front stairway and that from the kitchen stairway is in common; that is, it is the same. For the purpose of making this understood, it may be well to say that one may go up the stairway from the front hall to the landing, some eight steps, and from thence down into the kitchen, or he can turn right face and go to the landing on the second floor. This part of the stairs is used coming up from the kitchen as well as from the front hall. However, the kitchen stairway is separated from the landing by a door. There is another door at the foot of this kitchen stairway. In coming downstairs, one may turn to the right, open a door, and go down into the kitchen; or, he may turn to the left, and go down the front stairway into the hall. Thus it will be seen that the combination stairway is a front and rear stairway together, with separate entrance from both parts of the house, — one from the kitchen,

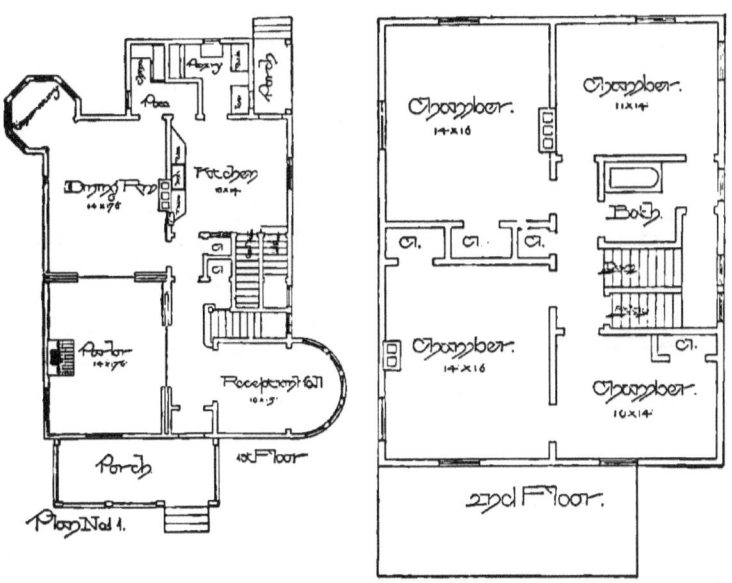

and one from the front hall. It must be confessed that there is a certain amount of compromise in an arrangement of this kind, but it is a saving of both space and money, and is tolerable on this account. By this plan everything is concentrated, and without the serious drawback which extra cost, or a smaller number of rooms, would imply to those who have only a little over two thousand dollars to spend for a house, without appurtenances. The head room for the stairway, coming up from the kitchen, is secured under the bath-tub in the bath-room immediately above.

The cellar stairway is clearly indicated as going down parallel to the kitchen stairs and under the front stairs. The cellar in this house should be under the kitchen, stairways, and the reception-hall; that is, it would occupy all of one side of the house. In this cellar plan the principles set forth in the previous chapter on cellars are carried out.

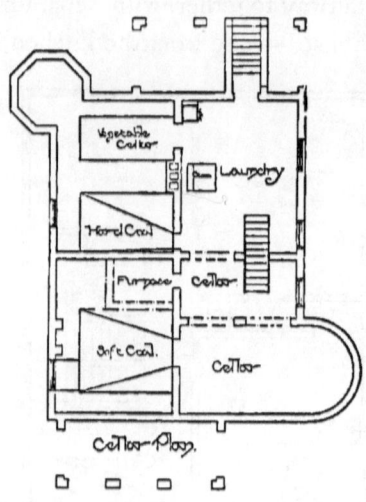

The parlor is thirteen and one-half by seventeen feet in size. It is connected with a hall by wide sliding doors, so that about one-half of this side of the room may be open. The grate opposite the sliding doors in the parlor would present a very beautiful view from the hall and stairway. The sliding doors between the parlor and dining-room are placed there more in deference to custom than through any personal sense of their fitness. Sliding doors do not have the quality of excluding sound or odors that is desirable. The ordinary hinged door is better in this respect. This room which would commonly be called a parlor would really be used as a living-room, excepting by those who use the dining-room or one of the second-floor chambers for that purpose.

Our dining-room has an independent connection with the front hall, so that we do not have to go through the parlor or the sitting-room to reach it. A little extra money, say seventy dollars, would place a conservatory at one side, at one corner, or at the end of this dining-room. Fifty dollars would give a bay window. As it is, we have two windows of the ordinary kind at one side of the room, and none at the end. A very good arrangement, when bay or conservatory is not used, would be to take one of these windows at the side and place it at the rear end, though near the outside corner of the room. This would give space between the windows and the china-closet door for a sideboard. The window at the side of the dining-room, if the other were moved to the end, should be in the middle of the wall space; that is, opposite the centre of the flue.

From the dining-room we go into the kitchen through the china-pantry, which is marked "passage." This china-pantry has a little window at one side, and at the end a separate apartment for chinaware, which is closed from the passage by means of glass doors. The doors leading from the passage into the dining-room and kitchen should be hung on double-swinging hinges.

There are those who would say that there should be no door from the kitchen into the passage leading from the dining-room to the front hall. It would probably be well to retain this door in this position, and have a bolt on the side of the door toward the hall. Thus the mistress of the house can close it, and keep it closed at will. Another thing that might be done would be to place a strong spring on this door which would always keep it closed. The windows in this kitchen should be placed about three feet from the floor, so that tables may be placed under them. There is a place for a gas-stove between the two windows, or even under them if desirable. The porch at the rear of the kitchen may be enclosed with lattice work, or, what is better, coarse louvered slats, like those of a shutter. In either event, it could be covered with screen wire, and made a part of the kitchen in summer. In the plan, however, nothing of this kind is indicated. The door which leads from the porch into the pantry is a small one, placed above the ice-chest, and is for the use of the ice-man.

The arrangement of rooms upstairs will be readily understood. Leading out of the hall is a store closet for bedding,

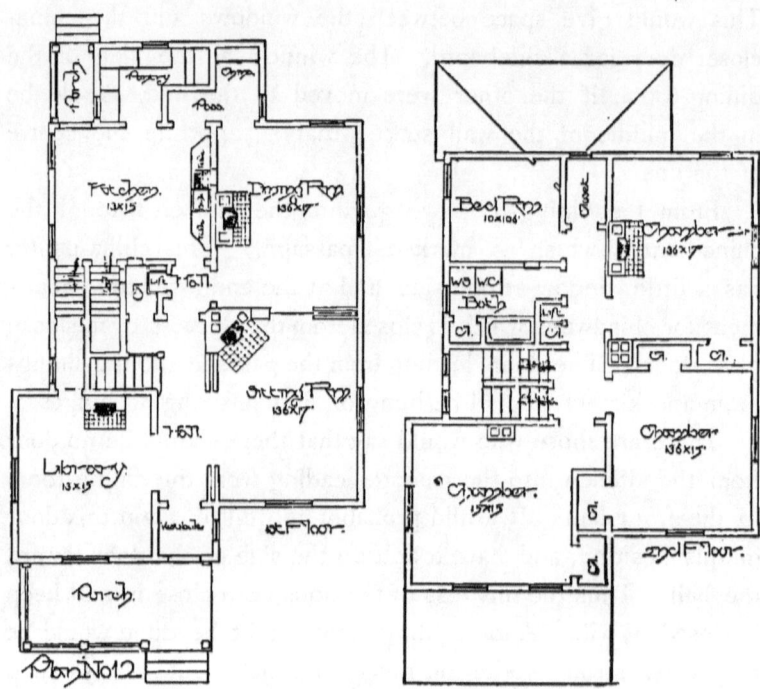

etc. It is located so as to be accessible from all rooms. From the front end of the hall a door leads into the stair passage to the attic.

Plan No. 12 is the outgrowth of Plan No. 11. In it there is a lift running from cellar to attic, as shown. The only important difference between it and No. 11 is in the size of the library. Cost, as per schedule "B," $2,600. Fig. 14 is an elevation: see page 147.

# CHAPTER XXI.

WHAT CAN BE DONE FOR $1,600? — THE CLOSET IN THE HALL. — A SMALL CONVENIENT KITCHEN. — CLOSETS IN THE BEDROOMS.

THIS house — Plan No. 13 — was finished at a cost of less than $1,600. This included, besides the house itself, a woodshed, well, and cistern. There is a cellar under the hall and parlor. The building has a brick foundation, and the woodwork begins two feet above the grade. The stud-walls of the exterior are lined, first with dressed sheathing, then with heavy building-paper, and finally covered with weather-boarding. The first and second tiers of joists are two by ten inches; the ceiling-joists of the second story are two by eight inches. All of the studding is two by four inches. The windows have box frames with iron weights and cotton cords. The first story is ten feet high, the second eight and a half feet. These details of construction are mentioned so that any one interested may know that it is a substantial, well-constructed building. The interior finish is of pine, part of which is varnished and the remainder stained and varnished. The front door and stairway are of quartered oak.

The front porch is 10½ feet wide and 7½ feet deep. It has a high roof over it, as will be seen by the elevation. The entrance, being at one side of the porch, gives more available space for uninterrupted use during the warm weather. The hall is 10 feet wide and 10½ feet long. The stairway has first two steps to a broad landing, and then a continuous movement to the second floor. If this landing were reduced in size by making the approach more direct, say turning directly to the left as one enters the door and going through a landing the width of the stairway before making the general ascent, there would be more available room in the hall. It is shown this way in the drawing, because it is the way the house was built.

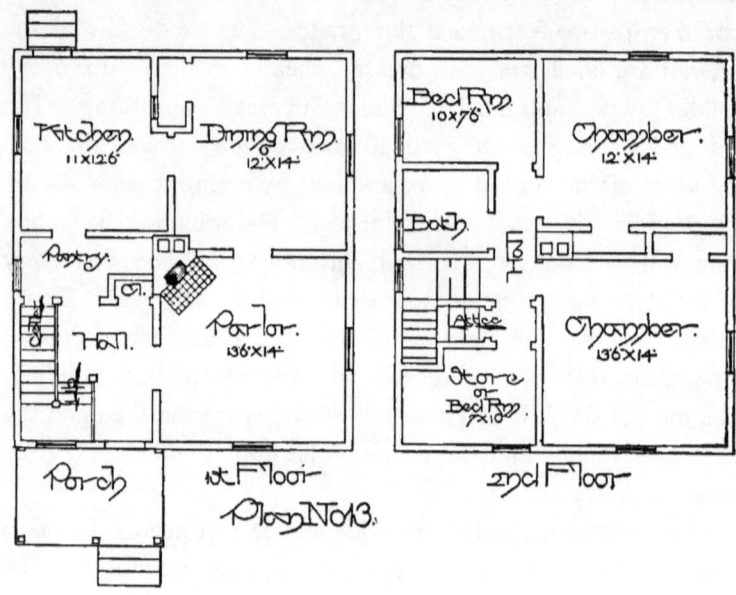

There is a closet in this hall. There are many houses built without a closet on the first floor, but it is certainly better that one be provided.

As will be seen, there are three rooms on the first floor, and four and a bath on the second. It is an easy house to care for, because there is no waste space, and all the rooms are readily accessible without extra steps. Waste room means waste of energy and waste of money in more ways than one — waste not only as to the unnecessary expenditure in the cost of building, but in carpets, and in the labor of sweeping and caring for them.

In the parlor at the right of the hall are two windows and a grate; one window is in front and the other at the side. The dining-room is similarly equipped. It has a large china-closet which connects with the table in the kitchen by means of a slide.

Fig 14.

There is also a door between the kitchen and dining-room. Eleven by twelve and a half feet is not large for a kitchen. The availability of kitchen space is not entirely dependent, however, on its dimensions, but rather upon the disposition of the wall-space and the conveniences which have to do with a kitchen. It will be seen that there is a space for the kitchen-range or stove near the flue which does not conflict with the use of any other part of the kitchen. Also there is a space between the door which leads into the pantry and an outside wall which gives place for a kitchen-safe, which may hold the kitchen utensils. It is out of the way and yet convenient to the range. The safe might be placed opposite the tables at the other end of the kitchen, if thought desirable. The kitchen window is placed about three feet above the floor. This gives wall-space

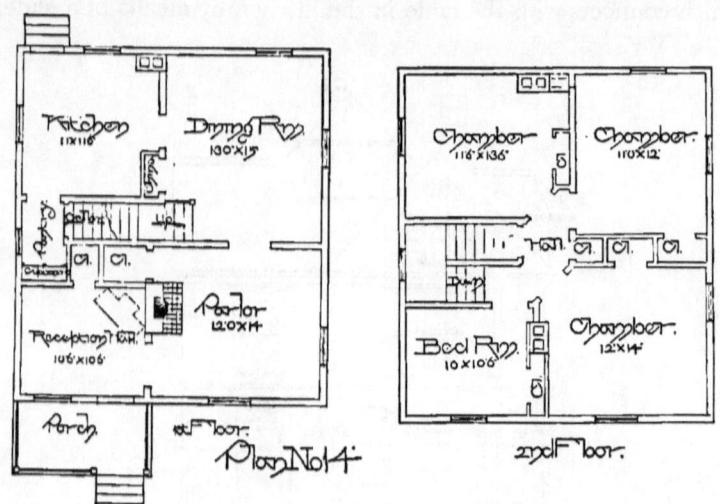

under it. Where a safe is not used, a cabinet, to contain pots, kettles, etc., can be placed there.

The pantry is quite convenient to the kitchen. There is an enclosed cupboard on one side which has doors and shelves above and below, and in the recess next to the dining-room wall is a place for open shelves. Near the pantry window is a dough-board and a place for flour. Here, also, is the entrance to the cellar. It will be seen that there is a door between the pantry and hall, which makes it possible to pass from the kitchen to the stairway or from the kitchen to the front hall without going through other rooms. The enclosed cupboard in the pantry makes it possible to keep it always tidy. There is a glazed door in the rear of the kitchen.

It may be noticed that there is not a large hall to be carpeted or swept on the second floor. This hall is well lighted by a window at the side. From here one can go into any of the

Fig. 15.

rooms on the second floor. As to the bedrooms, there is a convenient place for bedroom furniture in all of them. There is at least a choice of two places for each bed, a space for a dressing-case where it will get the best light, and room for a wash-stand. There is a closet in each bedroom, of ample capacity.

The right-hand house in Fig. No. 10 shows the exterior of Plan No. 13.

Plan No. 14 is another edition of Plan 15. The room lettered parlor is properly a sitting-room. By dispensing with the grate in the reception-hall this house could be built, as it was at one time, with a stairway meeting the one coming up from the dining-room and passing from thence to the second floor. The elevation of this house shows it with an attic,

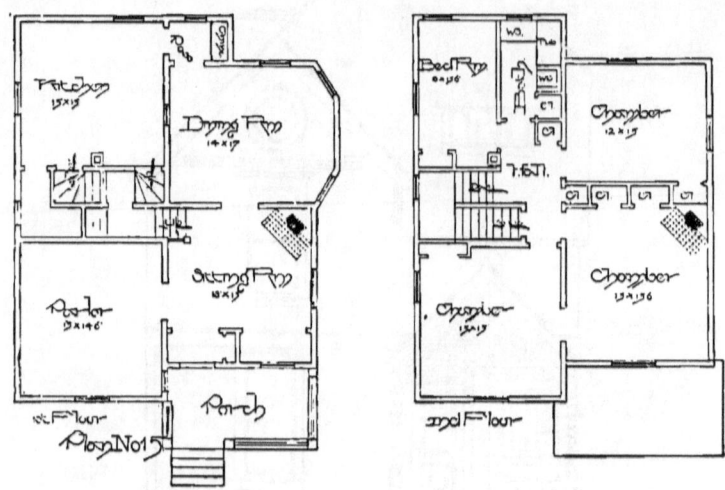

though the plan does not contemplate this arrangement. Without the attic and with a lower-pitched roof, this building, without appurtenances, can be finished for $1,500.

Fig. 15 is an elevation of Plans No. 14 and 15.

Plans No. 13 and 15 belong to the same class. No. 15 is more elaborate in its details, and larger. From the sitting-room one passes to the landing where it meets a stairway coming up from the kitchen. From thence there is a common passage to the second floor. On this floor are four bedrooms, a bath-room, and a liberal supply of closets. One of the front chambers is supplied with two, and the hall with two. There is one in the bath-room, and each of the other rooms. The cellar and attic of this house are plastered. The building, without appurtenances, as per schedule " B," cost $2,550.

Fig. No. 16 is an elevation of Plan No. 15.

## CHAPTER XXII.

OUTGROWTHS OF ONE IDEA. — EVERYTHING COUNTS AS A ROOM. — ONE CHIMNEY. — CONVENIENCES OF A CONDENSED HOUSE. — COST FROM $1,600 TO $2,800.

PLANS Nos. 16, 17, and 18 are all outgrowths of the same idea. It is the most economical general scheme for a house that is represented in this collection. In No. 16 there is not more than forty-eight square feet of hall space in the entire house. This is on the second floor. This plan was devised under an extraordinary pressure for a roomy house for a relatively small sum of money. Everything is made to count for a room. Twelve sets of plans of this general kind were made for as many different owners of houses during one season. This statement is made for the purpose of indicating its popularity. We will look through No. 16 with some respect to detail.

It is a one-chimney plan. There are three grates with independent flues in the three principal rooms on the first floor, and two grates with their flues on the second floor. One among other points of economy is the stairway arrangement. It is a combination, front, rear, and cellar all in compact form. There are two doors between the kitchen and the landing of the main stairway. In this respect it is like other combination stairways which have been described. The front and rear stairway come to the same landing, and from thence to the second floor. The front stairway is provided with a railing, baluster, etc., and the one from the kitchen is within an enclosure. There may be portières between the landing and the reception-hall. Thus one may pass from the kitchen to the second floor without coming into view from this room. The cellar stairway goes down under the main stairway. The combination idea is carried out again in the pantry and china-closet. This pantry and its arrangement in detail are fully described in Chapter VI., and illustrated in

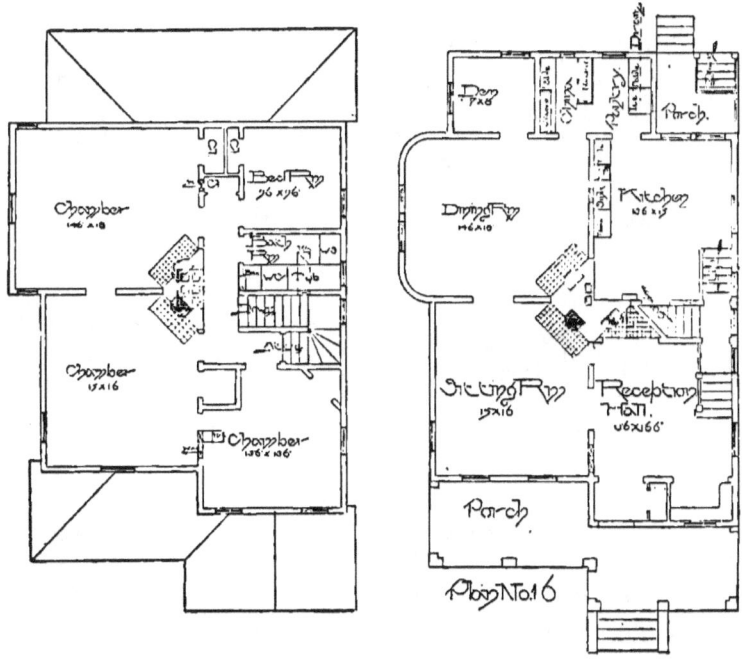

Fig. 4. The vestibule next to the reception-hall is the one referred to in Chapter V.

On the second floor are four bedrooms and a bath-room, which is immediately over the kitchen. There is a straight run of pipe in a pipe duct on the inside wall.

Fig. 17 is a photographic view of the exterior. It is an ultra shingle design.

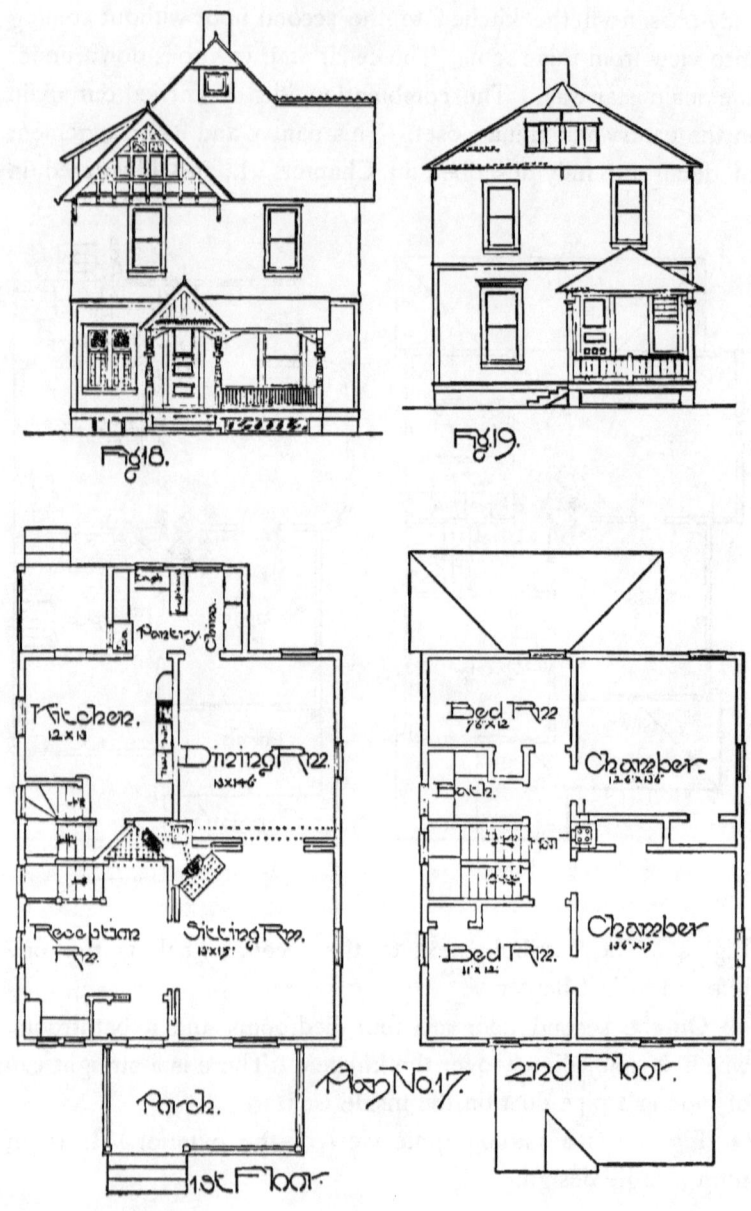

FIGURE 17.

Fig. 18 is an elevation of Plan No. 17. Fig. 19 of Plan No. 18.

No. 17 is the house in which the general plan was first worked out, and, in some respects, it shows that the idea was then in an experimental stage. However, it indicates a house of moderate size on this plan, whereas No. 16 is a large house. No.

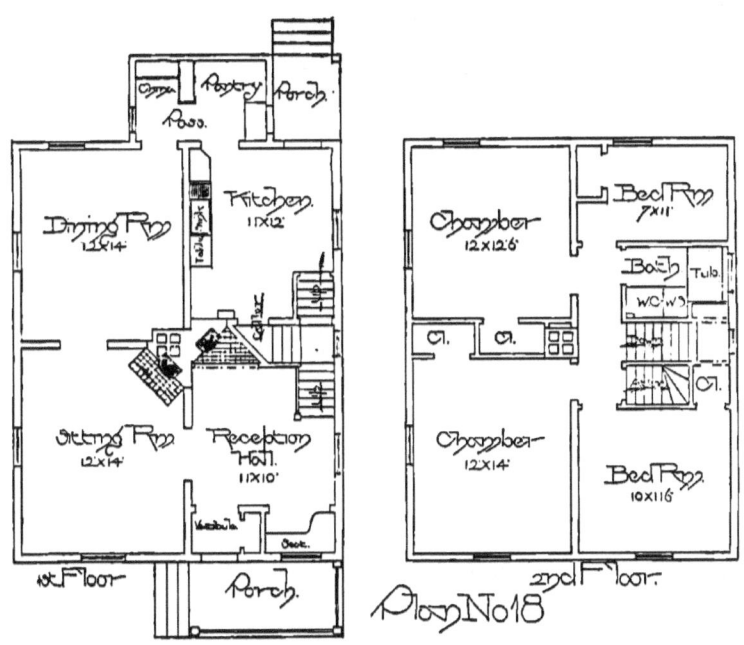

18 is the small size of the same plan. It has been built many times as a rental house. With the furnace it is under lease, in one instance, for five hundred dollars a year. In other cases, without a furnace but including plumbing with the use of city water only, the rent is thirty-five dollars a month. Any of these plans can be worked into a double house by putting the bathroom on the outside, and adding to the amount of window space

front and rear. The following is a list of costs, without appurtenances, as per schedule " B " : —

No. 16, as a shingle house, $2,800; No. 17, $2,200; No. 18, $1,600.

The latter figure includes soft-wood finish throughout. Other sizes of this house have been built where the general construction aggregated $2,400.

# CHAPTER XXIII.

ONE-STORY PLANS. — DESCRIPTION OF FLOOR PLANS. — BATH-ROOM NEXT TO KITCHEN FLUE. — KITCHEN, PORCH, AND PANTRY. — THE EXTERIOR. — ENLARGEMENTS ON THIS PLAN. — OTHER ONE-STORY HOUSES.

THIS house — Plan No. 19 — has been built for $1,400. It is a one-story cottage, containing five rooms, a bath-room, and a pantry. Such a house is suited to young people of moderate means, or possibly to older ones, where there are no children, or where the housekeeper does her own work. It will be seen that it gives more of the conveniences of a larger house than are usually found in a cottage of this size.

From the porch we pass into a little vestibule, which might be made larger by throwing into it the closet which opens from the sitting-room. From the vestibule we go either into the parlor or the sitting-room. This parlor could be used as the living-room of the house, and the sitting-room as the dining-room, and still meet all the conditions of good housekeeping. Off from the sitting-room is a projection, which could be very comfortably arranged as a window-seat. It could be used as such during warm weather, and as a place for plants in winter. In the corner of this room is a closet, which may be connected with the kitchen by a slide. There are sliding doors between the sitting-room and the bedroom. In the front part of the bedroom is a large closet. It is possible that many would prefer to have a window at this point, and have a smaller closet elsewhere; say, in the corner next to the sliding-door partition. The placing of a closet next to the rear wall would leave no place for a bed as the rooms are now arranged. If the door from the parlor to the bedroom were omitted the head of the bed might be placed against the sliding-door partition, and the

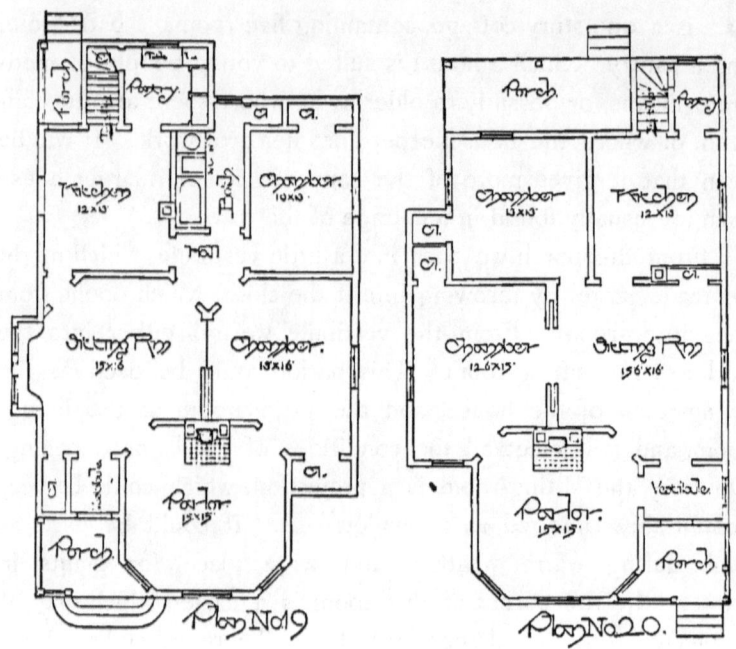

closet cut out from the rear bedroom, with an opening leading into the front bedroom.

From the sitting-room, or from the front bedroom, we pass into a little hall; and from the hall into the kitchen, the bath-room, or the rear bedroom. Over each of the five doors leading into this hall there should be a transom; thus it would be well lighted. The placing of the hall in this way makes all of the rooms surrounding it independently accessible. The rear bedroom has a place for a bed, a large closet, and a wall space for necessary furniture. The availability of a bedroom is not always dependent upon its size. A room may be large, and yet not contain wall space for the furniture. A large bedroom may have a small closet. This bedroom has a large one.

The bath-room comes next to the kitchen flue. This is important when we consider that the kitchen flue is frequently the last one in the house to get cool. As here arranged, the pipe connections with the bath-tub would all be short; they would all be near this flue, and on the inside wall. Hence the conditions would be against freezing. There is a hollow thimble in the pipe connections between the kitchen flue and the bedroom. The bath-room might connect with the same flue or flue-stack. Connecting with the bath-room there is a large linen-closet, which is about the proper size and form for folded bed-clothes. It is near the bath-room window, so that when the closet-door is open the contents will be plainly in view.

There is a large window in one side of the kitchen, which should be placed three feet from the floor, so as to admit of a table being set under it. If the kitchen stove were placed next the wall separating the kitchen and sitting-room, it could be piped across to the kitchen flue, and in that way leave the wall space adjacent to that flue and near the bath-tub for the kitchen sink. This would bring all the plumbing work together. At one side of this sink could be placed a well-pump, and a cistern-pump at the other.

In the rear of the kitchen are a porch and a pantry. We go down cellar directly from the kitchen. Over the headway of the cellar stairs could be placed a closet for various stores, such as canned fruit. This closet, of course, would be connected with the pantry, as shown. The necessity for head room in going into the cellar would make it necessary to place the floor of this closet three or four feet above the pantry floor.

On the side of the pantry opposite this closet are two cupboards, with doors and shelves above and below. There is a place for a flour-bin or flour-barrel under the dough-board, and space for an ice-box next to it. This box should have a drain connecting with the outside. It is intended to have the cellar under the kitchen and bath-room, though it might be extended under the sitting-room also. This part of the cellar might be used as a fuel-room, and thus dispense with wood and coal sheds. With the fuel and water in the house, the housekeeper would be saved much work. Where a kitchen sink is provided, it would be unnecessary even to carry out the dish-water.

Fig. 20.
FRONT ELEVATION.

There are two flue-stacks in this building. A base-burner would warm the sitting-room and bedroom and temper the air of the parlor. A grate fire in the parlor would complete the work of heating that room.

The cut of the exterior, Fig. 20, tells its own story. The porch has turned columns, and a frieze decorated with scrollwork. The window seat may have a window at each end, as shown in the floor-plan, or panels, as indicated in the elevation. There is a gable at the side and over the window seat, which extends the full width of the sitting-room.

Plan No. 20 is a development of Plan No. 19. Without appurtenances it cost $1,200.

Plan No. 21 is an enlargement of No. 19. The pantry

and china-room are arranged differently. The doors leading into the china-room are glazed in their upper panels with cathedral glass. This obscures the view, and gives sufficient light. These doors were hung on double-spring hinges, so frequently mentioned. Over the dining-room and chamber are

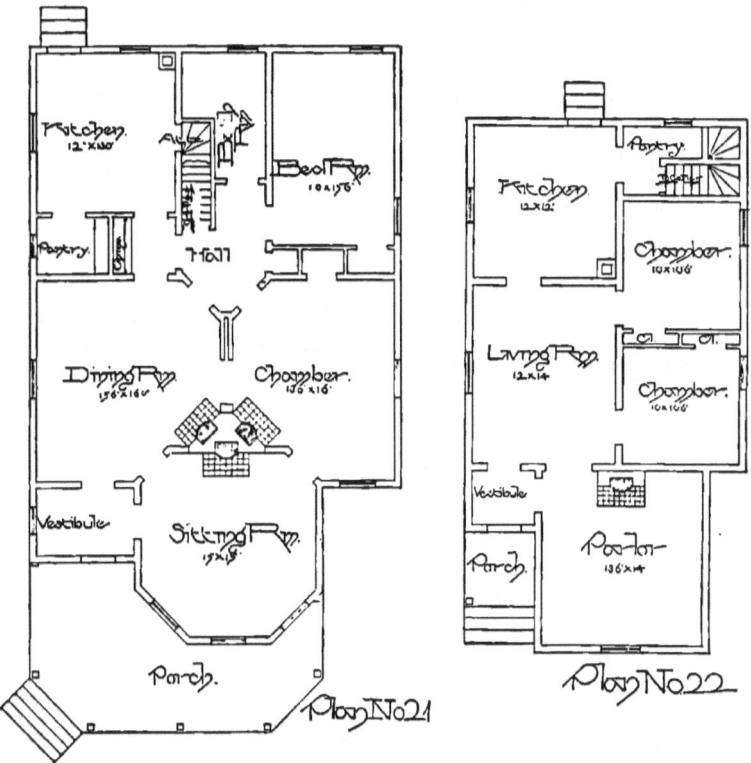

two finished bedrooms. They are arranged in the high part of the roof, and, with dormers, would have only a small part of the upper corners clipped. There are two grates more than shown in Plan No. 19. The stairway arrangement may be reversed, so that one goes to the second floor from the hall rather than from the kitchen. This house cost, with two finished rooms on the second floor, without appurtenances, as per schedule " B," $1,700.

Plan No. 22 can be built and finished for $800. The gable arrangement would be about the same as in Fig. No. 20.

Plan No. 23 was built, including everything that went on to the lot, for $1,600.

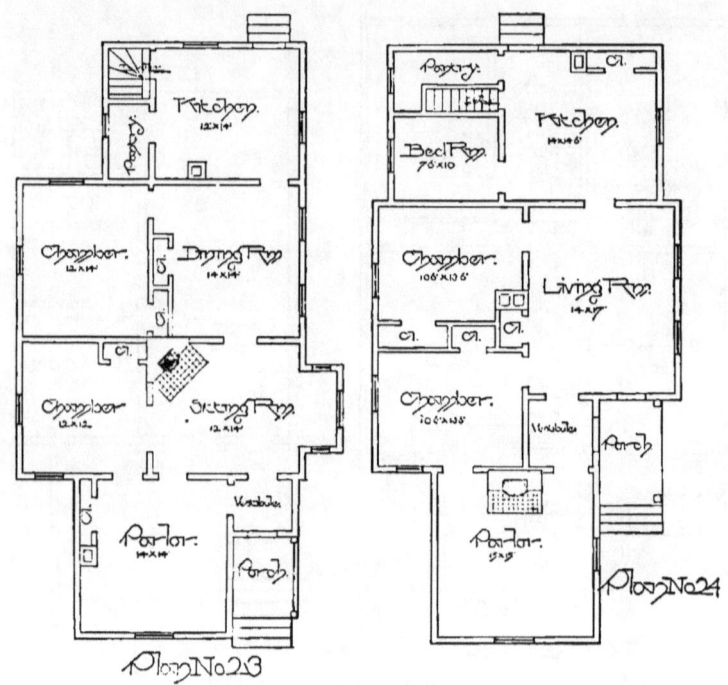

Plan No. 24, as per schedule " B," cost $1,100.

Plan No. 25, without appurtenances, cost $1,400.

One-story houses cost more for the accommodations which they afford than two-story buildings, for the reason that it takes the same foundation and roof for a one-story house that it does for one of two stories of the same area on the first floor. In fact, it usually takes more foundation and roof for a one-story house than it does for a two-story, for the reason that it covers more ground space than would be required for the same or a larger number of rooms in the two floors.

No. 26. This is a peculiar type of a one-story house. There is a servant's room over the kitchen. It is a very com-

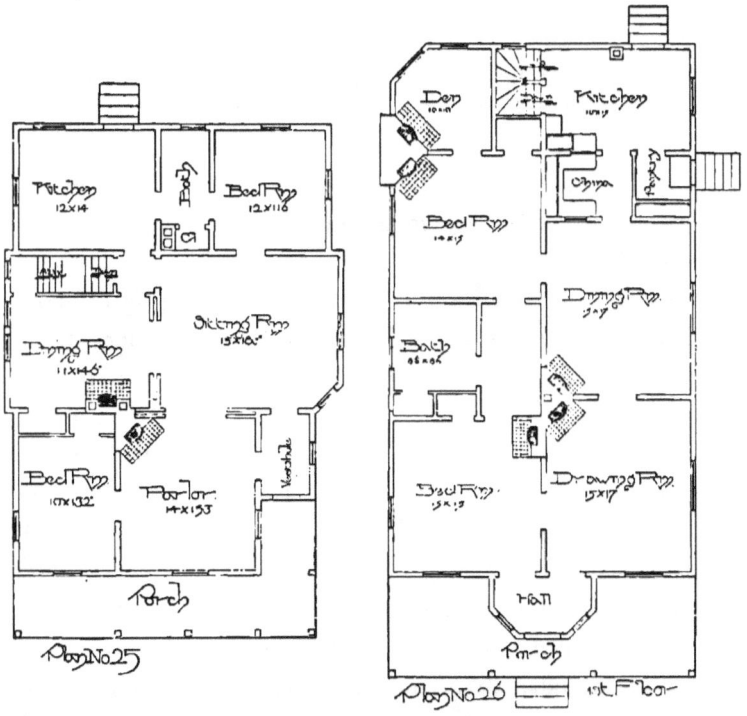

fortable arrangement. The bath-room stands between the two bedrooms. There is a grate in each of the rooms on the lower floor. The kitchen-sink arrangements are not altogether satisfactory. It is a plan which will never be very popular. It is designed to be finished with shingles for the outside wall. The structure will cost about two thousand dollars, as per schedule " B."

# CHAPTER XXIV.

### SIDE-HALL PLANS. — PLANS WITH BEDROOM ON FIRST FLOOR.

PLAN No. 27 is a side-hall plan with a bedroom on the first floor. The parlor and sitting-room have views directly to the front. The dining-room has a bay end, and a good china-passage to the kitchen. There is a rear side-hall which is desired by a good many people in building a large house. On the second floor are four principal chambers, which are entirely cut off from the rear bedroom, by bolting a door into the rear hall. The bath-room is measurably detached from the rest of the house, which fact will have the quality of satisfying people who are suspicious of all plumbing. This building, without appurtenances, according to schedule " B," cost about three thousand dollars.

Plan No. 28 has over two hundred dollars' worth of porch attached to it. It is a side-hall plan, with the entrance to the front. In it the combination stair idea is carried out in a way previously mentioned, but not before illustrated. The rear stairway is direct as to the servant's room, and combined with the central stairway only for entrance to the main part of the house on the second floor. The arrangement of rooms on the first floor makes this plan suitable for use by people who entertain in a small way. This is the plan to which reference is made in the special kitchen article, excepting that there is a change in the position of the cellar stairway. There are two closets and a wash-stand in the hall which connects the kitchen

PLANS OF FIFTY CONVENIENT HOUSES. 165

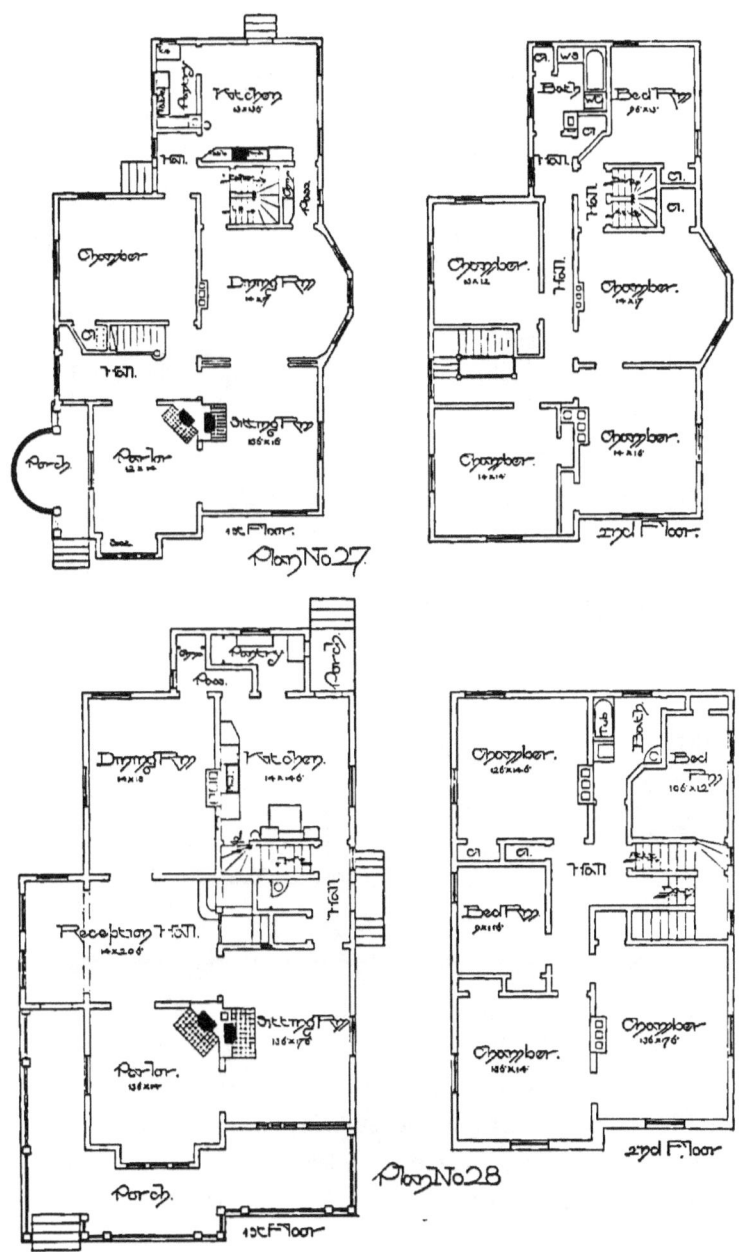

and sitting-room. This building, without appurtenances, as per schedule " B," cost between $2,800 and $2,900.

In Plan No. 29 the hall is in front, yet the entrance is at the side. The stairway is at the rear end of the hall. A little door is shown at the rear of the vestibule, leading under the stairway. The closet is not very high, yet it is high enough to use as a

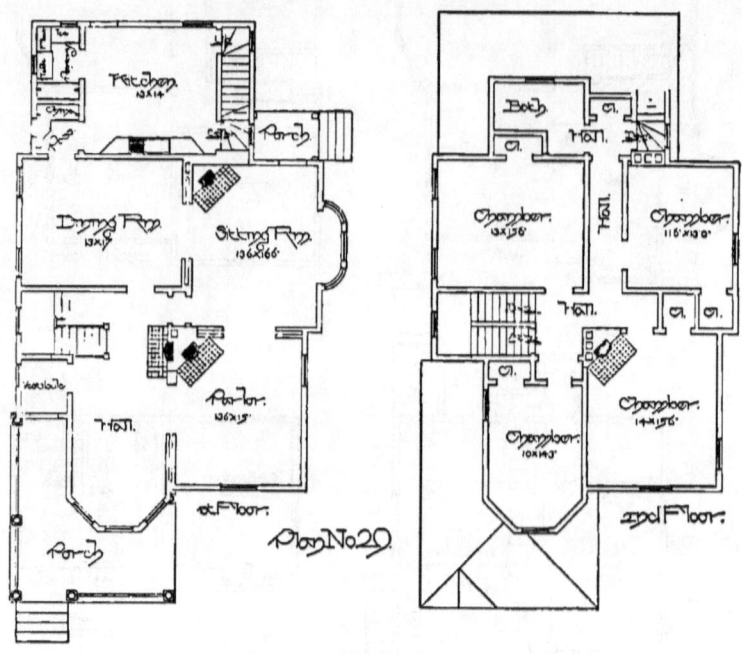

place to store a baby carriage or a small tricycle. The arrangement of the entrance and the stairs admits of the use of the hall as a room. In the house as constructed, there is a window seat in the octagon end. There is a double railing coming down into the hall. A part of the stairway is open on each side. Opposite is a grate. There are also grates in the parlor and sitting-room. By a little change in the kitchen arrangement, a bedroom could be placed back of the sitting room, and the rear and cellar stairway would occupy measurably the same position as now. The kitchen would have to be a little narrower, and, if desired, might be longer. The pantry and kitchen could both be pushed a little to the left of where they now stand. In this

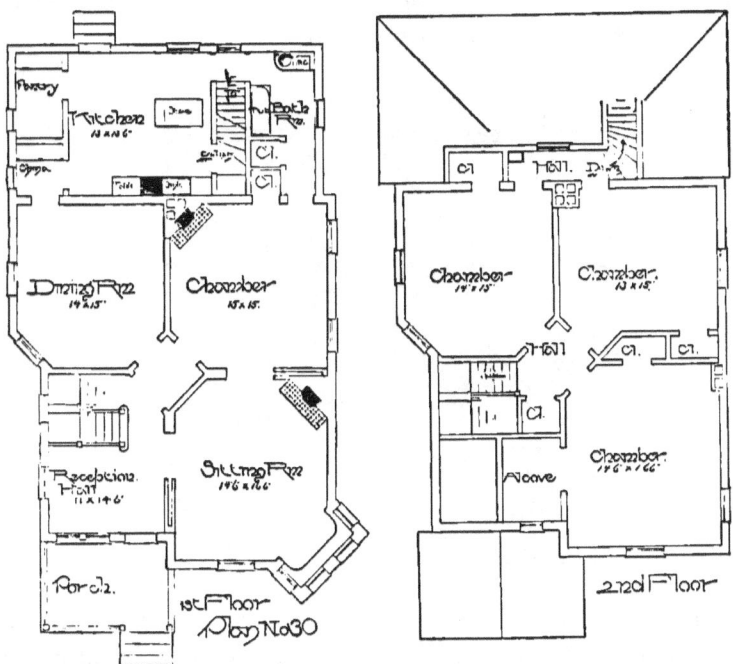

way space for a bedroom could be provided back of the sitting-room, with possibly only a small projection to the right. The rear vestibule could be cut out of the corner of the bedroom. To prevent this from injuring the appearance of the room, a corresponding space, to the left of this vestibule, could be arranged into passage and closets for the bedroom and sitting-room. In this event the rear bedroom wall would extend past the rear kitchen wall. Attention is called to the size of the closets on the second floor. By a slightly different arrangement of the bath-room an additional bedroom could be provided. There is a large attic over the front part of this house. The entire side walls are covered with shingles dipped in stain. There is a mild form of octagon tower over the front chamber. The building, as here planned, cost $2,600, without the appurtenances mentioned in schedule " B."

No. 30. Plans with bedrooms on the first floor are frequently wanted. This requirement makes an ugly problem. It increases the number of rooms on the first floor, and oftentimes leaves a less number to be provided on the second story. In this plan, including the bath and reception-hall, there are six rooms on the first floor and three on the second, hence a good deal of waste. There is a sink in the rear hall, second floor, with water supply over it, to obviate the necessity of carrying slops down stairs. Cost of building in brick, $3,000.

Fig. 21 is an elevation.

## PLANS OF FIFTY CONVENIENT HOUSES. 169

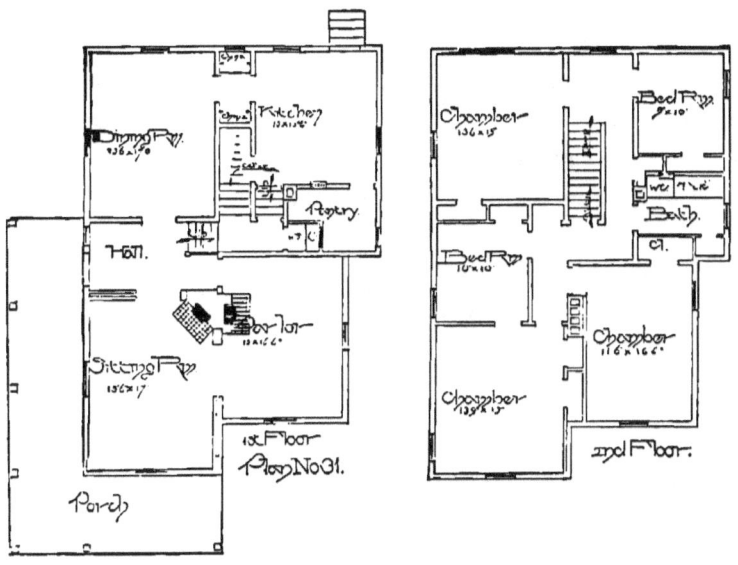

Fig. 22.

No. 31. This plan is of the same general character as No. 27, but is somewhat contracted. There is a wash-stand in the little room on the stair landing, a few steps above the reception-hall floor. This building, without appurtenances, cost $2,400, as per schedule " B."

Fig. 22 is an elevation of this plan.

## CHAPTER XXV.

MISCELLANEOUS COLLECTION. — SHORT DESCRIPTIONS OF ELEVEN HOUSE PLANS. — VARYING COSTS. — SQUARE PLANS. — ONE-CHIMNEY PLANS. — REAR AND SIDE HALL.

A GREAT many people like a side-hall entrance, as well as one in front. Plan No. 32 gives it. On the second floor there are a large number of bedrooms. The rear stairway comes up in a manner to separate the servant's room from the front part of the house. A double store-closet is shown on the rear of the second floor. The front part of this closet may be left unlocked and the other portion made secure. The bath-room in the rear has direct connection with the water pipes as they come up from the kitchen. All the bedrooms have the proper plan for furniture. This house, without appurtenances, as per schedule " B," was built for about $4,000.

Plan No. 33 was used three times in one season, in slightly differing forms, at a cost varying from $2,800 to $3,600, without appurtenances, as per schedule " B." In the matter of floor space it is not an economical house. It makes a very pretty arrangement of rooms on the first floor. There are five good bedrooms and a bath-room on the second floor. The rear part is measurably separated from the front by a door. A projecting bay window from the family bedroom is shown.

Plan No. 34. This is another plan that was made to order. It is an economical arrangement, and, in many respects, very convenient and satisfactory. The single stairway, passing from the dining-room, will be the least satisfactory feature about the whole house to the majority of people. However, the idea in this connection is a good one. It is economical in that it dispenses entirely with the hall. Furthermore, this stairway starts from a room which will be used less than any on the first floor.

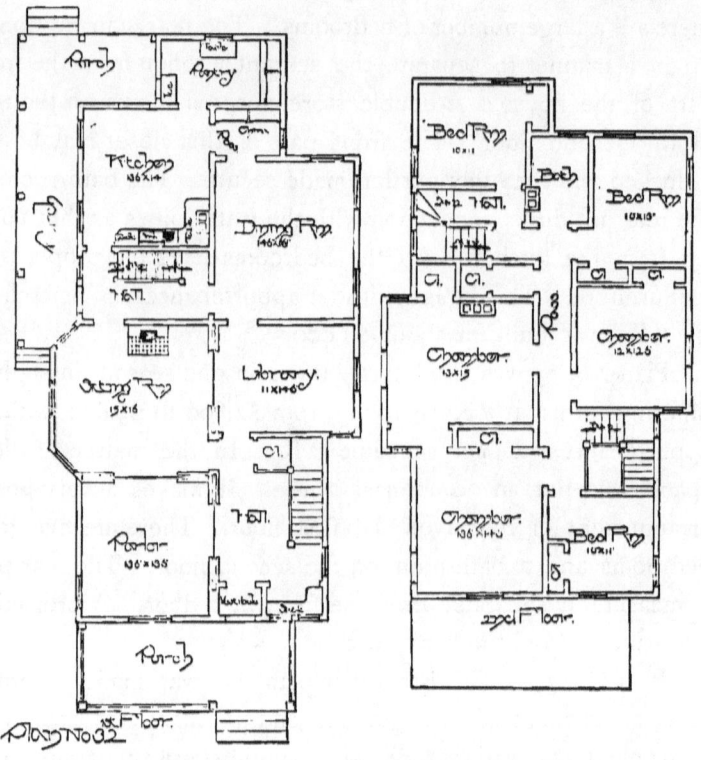

Few people will be inconvenienced by the use of the dining-room as a hall. Part of this stairway goes into a hall leading to the kitchen. The china-room and pantry arrangements in this house are very satisfactory. On the second floor are five bedrooms and a bath-room. The hall is lighted by a dormer over the stairway. This building, without appurtenances, would cost about $2,500, as per schedule " B."

Plan No. 35 is a house with a side entrance for small boys, which is sometimes wanted. This plan meets such a requirement. In the rear hall a coat closet is provided; also a rear

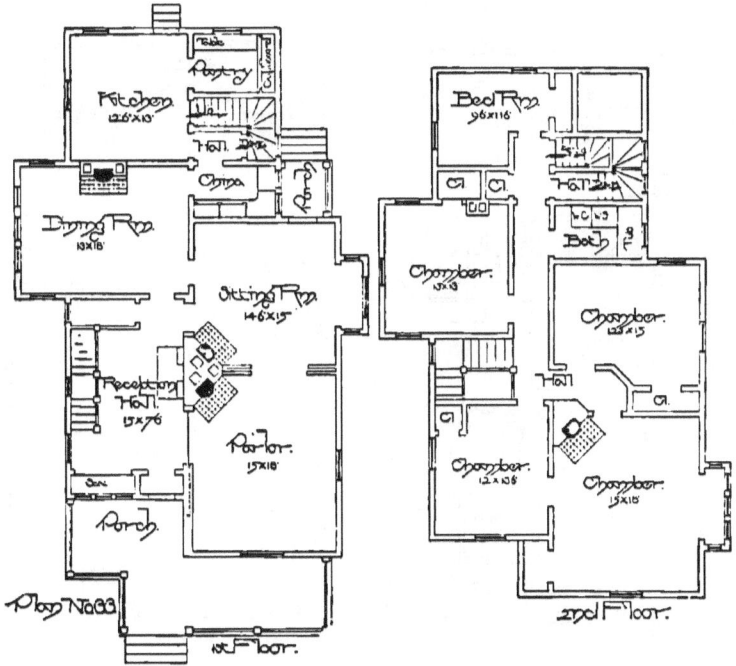

stairway. The vestibule in front of the reception-hall is sufficiently large to admit of the placing of hat rack and other vestibule furniture. The stairway is a pretty feature, though not satisfactory to all. There is a closet in connection with the music-room. In actual construction one was provided from the kitchen. The second floor is self-explanatory. It was built, as per schedule " B," for $2,500.

Plan No. 36. The requirements of the occupants of this building are peculiar. A large number of bedrooms are required. Other than bath and bedrooms, there are only the dining-room, parlor, and kitchen. There is no cellar. There is a combination stairway. One run starts from the front, and the other from the

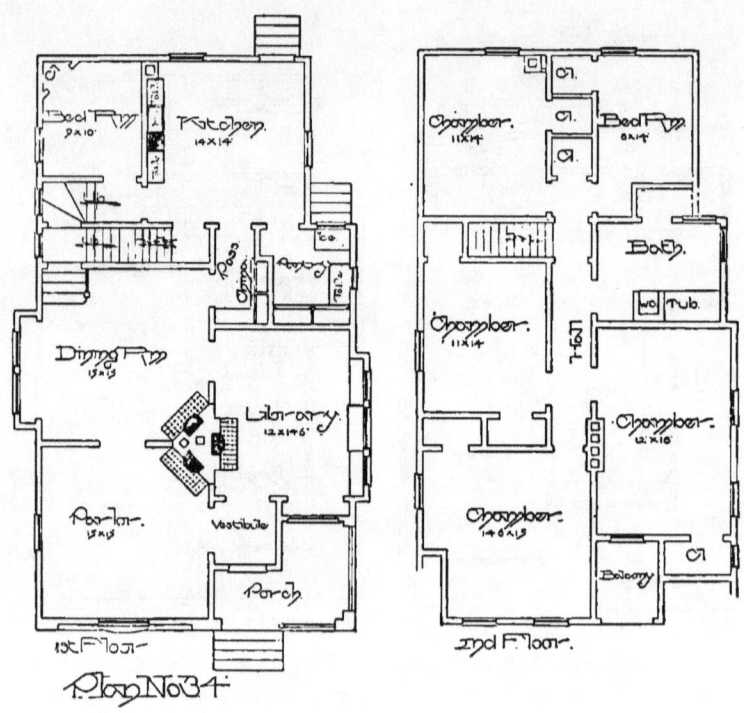

rear. The landing is in the centre on the second floor. Cost of this building, $2,000, as per schedule " B."

In No. 37 the stairway is back of the reception-hall. It is distinctively in the centre of the house, and is accessible from all rooms. There is a passage through two doors from the kitchen to the front part of the house. There is also the usual

## PLANS OF FIFTY CONVENIENT HOUSES. 175

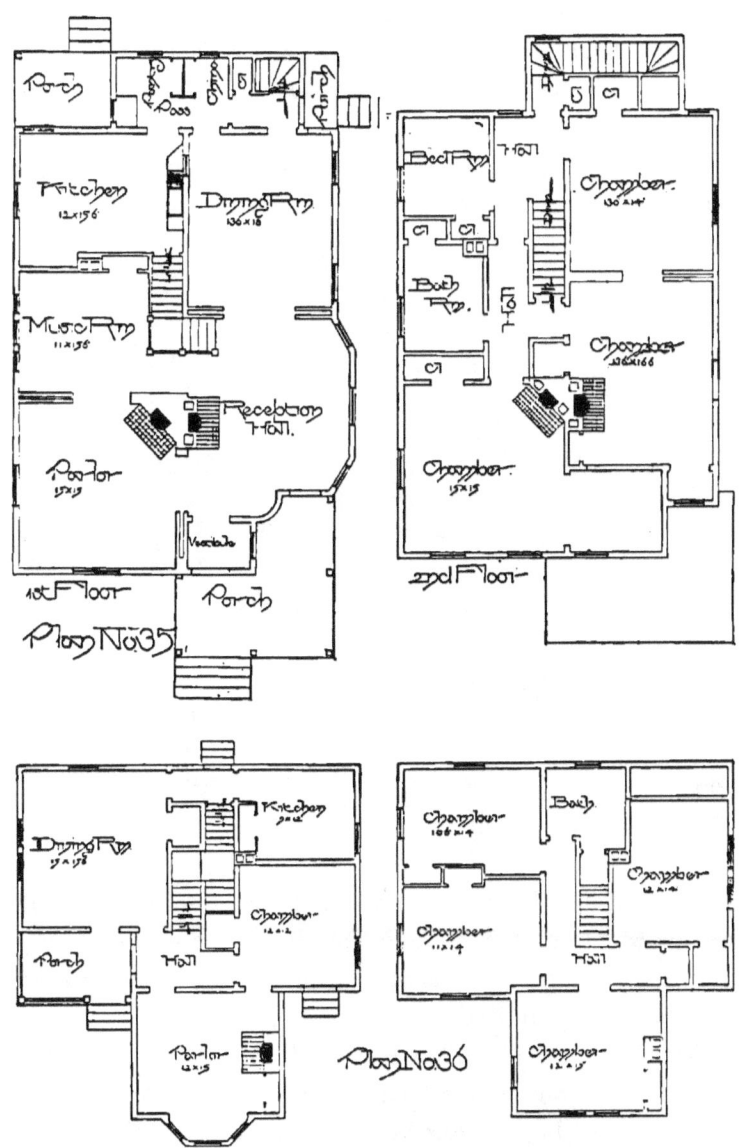

pantry passage. On the second floor there are four good bedrooms, a linen closet, and a bath-room. The cost of the building, without appurtenances, would be about $2,100, as per schedule "B."

Plan No. 38 is another square, one-chimney plan. The house is broad enough so that it gives a little better bath-room

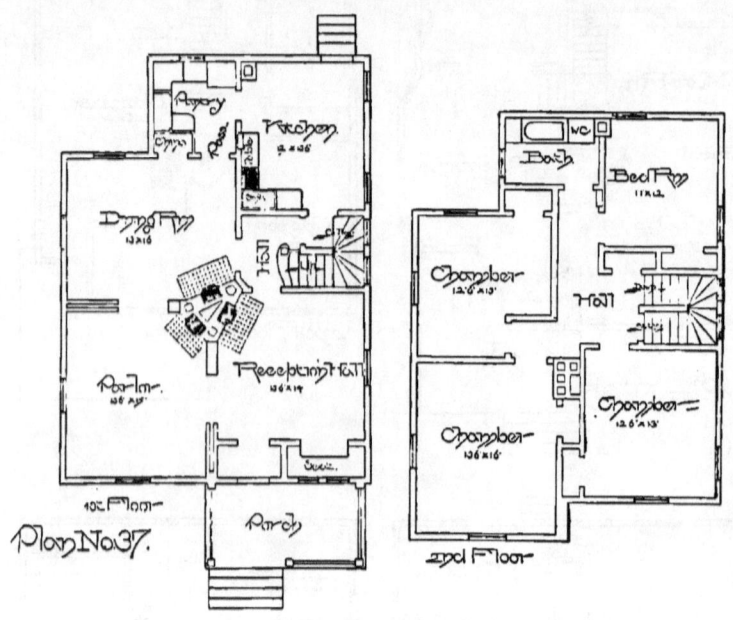

arrangement than is shown in some of the narrower plans. The great drawback to this house is that there is only one stairway, and that in front. If a cellar is wanted, the stairway can go down under the main stairs.

Plan No. 39. This plan has six bedrooms on the second floor. The hall on the first floor has two closets in front. There is a projecting bay window from the first landing of the front stairway.

This house was built for a minister. The library room is shown. Projecting from it is a window-seat. On one side is a large fireplace. The dining-room is separated from the front part of the house by a hall. Both sitting-room and dining-room have bay ends of a form to give a view to the street in front.

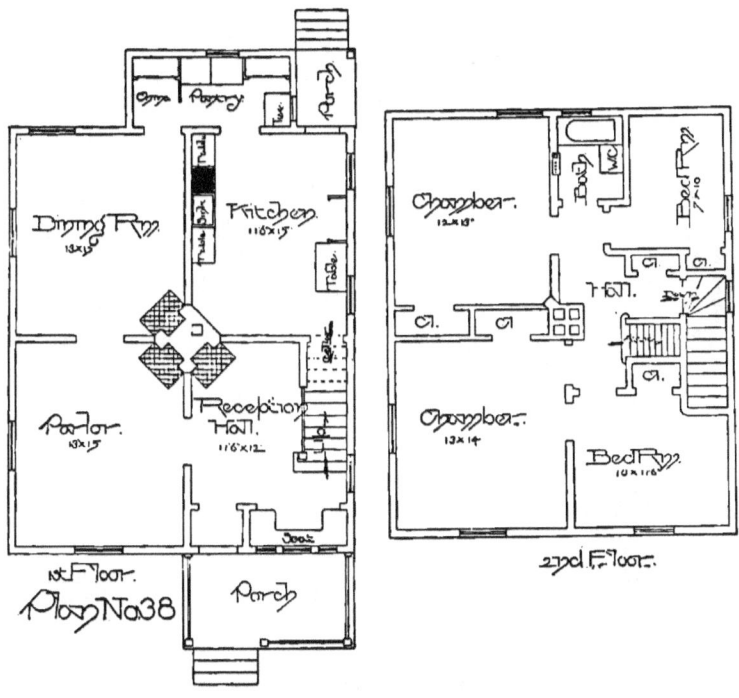

The side-hall communicates with the kitchen as well as the dining-room. In this hall is a closet, presumably for the boys. There is a liberal supply of closets on the second floor. The servant's room is cut off from the other part of the house. The attic is plastered. This building, without appurtenances described in schedule " B," cost $3,500.

Plan No. 40. The rear hall with the side entrance is the thing which will commend this house, as far as its floor plan is concerned. It is an old-style plan, and is wasteful of room. The building cost about $3,100, as per schedule " B."

Plan No. 41 is an eight-room house with a simple stairway. The outside walls are of brick. It has a side entrance. The

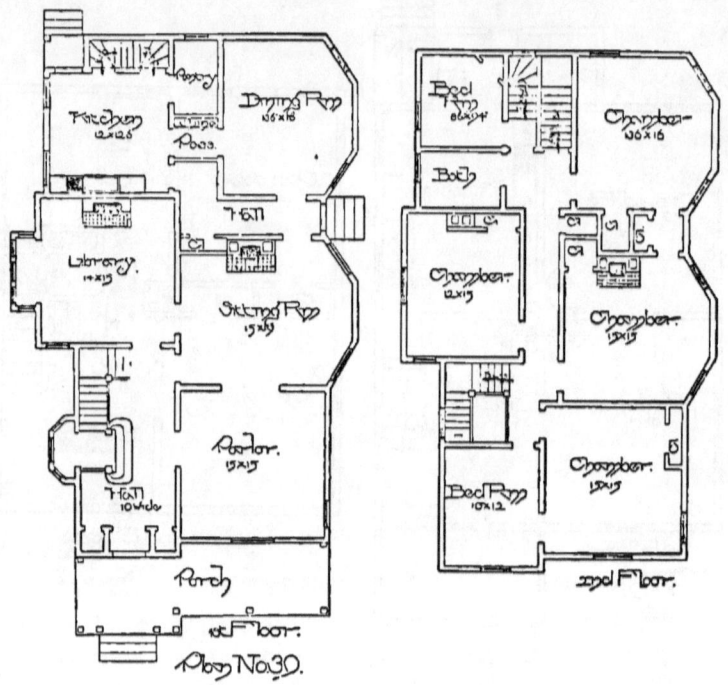

plan is a fairly good one. There are two closets on the first floor, opening from the hall. There is an abundant supply on the second floor. The building cost $3,400, as per schedule " B."

Plan No. 42 belongs to the centre hall type, which is less common now than in years past. The parlor, as here lettered,

## PLANS OF FIFTY CONVENIENT HOUSES. 179

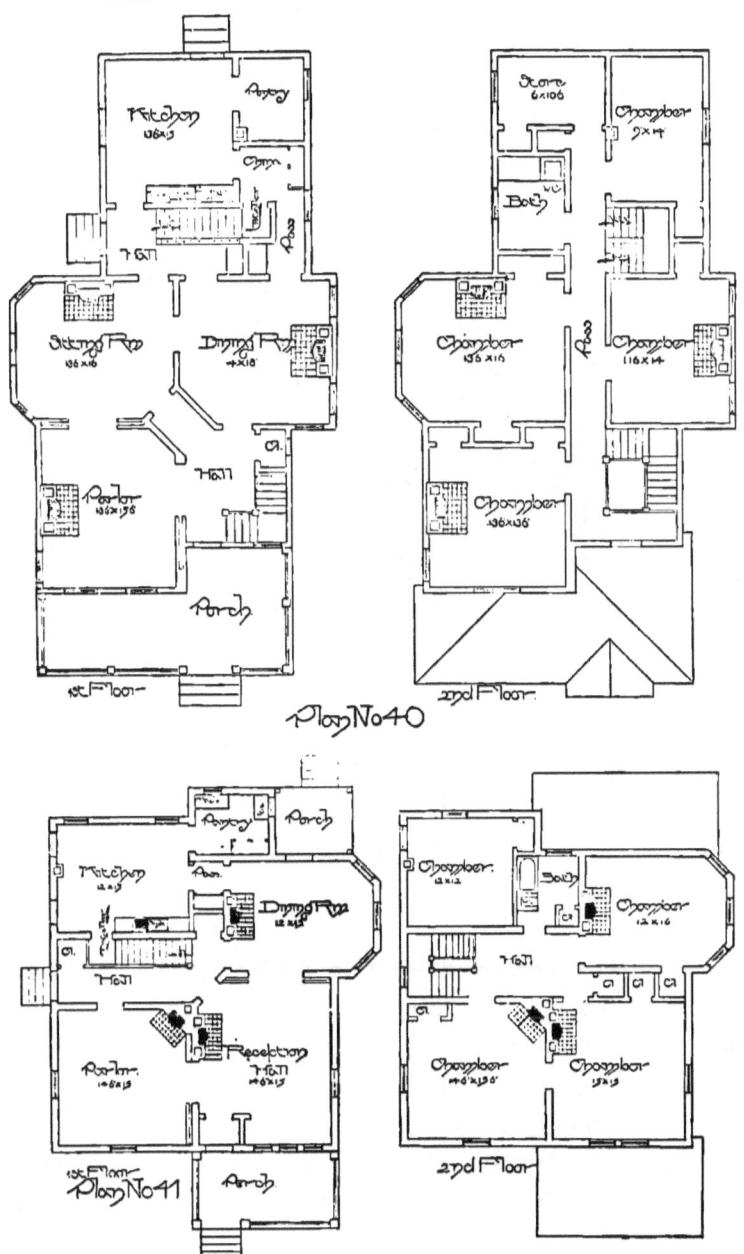

is in reality the sitting-room. A bedroom is shown on the first floor. In each of the four principal rooms a grate is indicated. A hall communicating with the second floor from the cellar is shown in the rear. The kitchen, pantry, and china-closet arrangements are such as have been fully described in other

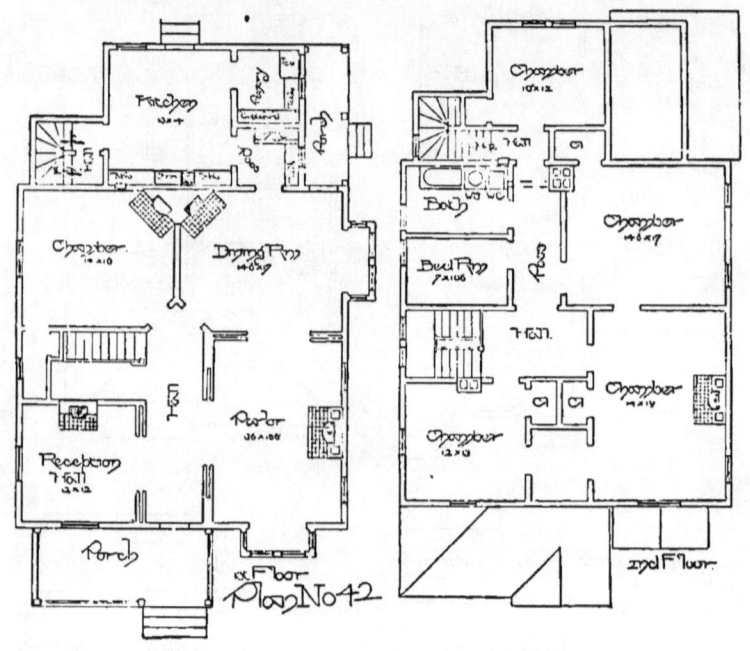

chapters. The side-porch, next to the pantry, affords means of putting ice into the refrigerator without coming into the room. The reception-hall and dining-room are connected by sliding doors. Five bedrooms and a bath-room and liberal closets are shown on the second floor. The front stairway to this floor is broad and easy. The details of the exterior of this structure were carefully rendered, and the appearance altogether satisfactory. An outline drawing of the front is shown. Small gables, similar in design to the one in front, show from the sides. The building, according to schedule "B," cost $2,800, without the appurtenances.

## CHAPTER XXVI.

EIGHT PLANS. — EACH SUITED TO FAMILY REQUIREMENTS. — DOUBLE HOUSES. — AN ELABORATE FLOOR PLAN. — A SHINGLE HOUSE. — A BRICK HOUSE.

PLAN No. 43, while not economical as to arrangement, is well suited to the requirements of the people who own it. There are no children. The lady does not employ a servant. The cost of the building would be about $2,200.

Plan No. 44. Double houses are not easy to plan where they are very long. This house was built, one part to live in and the other to rent. The living part has an entrance to the front; and the rental part one, removed from it, at the side. The centre partition is lined on both sides with sheathing lath; that is, sheathing with dovetails cut into it, so that the plastering will stick to it, which makes it solid, and, to a certain extent, deadens the sound. The lettering of the plan clearly indicates its arrangement. The cost, without appurtenances, as by schedule " B," is $5,000.

Most of the plans given that are only two rooms deep may be made into double houses by enlarging the amount of window space front and rear, and placing the bath-room side of the house on the exposed side. This gives direct light.

Plan No. 45. This house is built on a plat of ground having about seventy feet frontage. The side-hall arrangements give two entirely independent rooms in front. There is a good closet in the hall. From here we pass to the dining-room,

FIGURE 24.

library, or parlor, and to the second floor. Only one stairway is used. The pantry and china arrangements are shown. We enter the cellar stairway from the pantry passage. The kitchen is planned according to the general principles previously set forth.

On the second floor are four bedrooms and a bath-room.

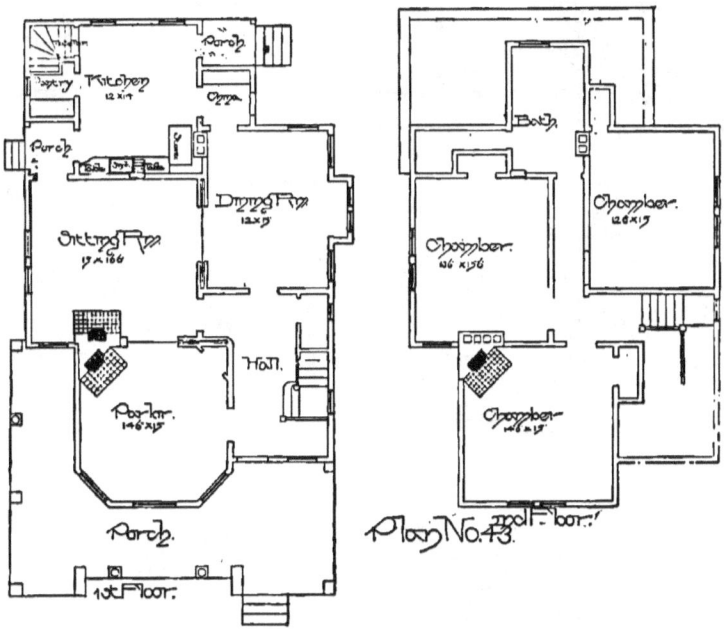

Each room, including the bath, is supplied with closets, and there is a linen closet in the hall. A stairway leads to the attic, in which there is an abundance of room for other chambers, should they be needed. ' The building, without appurtenances, according to schedule "B," cost $2,100. Fig. 24 is a photographic view of exterior.

Plan No. 46 is not greatly different in its general arrange-

184        CONVENIENT HOUSES.

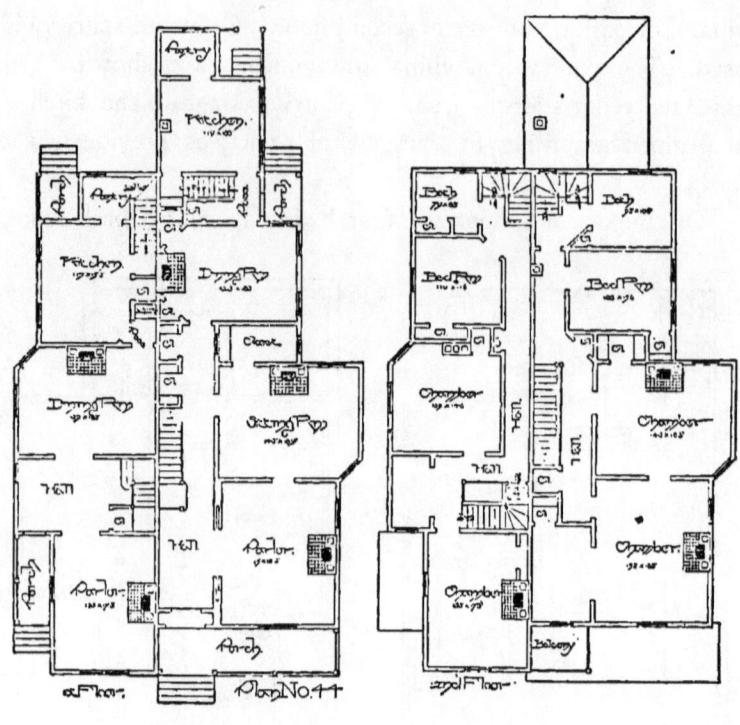

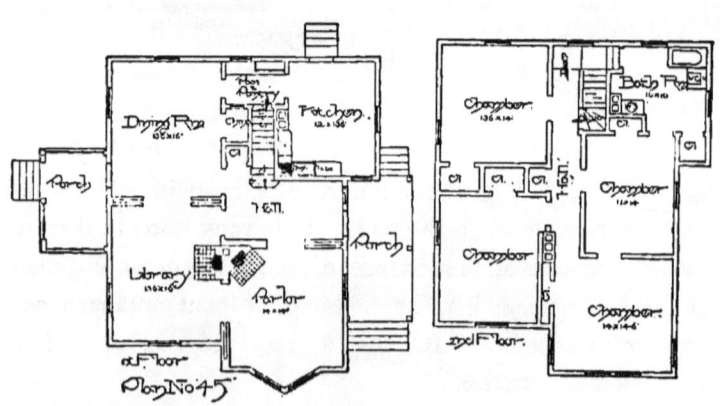

ment from others that have been shown. The details, however, are more complete, and it is generally more satisfactory than other houses of the same type. The vestibule arrangement in the front hall is very satisfactory. There is a window-seat under the stairs. The china-room arrangement is convenient. It has an open stairway running out of it to the rear of the second story.

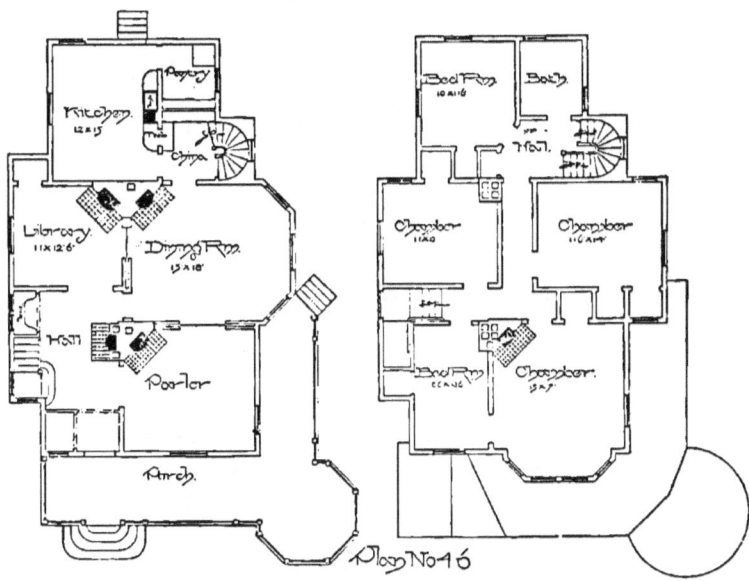

There is a laundry in the basement, and large closets on the second floor.

Fig. 25 is an elevation. It is a very picturesque house. Cost, as by schedule " B," $3,400.

Plan 47. This house was designed for a west frontage. It has a porch in front, a pagoda extension on the south side, and a carriage-porch on the north side. There are a set of storm doors and double inside doors. The reception-hall is thirteen by fifteen feet in the clear. At one side of this hall is a grate.

There is an archway over the front window. On each side of the mantel are shown seats, which may be treated as a part thereof.

The stairway may be seen from this reception-hall. It is separated from it merely by an open-work screen. The parlor connects with the reception-hall by sliding doors. It has a large window in front, and two smaller ones at the side.

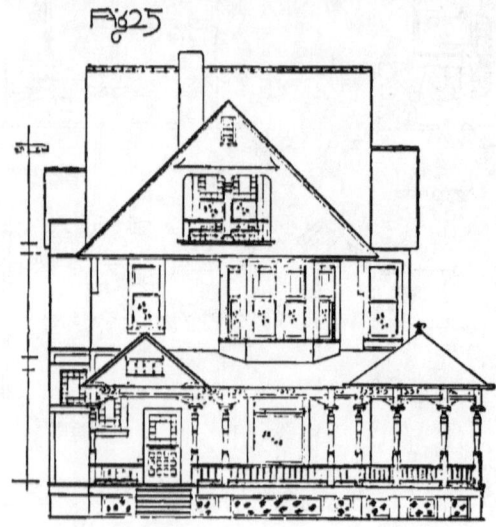

Fig. 25

The parlor connects with the sitting-room by sliding doors, as shown. There is a similar sliding door connecting the stair-hall and sitting-room. Thus the reception-hall and stair-hall, sitting-room and parlor, may be thrown together.

There is a bay end at the south side of the sitting-room. Sliding doors are not indicated between the dining-room and sitting-room, or between the dining-room and hall. They could be so placed, if desired.

There are two doors from the sitting-room to the dining-room, one on each side of the fireplace. There is sufficient wall space in the dining-room that these doors may be folded out of the way. The library connects with the stair-hall and rear hall.

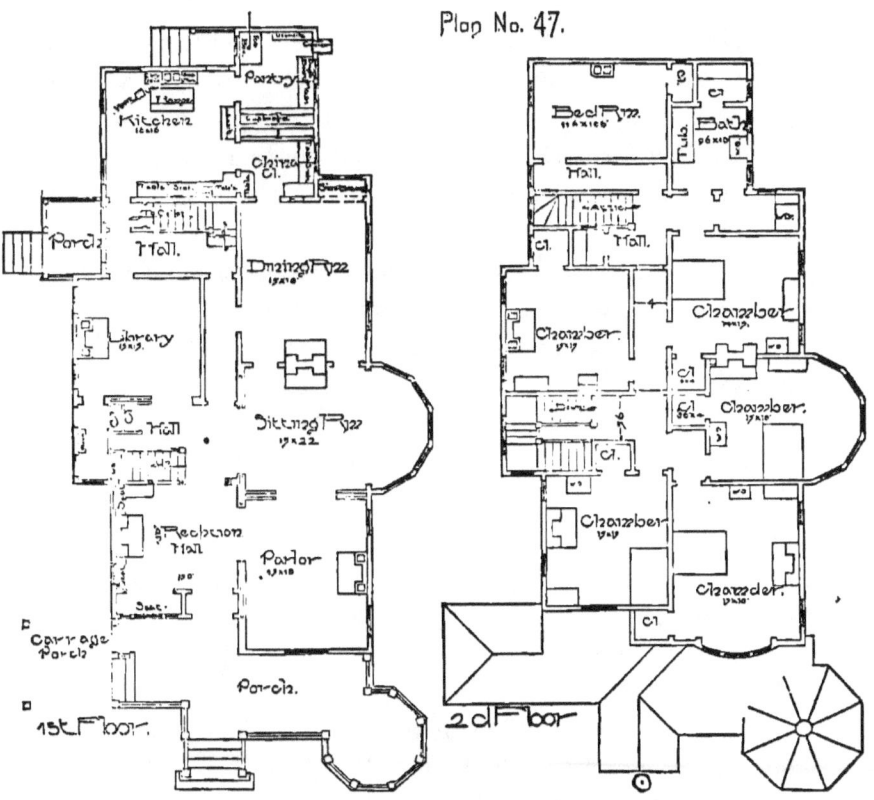

Plan No. 47.

There is a large closet room under the stairway. In it is a small closet, and places for a chest of drawers, and a wash-stand. This would be particularly useful in case the library were to be used as a bedroom.

There is a door separating the rear from the front hall.

There are two doors between the kitchen and the rear hall. The passageway between these doors is lighted by a window.

The sideboard in the dining-room is built into one end of this room. The windows are placed about five feet above the floor, and would look well of stained glass.

The kitchen is sixteen by sixteen feet. On one side are a table, sink, drain, and table, successively arranged as here named. In the china-closet is an extension of the last-named table. There is a slide which cuts off communication between the china-closet and the kitchen when this table is not in use. In the china-closet are another sink, table, etc., which could be used for washing and caring for the china, glass, and silver that one does not care to take into the kitchen.

There is good ventilation in the kitchen. Back of the range are shown two flues. A dry-box is placed on a level with the top of the range, and has openings in the bottom and into the flue. In this way, any articles placed therein will be readily dried and ventilated. The warm air from the range passes through the box and into the flue.

In the pantry are a dough-board and flour-bins, a cupboard for stores, and one for utensils. There is space for an ice-box or refrigerator next to the rear porch. It has a drain connection with the outside.

The landing of the front stairway is in the front of the building, as shown. The rear stairway is separated by a door from the rear hall. In the bedrooms, the beds, dressing-cases, and wash-stands are indicated on the plan. The front chamber has a circular window in front. Each room can be entered from the hall without going through any other room. There is a grate in each chamber. The closets are all very large; in each of the front rooms they are three and one-half by four and one-half feet. In the south-side chambers one is three and one-half by four feet, and the other is four by four feet. In the rear hall there is a large closet which may be used for general purposes. In all closets on this floor there is abundant room for drawers, hooks, shelves, etc.

The bath-room arrangement is somewhat different from that

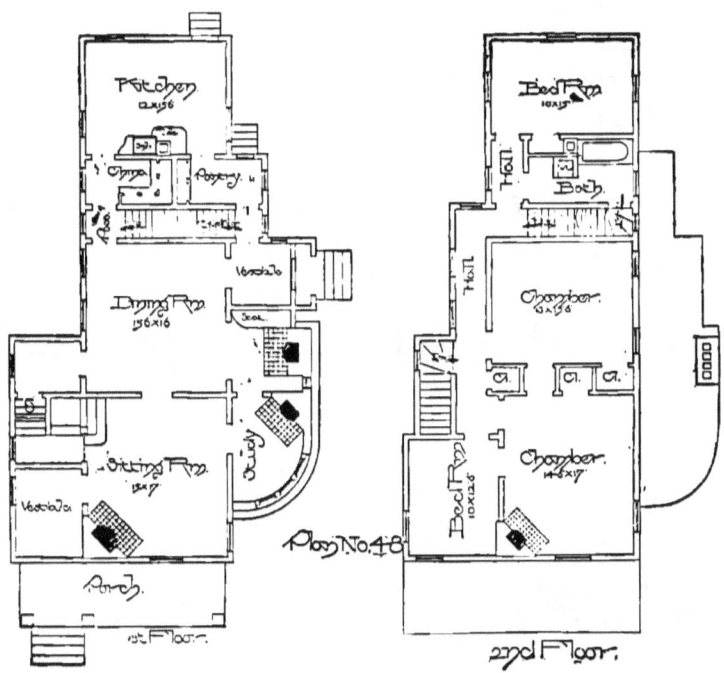

in general use. It will be noticed that the water-closet is separated from the bath-room proper, though connected with it by a door. One can enter either the bath-room or this water-closet room from the rear hall. In the bath-room is a large closet in which may be arranged a chest of drawers, and, if desired, a ventilated receptacle for soiled linen. This closet is lighted by a window. Cost, as by schedule "B," $10,000.

Plan No. 48 is of a house well suited to the requirements of the people who live in it. Fig. 26 is a view of the exterior. It is a shingle house of a severe type. The side projection is a combination of brick and stone. Cost, without appurtenances, $3,400.

Plan No. 49, without appurtenances, has been built for

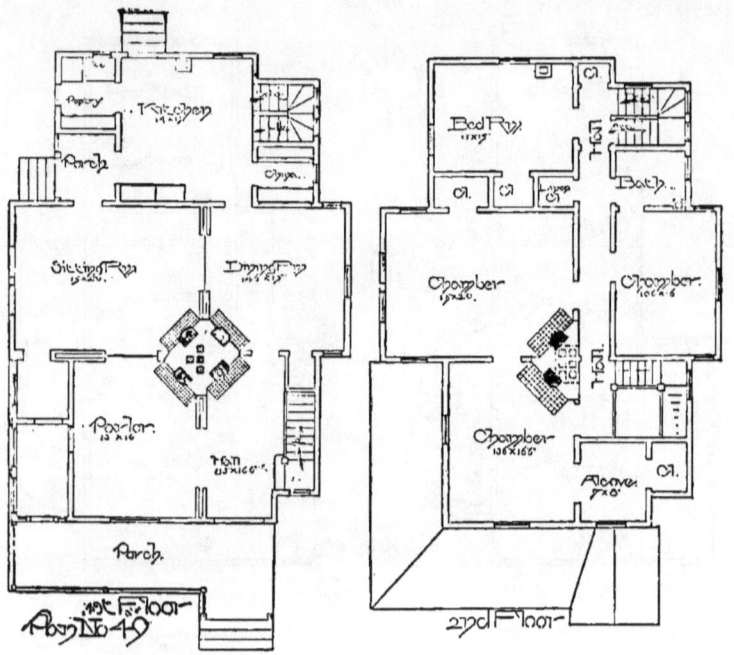

$3,400. It is finished in both stories in hard wood, has a front and rear stairway, and a side entrance. A central chimney contains four grates. The closet arrangement is as good as in any plan in this collection.

Figs. 27 and 28 are elevations. Fig. 28 shows how the conservatory at the side is finished so as to appear with, and as a part of, the porch.

FIGURE 26.

Front. Fig. 27.

Side. Fig. 28.

Plan No. 50. This is a plan of a brick house, built, without appurtenances, as per schedule " B," for $10,000. The external walls are of selected dark cherry red brick, laid in red mortar. The stone work, where exposed above grade, is of Ohio red sandstone, quarry face. There is very little detail to the exterior. The general style of design is quiet and unobtrusive. Red sandstone is selected to go with the brick-work

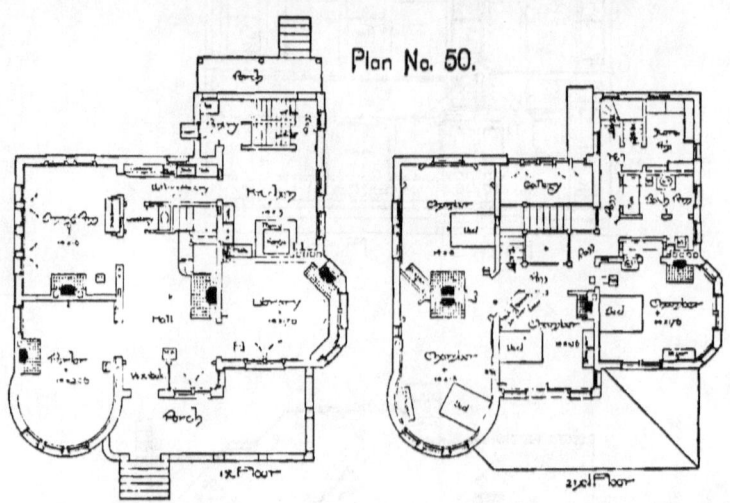

Plan No. 50.

in order to present a solid mass of color, rather than a variation between a light stone and brick work. The interior is complete in all its details; the attic is finished as well as the parlor; all is of quartered oak. Over the butler's pantry, in the rear of the hall, is a balcony. Above this balcony is a large window, twelve feet wide and ten feet high, divided with narrow mullions, and glazed with artistic patterns of stained glass. At one side of the hall is a large fireplace, with panelled wood-work above to ceiling. The sides of the hall are wainscoted to the height of six feet with small panels.

The ceiling is of oak. The dining-room and library are finished the same as hall, with oak ceiling omitted. Other details of the plan, in the light of what has been said in previous chapters, are self-explanatory. All has been planned according to the general principles set forth. The butler's pantry is arranged so that all china and glassware are cared for in that room rather than in the kitchen. Fig. 29 is an exterior view of this plan.

Fig. 29.

# PRACTICAL HOUSE-BUILDING.

## CHAPTER XXVII.

PRACTICAL POINTS. — WATER. — LOCATION OF HOUSE ON LOT. — DRAINING THE CELLAR. — MASON WORK. — FOUNDATIONS. — WALKS. — PIERS. — FLUES. — CISTERNS. — DAMP COURSE.

IN this section of the book it is proposed to consider, in as plain a manner as possible, the construction of all the details of a house.

### LOCATING THE HOUSE.

First is the placing of the house on the lot. If it have an east or a west front, it is common to set the north side of the house within a few feet of the north line. On a small lot this gives more south and sun exposure. The distance the house is set back from the front of the lot depends largely upon what one's neighbors have done or may do. In the case of a north or south frontage, the west side of the house is usually placed to the west line. This brings the east side of the house in the afternoon shade. Under any circumstances, there should never be less than eighteen inches of space beyond the north or west wall. If the projection of cornice is greater, there should be more than this.

### WATER.

The next thing to do when one begins to build, is to provide water for the builder. This is from the city water service, if any; otherwise from a well. If a driven well is used, it is best to locate it on the inside of the house, near the kitchen sink, and allow the builder to provide a common pump for use during building operations. The cistern and well pumps should go into the plumber's contract. It is not necessary that all the plumbing contract be let at the time the city water service is supplied. The method of letting contracts is explained in another part of the book.

### EXCAVATING.

In excavating for a house, the loam, or upper strata of earth, should be separated from that which comes below. After the walls are placed, the openings around the outside should not be filled at once; certainly not until the wall is dry and the mortar set. After this, the grading and filling should begin. The grade line of the house should be slightly above that of the sidewalk, and there should be a general slope to it. If there is an alley in the rear, the slope should be divided to reach it, if possible. The drainage, excavating and filling connected with the plumbing, gas supplies, etc., should be done early in the building period. Thus the entire surface becomes compact and natural by the time the building is finished. If it should become apparent that there will be superfluous earth, it should be removed from the lot.

### DRAINING.

Where there is a clay soil, and in sections of the country where cellars are inclined to be damp, they should be drained. This is done in various ways; usually by running an open farm tile around and below the level of the cellar wall, which should have connection preferably with a dry well; but if nothing better presents itself, with the sewer drain, although a connection of this kind is not safe. The air which will come into this drain from the sewer will contaminate the soil, and in that way affect the health of the occupants of the building. In some instances a sewer connection from this drain is necessary, but only then should it be used.

Another method of draining a cellar is to excavate below the level of lowest mason-work, and fill in a depth of about twelve inches with broken stone, which is given a drain connection with proper outlet. The space between stone particles acts as a drain.

### MASON-WORK.

The mason-work should be of brick or stone. First, we will consider that of brick, which is common to frame houses and is sometimes used for brick buildings. The foundations, walks, piers, and flues should be of hard burned brick. All should be laid wet, excepting in freezing weather, with lime mortar. The outside exposed brick should be preferably of a dark cherry-red color, laid in white or red mortar. The latter is in most general use. The joints for exposed work should be in form as indicated in Fig. 30; in mason's parlance, these are called "rodded joints." 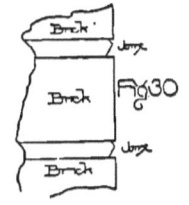 The joint is first cut down from above, with trowel, then the rod is placed along the upper edge of the joint, and the mortar is cut away with a knife in the form indicated. Then the vertical joints are trimmed in the same way; thus no mortar projects beyond the face of the brick. This form of joint is desirable for all kinds of exposed work, where one desires better work than is usual in foundations and other exposed brick work. Brick work should have struck or common joints in the cellar and outside exposed walls, only where small cost is of great importance. Brick work should be left rough where it is desired to plaster. Foundation walls and piers usually continue from sixteen to thirty inches above grade; twenty or twenty-four inches is most common. On this is placed a sill in most frame houses. Outside walls and piers generally begin from eighteen to thirty inches below grade line, where not influenced by the cellar. In an ordinarily cold climate the freezing line is four or five feet. Eighteen inches or two feet is usual, however, in the construction of frame buildings, and the results are not unsatisfactory. A damp-course of slate or hard limestone is sometimes placed just above the grade line, to prevent the passage of moisture from the brick wall below to that above. These general statements as to brick work apply alike to that used in brick and frame buildings, as do also the statements as to interior walls, chimneys, etc., which follow.

To prevent the passage of moisture through brick walls below grade from the outside, a coating of Portland cement is sometimes used. Coal-tar is also used, but is not as good as the cement.

## CHAPTER XXVIII.

BRICK FOUNDATIONS. — LAYING BRICK. — COLORED MORTARS. — COLORED BRICKS. — BRICK VENEERING. — HOT-AIR FLUES. — DETAILS OF BRICK CONSTRUCTION. — CHIMNEYS AND FLUES. — HOLLOW WALLS. — CELLAR. — ASH-PITS. — GRATES.

A BRICK wall under a frame house is ordinarily nine inches thick; that is, it is called a nine-inch wall. In reality, it is the thickness of the length of a brick. Under these walls are placed footings. For a two-story frame house there are usually two footings of two courses each projecting two inches. Thus a nine-inch wall would have the bottom footing seventeen inches wide. In ordinary American brick work there is what is called a bond to each seventh course. The bond is made by laying the brick crosswise the wall rather than lengthwise. In that way it ties or bonds the wall together in the direction of its length. Below grade, where the brick work is not exposed, the bond is made by laying a continuous course of brick in this way. Above the grade, the bond is made by laying each alternate brick across the wall. This is called a header and stretcher bond. The stretcher is the brick which lies lengthwise the wall in the common way, and the header is the one which shows its head and runs crosswise the wall to form the bond. Thus there is a continuous row of alternating headers and stretchers in the bond course, which occurs, as said before, each seventh course. Another bond, by some brick-layers called the American bond, does not show on the outside. The corners of the inside of the outer row of bricks are clipped, so that the bond brick runs part way into the outside course, and thus is out of sight. It is an artificial arrangement and not satisfactory; it is not good construction. The header and stretcher bond is the best for exposed work, where both appearance and solidity are to be considered. There are other forms of bond, — the old English and the Flemish, — but they need not be considered here.

All brick should be thoroughly "slushed" with mortar; that is, all spaces between brick should be thoroughly filled. The ideal condition would be to have all brick excepting the exposed faces entirely surrounded by mortar.

The selection of the brick for the exposed fronts in a frame as well as a brick house should be made before the brick work is begun; at least a large supply should be selected and piled up. While the brick cannot all be of the same shade, different shades can be selected for different walls — a lighter shade for a north wall, and a darker for a south wall, a different shade for an east and a west wall. Very slight variations can be made in the ells and projections. This would apply to pressed, stock, or common brick, though pressed brick is usually selected before delivery.

The best color for exposed work is a dark cherry red. The best-appearing work with indifferent brick can be made with the use of a reddish brown mortar. The use of this kind of mortar is increasing. White putty mortar is made in the ordinary way, excepting that white sand, similar to that from Lake Pontchartrain, rather than gray sand, is used. It contains more lime than ordinary mortar. The mortar is said to be richer.

Black brick are made by heating and then dipping in coal-tar. Enamelled, glazed, and colored brick can be purchased in the larger markets as desired. Various forms of ornamental brick work are possible even where only the common brick are used. Moulded pressed brick are quite common, and the results of their use very satisfactory.

Brick veneering is not unusual in sections of the country where brick is very expensive and the effect of a brick house desired. It is a four-inch brick wall anchored to a frame structure. The anchoring is sometimes accomplished by driving twenty-penny nails into wood-work in a way to project into joints.

Hot-air flues in brick walls are sometimes tin-lined, though this is not necessary when they are smoothly plastered, providing it is possible to make them eight inches square. If they cannot be made deeper than the width of a brick, four inches, they should be tin-lined. A four-inch hot-air flue can be placed in a nine-inch wall by setting the two outside rows of brick on edge.

Hollow walls have not been regarded with great favor during recent years, for the reason that it is difficult to secure their proper construction. A hollow wall is usually twelve inches in thickness, with the middle course of brick omitted excepting at the corners and adjacent to openings. Suitable ties are placed across the open space.

### CELLAR.

It now is in order to consider various features of interior brick work and details which come in connection therewith. Cellars are usually from seven to eight feet deep. As this does not give all the height necessary for furnace or other heating apparatus, it is usually pitted; that is, it is let down into the cellar floor, and a brick area built around the opening to the furnace-door. Because of the necessity for pitting the furnace, the walls of the house adjacent thereto should continue eighteen inches below the level of other walls.

Walls inside of cellar should continue to the top of joist. This completely separates the different compartments of the cellar, or from that part of the house where there is no cellar.

There should be a man-hole opening to the parts under the house where there is no cellar.

Lintels or wooden supports should be provided over all openings in cellar, and over all openings in inside brick walls.

Wooden brick should be provided and built in where it is necessary to attach wood work to brick work. Usually this is about two feet six inches apart in a vertical or horizontal direction. The wooden brick should be the thickness of the brick itself and the mortar joints; that is, there should be no mortar above or below a wooden brick. Iron ventilators should be provided; one in each outside wall under each room where cellar windows are not provided. Windows are not usually provided where there is no cellar.

### CHIMNEYS.

It is known that wood-work should not come directly in contact with chimneys. The framework should never rest on a chimney. There are reasons for this other than those which have a regard for safety from fire, one of which is that the chimney is not liable to settle. If it does not, the shrinkage of the wood-work, which in a two-story frame house will sometimes amount to two inches in the height of the building, makes a high place around the flues, where the frame comes in contact with or rests on the chimney. All chimney-stacks should extend above highest point of ridge of roof, and the extreme tops should be laid in Portland cement. All the exposed brick of the chimney should be hard-burned. If due regard were paid to these points, there would be no rickety chimney-tops. All flues should be thoroughly plastered on the inside. If chimneys were plastered on the outside, wherever they come in contact with the wood-work, the complaint of fires from defective flues would be hushed.

Fig. 31 illustrates the common form of constructing a chimney breast where a grate is to be used. The flues are eight and one-half inches square. A passage to the ash-pit is shown. The grate opening is two feet wide; the jambs on each side are one foot six inches wide; thus the entire width of the breast is five feet. Other dimensions as indicated. Where there are grates on two floors of the house, one above the other, or where it is desirable for any reason to have a flue pass around a grate, it is necessary that the breast should be five feet wide. It is clear that the grate from below must have its own flue out to the top of the chimney. Thus the grate flue from the first story must pass around the grate of the second story, if there be one. If there is no grate above, or if it is not desired to pass a flue around the first-story grate, the chimney breast need be only four feet wide; that is, it would have the usual two-feet opening to the grate, and twelve rather than eighteen inch jambs on each side. On one side of the dotted line is indicated flue construction for a brick wall, and on the other for a wood wall.

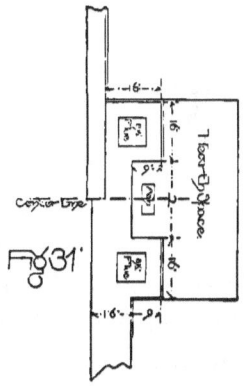

The hearth should rest on what is called a trimmer arch, which is made of brick. It springs from the chimney breast to the header of wood in front. It is four inches in thickness. It is laid in the ordinary way, and at the proper time is filled on the top with concrete by the mantel-setter. In case a grate on the second floor connects with the ash-pit, one of the flues at the side is used for this purpose.

Fig. 32 indicates a common form of corner grate. The flues in this as well as Fig. 31 are drawn close together and come out through the attic and roof in a smaller stem. There should be distinct separation of flues.

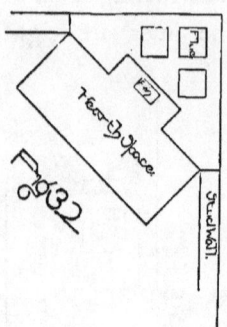

Ash-pits are frequently made of four-inch brick walls strengthened by brick pilasters. These pits are usually from three to four feet in depth and the width of the chimney breast, and nearly as high as the depth of the cellar. Where more than one grate empties into an ash-pit, it is common to divide it into compartments, one for each fire. The top of the pit is crowned with a brick arch. Ash-dumps are sometimes provided for the grate, depending, of course, upon the kind of grate used, and ash-pit doors of iron for the pits themselves.

### OUTSIDE CELLAR-WAY.

The side walls of an outside cellar-way should continue to the bottom of cellar. It should be floored the same as the cellar itself.

### AREAS.

Areas of brick should be provided around all cellar openings that continue below grade. The bottoms of these areas should be floored with paving-brick. This is better than cement, as it admits of natural drainage.

## CHAPTER XXIX.

STONE MASONRY. — CUT STONE. — TERRA COTTA. — PRIVY VAULTS. — CISTERNS. — FILTERS FOR CISTERNS. — BRICK PAVEMENTS. — CEMENT PAVEMENTS.

STONE foundations for dwelling-houses are usually made of native stone, and anything that may be said here must necessarily conform to general rather than special conditions. The best stone that can be used for this purpose is hard, non-absorbent limestone. There are many varieties of stone conglomerates throughout the country which are valuable for foundation uses. Stone should be laid up in lime mortar in the direction of its natural bed in the quarry, with a sufficiency of bond stone. For ordinary dwelling-house work there should be at least one footing eight inches in depth, and six inches projection on each side of the wall. Stone walls for foundations are usually made not less than eighteen inches in thickness. It is not easy to lay a good stone wall less than eighteen inches in thickness. While the same number of cubic feet of stone work may cost less than brick work, a stone foundation ordinarily would cost more than one of brick for the reason that a brick wall does not have to be so thick. It usually takes about half the number of cubic feet of brick work that it does of stone work to answer the same purpose. Where stone is available at low cost it is best to use it. Interior brick walls may rest on stone footings. The inside of stone walls should be neatly pointed after other work has been finished. Stone work above grade may be finished in many ways — random range work, rubble work, regular course range work, etc. After the other work has been finished, the mortar should be raked out a short distance and a finish joint added.

### CUT STONE.

Cut-stone work is too large a subject to consider in detail. There are several points which cannot be overlooked. There should be drips cut under all projections, so that the water will not run down the other stone or brick work and stain it. A drip is merely a little V-shaped channel cut on the under side of the stone work. They are found on the under side of most window-sills. In door, window, or other openings, the stone work should underlie or overlie all wood work at least two inches. This may be explained by stating that the stone window-sill should underlie the wood sill two inches, and the window cap should overlie the wood cap at least two inches. Generally speaking, coping should project on each side of the wall about two inches. Sills should extend at least one inch beyond the face of the wall. Window-sills should be no less than five inches in thickness. Door-sills should generally be about seven or eight inches, and extend at least one inch beyond the face of the wall, and through its full thickness. The water table of the stone foundation usually forms the window cap of the cellar windows, and the cap course, which comes at the grade line, the cellar window-sills. In this case it is necessary that the stone should run farther into the wall where the openings occur.

Stone steps are not over six and one-half to seven and one-half inches in thickness, with from nine to twelve inch treads. They underlie and lap about one inch, and have walls, the same material as the foundation, for lower supports. These walls should go to the full depth of the house walls with which they come in contact. Thus there is no danger of settling. Stone steps are frequently used in the front of the yard from the sidewalk to the grade level where there is considerable elevation. In such cases it is necessary to use stone side pieces for the steps, to prevent caving and to make a neat finish. Where flagging is cheap, it is well to use it for walks and porch floors.

### TERRA-COTTA WORK.

Terra cotta is the perfection of brick-making. It is the only building material which is not affected by changes of temperature, or other natural or artificial conditions to which the building may be subject. It may be described as being a very plastic material; that is, anything can be done with it. It can be worked into any form that is desired, excepting long lintels, and even in that case there are means of arriving at the desired result and giving a lintel form in a very proper manner. Ornamental terra cotta is modelled by artists before being burned, and the best results may naturally be expected.

### PRIVY VAULT.

The size of the privy vault is usually three and one-half by four and one-half feet, elliptical, and from ten to twenty feet deep, according to the character of the soil. Usually it is walled up with four-inch dry brick wall. Piers should be provided at corners for privy building. In some instances it is required that the privy vault should be made water-tight. In that case it should be built the same as a cistern, with round bottom and cemented interior surface. When it is desired to connect the privy vault with the sewer, it should be cemented in the manner just described, with a siphon vitrified pipe connection with the drain to the sewer. The siphon prevents solid rubbish, which may be thrown into the vault, from getting into the drain and clogging it.

### CISTERN.

The cistern is generally located near the rear kitchen wall, say ten or twelve feet therefrom. The walls, arch, and neck are usually four inches in thickness when capacity of cistern does not exceed one hundred and twenty-five barrels. Otherwise the brick work mentioned should be eight inches in thickness. The brick should be laid in domestic cement, and smoothly coated with Portland cement. It should be connected with the down spouts of the house by means of vitrified drain-pipe, the same as described in connection with plumbing work, though it has no connection therewith.

The following table gives capacity of cisterns of various sizes.

CAPACITY OF CISTERN IN GALLONS FOR EACH TEN INCHES IN DEPTH.

| DIAM. IN FEET. | GALLONS. | DIAM. IN FEET. | GALLONS. | DIAM. IN FEET. | GALLONS. |
|---|---|---|---|---|---|
| 2 | 19.50 | 6½ | 206.85 | 12 | 705.0 |
| 2½ | 30.50 | 7 | 239.88 | 13 | 827.4 |
| 3 | 44.60 | 7½ | 275.40 | 14 | 959.6 |
| 3½ | 59.97 | 8 | 313.33 | 15 | 1,101.6 |
| 4 | 78.33 | 8½ | 353.72 | 20 | 1,958.4 |
| 4½ | 99.14 | 9 | 396.56 | 25 | 3,059.9 |
| 5 | 122.40 | 9½ | 461.40 | 30 | 4,406.4 |
| 5½ | 148.10 | 10 | 489.60 | 35 | 5,990.0 |
| 6 | 176.25 | 11 | 592.40 | 40 | 7,831.0 |

## FILTERS.

There are various ways of forming a filter. One is to have a small cistern of eight or ten barrel capacity, located between the main cistern and house. It should be divided by a brick wall laid in mortar, but not cemented on either side. The water enters on one side, passes through the brick wall in the middle, and from thence to the cistern beyond. Another plan is to cement the wall, leave an opening at the bottom, and pack the side on which the water enters with charcoal, sand, and gravel. The water passes through this packing and the opening below to the other side of the filter, and then to the cistern. Still another plan is to build the partition as first described on the inside of the cistern proper. All of the water passes to one side of the divided cistern, and through the partition before being drawn out. Thus it has to pass through the brick before it is to be drawn out. Still another filter is made by building what is called a beehive in the bottom of the cistern. It is a beehive form of brick work, with the pump pipe leading to the inside, so that all water has to be drawn through the brick beehive before it is pumped out. According to this plan, as well as the others mentioned, the water is strained through the brick.

It is best that the cistern and independent filter, when used, should be provided with iron rims and cast-iron covers. It is good practice to connect the cistern with a dry well, which is constructed the same as an open vault excepting that the top is arched. This dry-well connection is by means of five-inch vitrified pipe laid in the same manner as sewer pipe.

There is a practice, altogether too common among builders, of connecting the cistern overflow with the vault or sewer. Nothing could be worse than this. The water is certain to be polluted.

## BRICK PAVEMENT.

Brick pavements are used for walks around the house, and sometimes for cellar floors. Cement floors, however, are better for cellars. Brick pavement of all kinds should be made of hard-burned bricks, laid on a six or eight inch bed of sand. The brick walk should not be laid until after all the grading and filling of the lot has been done. It is best to leave the brick walks out of the general contract, so that this work can be delayed until after the house is finished. It is a good thing to have the sodding and the paving in the same contract. The contractor who attends to the sodding can work the two together to a better advantage than if the walks were placed and the sodding done afterwards.

## CEMENT PAVEMENT.

Cement pavements are used for walks around the house, and for cellar floors. Cement is more expensive than brick. The surface to be covered should, first, be levelled, then saturated with water; after which is laid a three-inch bed of cement concrete, made of gravel, sand, and cement in proper proportions. Upon this is placed a three-fourth-inch layer of cement mortar. Ordinary American, hydraulic cement may be used for concrete, but for the three-fourth-inch layer nothing but best Portland cement should be considered. Sometimes the cement work in the cellar is done by the plasterer. Outside cement work for walks requires special skill. In most large cities there are those who make a business of doing this work. They have different formulas and methods of reaching the proper results.

# CHAPTER XXX.

CARPENTER WORK. — FRAMING. — SIZE OF TIMBERS. — HEIGHT OF STORIES. — JOIST. — STUD WALLS. — OUTSIDE SHEATHING. — BUILDING-PAPER. — ROOFS. — OUTSIDE FINISH. — OUTSIDE SHINGLE WALLS. — OUTSIDE CASINGS. — WINDOWS WITH BOX FRAMES. — HINGED OR PIVOTED WINDOWS. — OUTSIDE SHUTTERS. — PORCHES. — LATTICE PORCHES.

### CARPENTER WORK.

IN considering carpenter work, we will first take up framing, and everything which pertains to the outside of the house. All material used for framing should be sound, square-edged material, free from imperfections tending to impair its use, durability, or strength. In different parts of the country, different kinds of lumber are standard for framing purposes. In the South and sections contiguous to it, yellow pine is used; in the North, white pine, hemlock, Norway spruce, poplar, and even hard wood. It is neither profitable nor desirable in this connection to indicate any particular material; it is natural to use the cheapest that is sufficiently strong for framing. The following table indicates the sizes of timber in common use in framing an ordinary dwelling.

| | |
|---|---|
| Sills, outside walls | $6' \times 8''$ |
| Sills, inside walls | $6 \times 8$ |
| Lintels, over openings | $6 \times 10$ |
| Girders, over piers | $6 \times 10$ |
| Plates | 4 thick |
| Rafters, 20 on centres | $2 \times 6$ |
| Horizontal purlins, or roof supports | $4 \times 6$ |

| | |
|---|---|
| Roof posts | $4'' \times 4''$ |
| Bridging | $2 \times 4$ |
| Joists, 1st tier | $2'' \times 10'' \times 16''$ on centres |
| " 2d tier | $2 \times 10 \times 16$ " " |
| " 3d tier | $2 \times 8 \times 16$ " " |
| " deck | $2 \times 6 \times 20$ " " |
| Studs | $2 \times 4 \times 16$ " " |

Rafters, or deck joist, 16" on centres, when to be plastered.

Sizes here given may not be adapted to all sections. There is no occasion for being arbitrary. The sizes may be conformed to the material which is ordinarily used.

Stories ten and a half feet high are generally considered the limit in an ordinary frame house at this time. Nine and a half and ten are more common. This is quite different from the general tendency to high stories a few years ago. Certainly, it is more rational.

## JOISTS.

Joists are usually dressed, so that they have about one-half-inch crown or curve on their upper surface, which would make the centre of the room about one-half inch higher than the sides. They should be trimmed so that all are of the same width and form. Double trimmers and headers — that is, double joist — should be framed around all chimney-breasts, well-holes, scuttles, and openings in the wall. In dwelling-house work they should be mortised and tenoned together, as should be the pieces connecting therewith. In very cheap work headers and trimmers are sometimes spiked together. This is not good practice. For very good work, where heavy weights are to be carried, trimmers and headers should be supported on wrought-iron strips. This, however, is not necessary in ordinary dwelling-house work.

Joists longer than eighteen feet should be twelve inches in

PRACTICAL HOUSE-BUILDING. 215

width. Those running adjacent or parallel to partition or other walls should be firmly spiked thereto. Double joists should be placed under all partitions and supports having no support from below. Where the weight is extra heavy, the double joists should be trussed by a two-by-four-inch stud, spiked in truss form, between them. There should be one row of truss bridging to each span or tier, size as indicated. Header should be framed across pipe duct, about eighteen inches therefrom.

### STUD WALLS.

See Fig. 33. Walls and partitions are usually of two-by-four-inch studding. In large houses it is best that the studding be two by six inches, and plates four inches in thickness and the width of the studding are commonly placed at the bottom and top of the walls of each story. Sometimes, however, the studding continues to the height of two stories, and the joists are supported on a one-by-six-inch "ribbon" piece let into the studding.

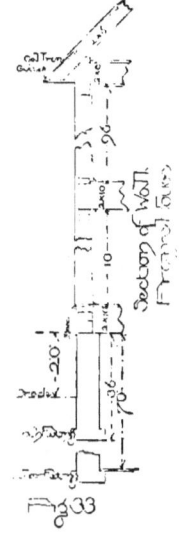

Trusses or supports should be framed over all openings. Sliding-door pockets or runways should be lined with flooring. All corners and angles should be framed solid and have two-inch projections for lathing. Studding four by four inches thick should be framed around all window openings and on three sides of the door openings; bridging, two by two inches, one row for each story. Grounds should be placed on the inside openings, and elsewhere for plastering. The pipe duct, fourteen inches wide, should be placed between studding from kitchen to attic floor. All outside walls of frame houses should be diagonally sheathed with seven-eighths-by-six-inch dressed sheathing. Tongued and grooved material is best for this purpose, although it is not in common use. All sheathing should be covered with six-pound sized building-paper.

Sometimes the insides of brick walls are furred. This means that they are lined on the inside with wood strips two inches in thickness, sixteen inches on centres, and then lathed and plastered. This prevents the passage of the moisture through the brick into the inside of the room.

Various forms of sheathing lath for inside sheathing of a frame house are now in use. This form of lath contemplates a seven-eighth-inch tongued and grooved sheathing on the inside with dove-tailed channels cut into its surface, which form key-room for the plastering.

### ROOF.

Most roofs can be formed with out-posts and purlins. All can be formed in this way where cost is not considered. An ordinary dwelling-house of the size given in these plans does not require separate posts and purlins. There should be double rafters around all chimneys and openings in the roof.

The roof should be sheathed with seven-eighths by four-inch material; where exposed to view, with five-and-one-half-inch beaded flooring. Where deck framing is required, posts and purlins are necessary, size according to weight to be carried.

Where shingles are used for roofing, they should be laid four and one-half inches to the weather for sixteen-inch shingles, with two nails to each. It is best that shingles should be dipped in stain, oil, or paint before they are put on the roof. The durability of shingles is not increased by being painted after they have been laid. The ridge finish of the shingle or slate roof should be of galvanized iron, with about four-inch lap on each side. It may be made as ornamental as desired. Wood should never be used for this purpose. Hips and ridges of slate or shingle roofs may be finished with tin or galvanized iron, lapped on each side about three and one-half inches. Gutters of galvanized iron set up on the first course of shingles or slate, with metallic support from above or below, are better than gutters of wood tin-lined.

Where slate covering is used, any size slate desired may be employed, bearing in mind that the bond should not be less than three and one-half or four inches. There should be two nails to each slate.

### OUTSIDE FINISH.

All lumber used for outside finish should be thoroughly seasoned, clear, smoothly dressed, and free from imperfections tending to impair its use, durability, strength, or appearance. Poplar is the ideal building material for outside finish. It takes paint better than other woods used for this purpose. However, pine
is generally used, for the reason that it is cheaper. Weather-boarding is usually laid with an inch lap four and one-half inches to the weather; three and one-half inches is better.

Drop siding, or German siding as it is sometimes called, makes a warmer and better wall than weather-boarding. It is usually six or eight inches wide, and in form and construction as indicated by Fig. 34.

Outside shingle walls are now quite common. Shingles are used for ornamental purposes in a large proportion of the houses that are built; in some instances they are used exclusively for outside covering. In such cases they are undressed, and are stained commonly with one of the proprietary stains now on the market. Before being placed they are dipped into the stain for about eight inches from their buts, and are laid in piles to dry. Any desired color may be secured, and there are instances where stained shingled walls have gone without any attention or expense for eight or ten years.

Dressed shingles are commonly painted. Their form may be as ornamental as desired. Outside shingles are sometimes laid five and one-half inches to the weather, but four and one-half is better. It is not uncommon at this time to leave all shingles unpainted and unstained. The effect is very agreeable when they become weather-stained.

### OUTSIDE CASINGS.

All horizontal trimmings and casings should be bevelled on the top to shed the water. They should run back under the shingled weather-boarding or other outside covering. There should be tin covering for all projections in excess of one and three-eighths inch. Ordinary window or door casings outside are usually three-eighths inch thick.

### WINDOWS.

All windows in the part of the house regularly occupied should have box frames. Pulley styles should be of hard wood, and the inside bead should be secured with round-headed screws. Sash for plate glass should be one and three-fourths inch thick; side rail, two and one-half inches in rabbet; bottom rail, three and one-eighth inches; and meeting rail, one and one-fourth inch in the rabbet. Sash for common glass may be one and three-eighths inch thick. Other sizes, as given. Sash for rooms finished in hard wood is better when of the wood in which the room is finished. However, where there is great variation this is not necessary. Quartered oak is the material commonly used for hard-wood sash. Almost any hard wood is more liable to warp than pine. All box frames should be provided with turned axle pulleys. Nothing but the best plaited cotton sash-cord should be used. Necessary weights should be provided.

In some of the plans where wide front windows are indicated, the design is called pocket head. There is a pocket above the head of the frame so that a high sash may be run into it. The sash may be pushed up into the pocket; that is, it runs into the wall above the head of the frame. Where the pocket-head window is used, it is necessary that there be a clear space above the frame for the sash to be run up equal to the height of the sash itself.

Hinged or pivoted windows have rabbeted frames which are usually one and three-eighths inch thick. They are used for the most part in unfinished cellars, attics, and unoccupied parts of the house, and preferably for pantry, store-room, and, occasionally, bath-room windows. They may be hung on hinges or pivots. Hinges are better, for the reason that fly screens cannot be used where the sash is pivoted. Sills should slant twenty degrees, with drip piece secured to outside. This prevents the storm from blowing water to the inside.

### OUTSIDE SHUTTERS.

Outside shutters are usually one and three-eighths inch thick, with movable slats; if more than six and one-half feet high, they should be made in three panels each. Arrangements are provided by various manufacturers of hardware for opening outside shutters from the inside of the room. They may be swung either from the sides or top at will. When they are suspended from above they act as an awning; they admit the air but not the rays of the sun.

Sometimes shutters are cut at the meeting rail, so that the upper or lower section may be opened as desired.

## PORCHES.

At this time it is not usual to provide special ceiling for porches. The rafters and all exposed material are dressed so that they may be painted or stained. Floor joists are not usually more than two by eight inches; sills, about six by eight. The floor should be inclined about one-eighth of an inch to the foot, and made of hard wood, tongued and grooved, not over two and three-fourths inches in width. Edges should be finished with nosings, which are rounded edges. The roof of the porch is usually the same as that of the body of the house. Gutters are similar to those on other roofs.

Railing and turned balusters are usual, excepting where an opening for passage is desired.

## LATTICE PORCH.

Framework of lattice porch is generally the same form as other porches. The covering is usually made with one-and-three-eighths-inch material, laid diagonal; openings, one and three-eighths inch. Door and hardware, same as used for other parts of the house, are generally provided.

## OUTSIDE STEPS.

Outside steps of wood usually have hard-wood treads made of seven-eighths-by-two-and-one-half-inch pieces, with three-eighths-inch space between; carriages should be two by ten inches, about sixteen on centres. Railing and posts for steps should be provided if necessary. Lattice should be placed under porches and outside steps, and between all outside piers. Outside lattice-work in yard may be of the same general design as mentioned for lattice-work porches.

General statements as to outside wood-work apply alike to brick or frame houses, with certain omissions that should be obvious to an intelligent reader.

# CHAPTER XXXI.

INSIDE WOOD-WORK. — FLOORS. — SOFT AND HARD WOOD FLOORS. — TABULATED STATEMENT OF INSIDE FINISH. — DIFFERENT KINDS OF WOOD. — DOORS AND FRAMES. — FLY SCREENS. — INSIDE CASINGS. — WAINSCOTING. — INSIDE SHUTTERS. — WOOD-WORK FOR PLUMBING. — KITCHEN SINK AND FITTINGS. — KITCHEN TABLES. — CELLAR-SINK FITTINGS. — WOOD-WORK FOR BATH-TUB. — WATER-CLOSETS. — WASH-STANDS. — TANK. — PICTURE MOULDING. — CLOSET FITTINGS. — BROOM-RACK. — CEDAR-CLOSET. — DRY-BOX. — CLOCK SHELF. — CHINA-ROOM FITTINGS. — PANTRY FITTINGS. — STAIRWAYS.

### INSIDE WOOD-WORK.

ALL material should be perfectly clear, first-class, thoroughly seasoned, kiln-dried, dressed material, free from imperfections tending to impair its use, durability, strength, or appearance. All inside finish excepting floors should be sand-papered. Where an especially good finish is desired, all should be scraped as well.

### FLOORS.

In preparing for floors, it is not unusual to make arrangements for preventing the passage of sound. This is done by deadening. The usual method is to nail strips about two inches and a half from the top edge of the joist, on which are laid one-inch boards. This leaves an inch and a half between their surface and the upper edge of the joist. This may be filled in with concrete, mineral wool, or other non-conducting material. Either is very effective in preventing the passage of sound from the floors to the rooms below. In a dwelling-house where two floors only are in common use, it is only necessary to deaden the second floor.

A permanent sheathing floor of the same material that is used for rough siding may be placed over all joists of first and second floors for a floor during the plastering of the house. This does not act as deadening, unless concrete or mineral wool be placed over it. It is well to have a floor of this kind for use during plastering. It also makes the lower floor warmer. It should be covered with building-paper before the finished floor is laid. Finished floors should extend throughout the first and second stories and the attic. They are commonly of pine or other soft wood. The material is tongued and grooved, secret-nailed, and should be smoothed off after laying. The boards should never be wider than five and a half inches, nor less in thickness than seven-eighths of an inch. They should be free from sap, large, loose, or black knots. Hard-wood floors may be of hard pine, oak, maple, or other hard wood that is readily obtainable or desirable. This material should not be more than two and three-fourths inches in width, nor less than seven-eighths of an inch in thickness, and should be tongued and grooved, secret-nailed, and smoothed off and scraped after laying. A better grade of pine flooring than that mentioned may be had if desired. It is best that all floors be laid after plastering. However, this is not the common practice. The carpenter should cut out flooring as directed, and prepare for hearths in proper places. Other inside dressed wood-work should never be placed in position until after the plastering is finished and dry.

The following table is from a specification in use by myself, and shows the kind of lumber, style of doors, finish of wood, painters' finish, and rooms supplied with plate glass, and the general style of hardware. The detail specification makes clear the points here outlined. The filling out of the blanks indicates the range and style of finish which frequently occur. The lettering of the doors and finish refers to drawings and details, a part of which are given in this connection.

| FLOORS. | KIND OF LUMBER. | DOORS AND FINISH. | THICKNESS OF DOOR. | PAINTERS' FINISH. | ROOMS WITH PLATE-GLASS. | STYLE OF HARDWARE. |
|---|---|---|---|---|---|---|
| **FIRST FLOOR.** | | | | | | |
| Front Hall ... | Qu. Oak. | A | 1¾ | – | – | – |
| Parlor ....... | " " | A | 1¾ | All Oil. | – | – |
| Sitting-Room.. | " Sycamore. | A | 1¾ | – | – | – |
| Library ...... | " " | A | 1¾ | – | – | – |
| Rear Hall .... | Gum. | A | 1¾ | – | – | – |
| Dining-Room . | " | A | 1¾ | – | – | – |
| Chamber .... | – – | – | – | – | – | – |
| Kitchen ..... | Plain Oak. | D | 1⅜ | – | – | – |
| Bedrooms .... | – – | – | – | – | – | – |
| Pantry ...... | " " | D | 1⅜ | – | – | – |
| China Room .. | " " | D | 1⅜ | – | – | – |
| **SECOND FLOOR.** | | | | | | |
| Front Hall ... | Gum. | E | 1⅜ | – | – | – |
| Chamber .... | Pine. | E | 1⅜ | – | – | – |
| " .... | " | E | 1⅜ | – | – | – |
| " .... | " | E | 1⅜ | – | – | – |
| " .... | " | E | 1⅜ | – | – | – |
| Rear Bedroom . | Poplar. | D | 1⅜ | – | – | – |
| Alcove ....... | Pine. | E | 1⅜ | – | – | – |
| Bath-Room ... | Qu. Oak. | D | 1⅜ | – | – | – |
| Rear Hall .... | Pine. | D | 1⅜ | – | – | – |
| Other rooms .. | " | D | 1⅜ | – | – | – |

It may be said, in general terms, in regard to the different kinds of wood used in finishing a house, that, all things considered, hard wood of one kind or another is preferable, for the reason that it stands the general wear and tear of house-keeping with less evidence of the struggle. Soft wood — pine or poplar — is only to be used because it is cheaper than the other. Quartered oak, quartered sycamore, cherry, maple, walnut and chestnut may be classed as the hard woods in ordinary use in finishing houses of moderate cost. Gum is difficult to class. It is neither hard nor soft. Others might be mentioned in this same connection. Pine and other resinous woods are mentioned as soft woods; as is also poplar, called in some sections whitewood. Any of these woods may be oil-finished, according to the general formula indicated elsewhere, or any of them may be stained. Birch stains very nicely.

### DOORS AND FRAMES.

Door-frames, when rabbeted, should not be less than one and three-eighths inch in thickness. Sometimes the strip is screwed to the frame. In that case the frame is often not more than one and one-eighth inch thick. One and three-eighths inch, however, is better. Front doors or principal entrance doors are frequently hard wood when all the others are soft wood. All outside doors are generally filled with glass in their upper panels. Sliding doors should be the same general design as other adjacent doors. One additional panel to each additional twelve inches in excess of width of other doors may be provided. Sliding doors should be hung from above. Hard-wood doors are usually solid. All excepting pine are best made of a veneer, one-fourth inch thick on a one-and-three-eighths-inch pine body, as indicated by Fig. 35. Sometimes doors are made in two thicknesses of hard wood. This is not as good as a single thickness. Three thicknesses are better. The only door to be recommended, however, is the veneered door. Such doors will not warp; others are liable to do so. Transoms may be hung on pivots, and should be provided with catches, and, if heavy or high, with adjustable lifts. Transoms are sometimes used in doors on the second floor, though this practice is less common

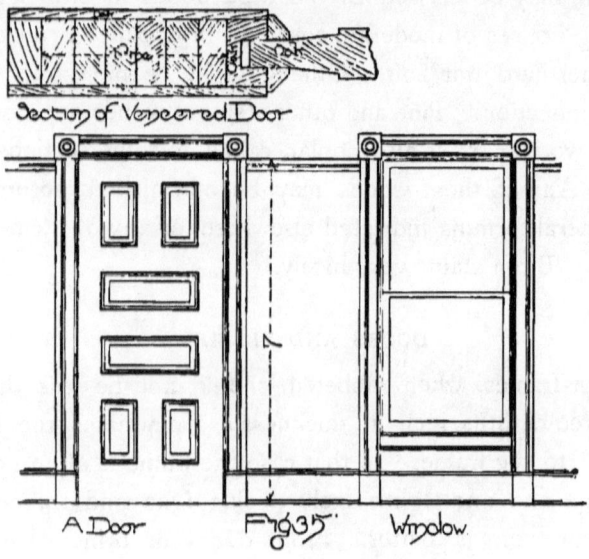

Fig. 35.

than in the past. Where doors with transoms are used, it is not uncommon to have the closet doors extend to the full height of the transom tops, and provide additional top panels. Doors six feet ten inches in height, or less, and not more than one and three-eighths inch in thickness, may be hung on two three-and-one-half by three-and-one-half-inch buts. If higher than this or wider than three feet, they should be hung on three buts or hinges.

Doors in unfinished cellars may be made of two thicknesses

of seven-eighths beaded flooring; frames the same as in rooms above. A seven-eighths batten door, with one-and-three-eighths-inch frame, should be provided for man-hole in cellar. Scuttle doors, where required, may be seven-eighths inch in thickness, battened.

Cuts 35, 36, 37 indicate ordinary style of inside door and window finish, the sizes and heights being marked.

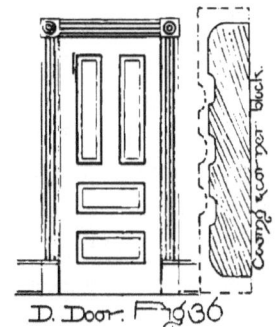

Doors from dining-room to china-closet and china-closet to kitchen should be hung on double-spring hinges, so that they will swing either way and come back to position. The slide from the kitchen to china-closet or dining-room should be hung the same as sash, with plaited cotton sash-cord, pulleys, and weights, and provided with lifts and bolt fastenings.

Frames should be provided for opening into bay windows, window-seats, alcoves, and pilasters.

Stop beads for glazed and sliding doors should be secured with round-headed screws.

There should be corner beads for external angles.

### FLY SCREEN.

In the modern house all outside openings, from cellar to attic, are provided with fly screens. They are now made by concerns who make it a business to do this work, and are much better than those made by the ordinary carpenter. They are arranged so that they will slide up and down on the inside or outside stop, and are finished in every way to correspond with the other wood-work of the house. They need not be more than three-quarters of an inch in thickness if properly made. A small strip is secured to the stop bead, and a corresponding groove is cut in the screen frame. A spring therein holds it firm, and admits of their removal without trouble or waste of time. Special hardware is provided for door and window screens.

### INSIDE CASINGS.

The commonest way of constructing casings at this time is indicated in Figs. 35 and 36, showing inside of doors and windows. This is one of the least expensive forms, and is adapted to all ordinary work. The casings are usually seven-eighths inch thick, the corner and plinth blocks one and one-eighth inch thick. The plinth block comes at the bottom of the casing. One reason that this form of casing is in such general use is, that the corner block conceals any slight shrinkage which there may be in the wood. Where there is a mitred or flush joint, the shrinkage is certain to show. Casings as elaborate as any one is inclined to pay for may be used. Window, door, alcove, and other casings are generally all of one design in a room. All girders and projections below ceilings should be cased.

### BASE.

The base-board around the room should be plain, so that it may be readily cleaned. Where it is ornamented, it adds nothing to the appearance of the room. There should be a base for all plastered walls. Generally they should be not more than eight inches high, seven-eighths inch thick, bevelled at the top and a quarter round at the bottom. A five-eighths-inch adjustable lip may be put on at the top, to take up the inequalities in the plaster. The closet base may be formed of a quarter round only if it is plastered and skimmed to the floor. It is well to have as little wood-work as possible in the closet.

### WAINSCOTING.

Wainscoting kitchen, bath, and other rooms is not as common as it once was. This is because wood-work is more difficult to keep clean than plastering. Wherever there is wainscoting, there must necessarily be joints. These are difficult to keep clean. Panel wood-work, or other form of decoration for wall or ceiling, may be used in rooms according to the disposition of the owner and the taste of the architect.

### INSIDE SHUTTERS.

Inside shutters are not so universally used in good houses as they were a few years ago. Draperies, though more expensive, are preferred, and are taking their place. Inside sliding shutters, arranged in several sections and constructed according to the general plan described for fly-screens, are in more common use. Rolling slats which roll into a pocket are to be thought of only in connection with an expensive dwelling. The common inside shutter is ordinarily seven-eighths inch in thickness, four panels wide, beaded, and cut at the meeting rail; and the four centre panels are provided with movable slats. The special designs of inside shutters mentioned are manufactured by various establishments throughout the country, and are advertised in various magazines and periodicals. Under any circumstances the owner will have to investigate proprietary goods and special furnishings for himself. They are not to be considered in a work of this kind.

### WOOD-WORK FOR PLUMBING.

All should be put up in a way to make plumbing readily accessible by the removal of screws. The pipe duct should be located as required in the kitchen, and pass from basement to attic floor. The inside measurement should be seven by twelve inches. It should be constructed of seven-eighths-inch lumber. In case of stud partitions, the duct may be let into the wall the full depth allowed by studding. The front will project into the kitchen. All should be of clear lumber, the same as other wood used in finishing. A ventilating opening, five inches in diameter, may be provided at the top of the duct. This may be connected with pipe and funnel, or other device, placed over the kitchen range. The carpenter should provide pipe boards for all pipe runs. The following, in regard to wood-work for plumbing, is from the specification of an architect:

KITCHEN SINK AND FITTINGS. — Wood rim, $\frac{7}{8}$ by $2\frac{1}{2}$ inches; skirt, $\frac{7}{8}$ by $6\frac{1}{2}$ inches; support on cleat at back, plain oak, $1\frac{3}{8}$-inch turned legs in front.

SPLASH-BOARD. — $\frac{7}{8}$ by 14 inches, scurfed back; $\frac{7}{8}$ by 2 inches, plain top.

DRAIN-BOARD. — Shall be 22 inches long by 21 inches wide, $\frac{7}{8}$ inch thick, 1 inch incline; channelled top; skirt, 3 by $\frac{3}{4}$, cleated with two cleats at bottom. One end shall rest on sink, side on wall cleat, other end on turned leg.

Full length of tables, sink, and drain.

TABLES. — There shall be two tables connected with drain and sink, each 21 inches wide, 2 by 6 inches long, $\frac{7}{8}$ thick; skirt, 3 by $\frac{7}{8}$ inches. Cleated back. Secured and supported same as drain.

OTHER SINKS: —

CELLAR SINK. — Provide $\frac{7}{8}$-by-3-inch supporting rim, $2\frac{1}{4}$ inches by $\frac{7}{8}$ inch top. $1\frac{3}{8}$ square legs.

BATH-TUB. — Case sides and ends with $\frac{7}{8}$-by-$2\frac{3}{4}$-inch oak board, tongued and grooved material, secret-nailed. Batten foot-casing, and put in in one piece with round-headed blue screws. Cap top.

SPLASH-BOARD. — Wainscoting same as tub casing, 6 inches high. Cap top in two members $\frac{7}{8}$ inch thick.

WATER-CLOSET. — Hinged flap and seat, each $\frac{7}{8}$ inch thick; skirt, $\frac{7}{8}$ by 5 inches; support on $1\frac{3}{4}$ turned legs in front, cleat at back.

Case water-closet tank, mould top.

WASH-STANDS. — Provide supports under marble top. Case sides same as specified for tub. Make cleated door in front of same material. Provide hinges and fastenings.

TANK. — A tank shall be placed in attic; capacity, 8 barrels. Construct with $1\frac{3}{4}$-inch ploughed and tongued material, with two $\frac{3}{8}$-inch rods, bolts, and nuts at each end, and cleats across top at middle.

In this house there shall be the following plumbing fixtures, to be fitted up as above: 1 kitchen sink, cellar sink, sink, 1 bath-tub, 1 water-closet, 1 wash-stand.

### PICTURE MOULDINGS.

Picture mouldings should be provided on all plastered walls excepting those of kitchen and pantries. It is usual to place the picture moulding on a line with the top of the door; that is, so that it comes just below the top of the corner block.

### CLOSET-FITTINGS.

Shelves should be seven-eighths inch thick, number and arrangement as desired.

The following is a schedule from closet-fittings. Provide hooks in closets as follows: —

One row to cleat on wall 5 feet 3 inches from floor.
One row under side of shelf.
One row to cleat on wall 3 feet 6 inches from floor in children's closets.

### DRAWERS FOR CLOSETS.

Drawers for closets are best made by a cabinet-maker. If not, they should be modelled in all respects after cabinet work.

Cedar closets are not as common as they once were. As people have more to place in them, there is less confidence in their efficacy. The following is from a specification: —

BROOM-RACK. — Provide in space as directed 1 broom-rack, with cast-iron broom-holder, for sweep-broom, whisk-broom; hooks for dust-pan and bucket.

MEDICINE-CHEST. — Provide in closet a medicine-chest 8 by 10 by 16 inches, with ⅜ panelled and hinged door. Approved lock.

Exposed wood-work thereof same as room in which closet is placed.

CEDAR-CLOSET. — Closet shall be lined, ceiled, and fitted up with red cedar.

DRY-BOX. — Secured on wall adjacent to kitchen range shall be placed a drying-box for scrub-rags, brushes, etc., 8 inches deep by 18 inches wide by 24 inches high, constructed with ⅞ material, inside measurements. Provide hinged ⅞-inch panelled door with fastening. Top, bottom, and shelves shall be perforated with ¾ auger-holes for passage of warm air through the box.

SOAP-BOX. — Constructed same as dry-box. Size, 9 inches deep, 20 inches wide, 30 inches high.

Door, ⅞ inch thick, panelled. Provide approved lock. Shelves, ⅝ thick, set into sides, 3 inches apart. Perforate bottom and shelves with ¾-inch auger-holes, and connect top with kitchen or vent-flue.

CLOCK-SHELF. — Provide 8-inch moulded clock-shelf, ⅞ inch thick, in kitchen.

VENTILATOR. CLOTHES-CHUTE. COAL-CHUTE. COAL-BINS IN CELLAR.

## CHINA-ROOM SPECIFICATION.

CUPBOARD (see drawing, Chapter VII.). — Shelves as directed below and above. Lower shelves ⅞ inch thick.

Lower doors ⅞ panelled, upper doors glazed.

Provide hinges and fastenings for all.

There shall be 8 inches space between ⅞-inch top of lower section and bottom shelf of upper section. Upper door shall not come below under side of this upper section shelf.

TABLE. — Construction same as in kitchen.

SINK.

DRAWERS.

## PANTRY SPECIFICATION.

CUPBOARD (see drawing, Chapter VII.). — As indicated. Doors below and shelves above, same as specified for china. No doors above.

DOUGH-BOARD. — Provide constructed same as tables specified for kitchen, except that it shall be supported on brackets.

FLOUR-BIN. — Shall be 18 inches deep by 24 inches high in front, 28 inches in rear, by ———— long, ———— compartments. Set 4 inches from floor. Top cleated and hinged. Lumber $\frac{7}{8}$ inch thick.

### FLOUR-BIN.

The flour-bin described in the specifications is the old kind with the hinged top. Another kind that has been used successfully is here illustrated.

The receptacle for flour is pivoted in the manner indicated by the section. The pivot position is indicated on the drawing by the point of the arrow. The dotted lines on the section indicate the position of the flour receptacle when it is open. It is pulled open by the hand. The knob is shown on the drawing of front. As soon as it is released

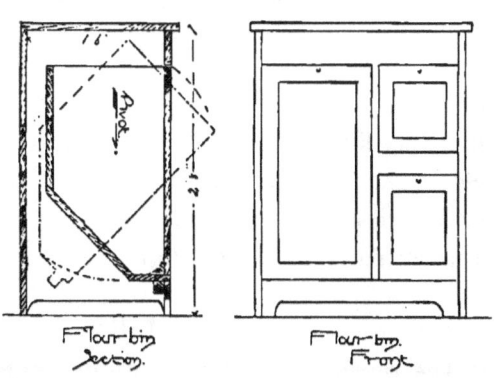

it falls back into a closed position. It is pivoted so that it remains closed unless held open. The front drawing indicates a flour-bin of this kind with three receptacles; the larger one for flour, and the two smaller ones for meal and graham. The marble dough-stone can be placed on the top of a bin of this kind. If there is no other room for the bin it can be placed in the lower section of the pantry cupboard, and can take the space ordinarily given one of the doors. The pantry cupboard is illustrated and described in Chapter VII.

### BOXES FOR PANTRY SUPPLIES.

These boxes are constructed on the same principle as the flour-bin, just described. They are pivoted and arranged in a row, and may be set on a pantry shelf. The drawing indicates eight of these boxes, four of them nine by twelve inches, and four five by three and three-fourths inches. These boxes are of tin, the frame only being of wood. The socket into which the pivot fits is open at the bottom, so that the box can be lifted off the pivot

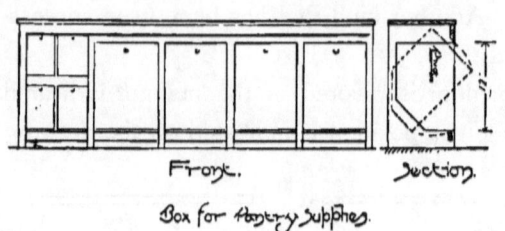

Box for Pantry Supplies.

and taken out and washed. An arrangement such as this takes very little room, and the boxes are always closed unless held open. They are so pivoted that they fall into a closed position as soon as released. Two of these boxes in a china-closet would be convenient to hold bread and cake.

### STAIRS.

The wood-work of the stairway should always be of hard wood. Where hard wood is used for entire finish, the stairway is best of the same variety. The treads should always be one and one-eighth inch in thickness, and never less than ten inches in width. The risers may be seven-eighths inch thick and never more than seven and one-half inches in height. Square or turned newel posts are in common use. Winders should not be used for the main stairway. Square turns at the landing should be made. Sometimes the rear stairway is of the same general style and design as the front. When it is an open stairway, it is necessary that this should be the case. A rear box stairway, the cellar and attic stairway, or, in fact, any box stairway, should have the treads and risers the same thickness and general dimensions as those mentioned for the front. However, they need not be of hard wood. They should always be provided with hand-rails. All lumber for cellar or attic stairways should be clear and dressed, and quite as well finished as that of any other part of the house. When the cellar is not plastered, the side lining for cellar stairways should be seven-eighths-inch flooring below the first-story plastering. This flooring should be dressed on both sides. The outside cellar-way should have dressed treads and risers one and three-fourths inch thick. The wall should be capped, preferably with stone, and the outside cellar door should be of iron. Where economy is necessary, one-and-three-fourths-inch oak coping and doors may be used.

# CHAPTER XXXII.

PLASTERING. — GRAY FINISH. — WHITE HARD FINISH. — BACK PLASTERING. — GAS-PIPING. — TIN WORK. — GUTTERS. — VALLEYS. — DOWN SPOUTS. — GALVANIZED IRON-WORK. — HOT-AIR PIPES. — THIMBLES. — PAINTING. — STAINING. — OIL FINISHING. — INTERIOR STAINING. — FLOOR FINISH. — GLAZING. — PLATE-GLASS. — BEVELLED GLASS. — CATHEDRAL GLASS. — HARDWARE.

IT is only within the last ten or fifteen years that it has been at all common to do two-coat work in plastering. Before that time three-coat work was almost universal. Most of the plastering done at this time is what is called "laid-on" work. The first two coats are put on at the same time. The last coat is put on after these are dry. The laths are nearly always of pine. There should be one nail for each contact with the wood-work; that is, four nails to each lath. The mortar should be made of the best quality of lime and sharp sand.

A sufficient quantity of hair should be used. The mortar should be floated, or made smooth, and straightened to receive the wood-work. The last coat should be put on after the other is thoroughly dry. It should be trowelled to a smooth surface, and when completed should be free from chip cracks, stains, and improper mixing of sand. Three-coat work, where each coat is allowed to become thoroughly dry, is better than two-coat work. The last coat is usually a white plaster-of-Paris finish, put on with the skim.

A gray finish is used more generally at the present time than in the past. It is put on in place of the white skim coat.

The natural color is a pleasant gray tint. It may be made smooth enough for papering. The skim coat, white or gray, may be tinted with fresco color at less cost than it can be papered. Paper becomes necessary on a white skim finish after a short time.

The hard white finish, which is not commonly used at the present time, is very satisfactory excepting for its extreme whiteness. This finish is made by the use of white sand and skim rubbed and floated down until only a sufficient amount of the lime or skim proper remains to cement the sand to the wall. The same kind of a finish with gray sand is very satisfactory.

Proprietary finishes for plastered walls are now used to some extent in the better class of work. They are very hard, of waterproof texture and of any color desired. The coloring of finish for plastering is ordinarily not successful. However, some of the proprietary colored goods before the public are very satisfactory when well put on. The one difficulty in the way of their use is in getting the plasterer to handle properly a thing with which he is not familiar.

Back plastering is common in very cold climates, and is done by plastering on the back of the sheathing between the studding. It is independent of the inside plastering.

Cement pavements in floors are considered in the previous chapter.

### GAS-PIPING.

Gas-pipes are placed in a house before lathing. The gas company which supplies the illuminating or fuel gas furnishes the inspection for each set of pipes. Below is given a form of specification in use by an architect in a natural-gas region.

### GAS.

ILLUMINATING GAS. — Provide and fix gas-pipe and fittings according to gas company's regulations. All pipes shall be concealed, excepting where it is desired to attach a burner. Cap pipes. Lights to be placed as indicated by table below.

FUEL OR NATURAL GAS. — Provide and fix pipe and fittings according to company's regulations. Company's certificate of approval will be required before payments are made. Cap pipes until mixers and burners are attached.

Valves and connections shall be provided preparatory to mixer and burner connections. Provide connection with street mains.

TABLE OF DISTRIBUTION.

| FLOORS. | ILLUMINATING GAS. | | NATURAL-GAS FIRES. |
|---|---|---|---|
| | CENTRE. | BRACKET. | |
| **FIRST FLOOR.** | | | |
| Parlor or Reception Room | – | – | – |
| Porch | – | – | – |
| Sitting-Room | – | – | – |
| Front Hall — newel | – | – | – |
| Dining-Room | – | – | – |
| Library | – | – | – |
| Chambers — each | – | – | – |
| Rear Hall | – | – | – |
| Bedrooms — each | – | – | – |
| Kitchen . . gas stove | – | – | Range. |
| Pantry | – | – | – |
| China-Room | – | – | – |
| Cellar | – | – | { Furnace. { Laundry stove. |
| **SECOND FLOOR** | | | |
| Chambers — each | – | – | – |
| Bedrooms — each | – | – | – |
| Alcove | – | – | – |
| Front Hall | – | – | – |
| Rear Hall | – | – | – |
| Bath-Room | – | – | – |
| Attic | – | – | – |

## TIN WORK.

It is now entirely possible to get first-class tin plate for architectural uses. The process is very simple. Require and pay only for a tin plate stamped with a reputable maker's name and brand. There is a general effort upon the part of tin-plate dealers to raise the standard of tin in this way; and there are now a number of manufacturers of integrity who are pursuing the course of branding a first-class tin plate. All tin work should be painted on the under side before it leaves the shop.

## GUTTERS.

In the matter of general utility the hanging gutter is ideal. It is below the eaves, where its overflow can injure nothing. It is easy to reach all parts of it in case of repair. If it is necessary to remove any of the shingles or other roof covering, the gutter need not be disturbed. There are those, however, who object to the appearance of a hanging gutter. A galvanized iron gutter made of No. 26 iron, in form as per Fig. 33, and which runs four inches above the overflow line at all times, may be placed on the first or second row of shingles or slate, and will give very good satisfaction. It is certainly much better than a wood tin-lined gutter.

## VALLEYS AND OTHER TIN WORK.

All valleys should be lined with twenty-inch tin. The connection between all roof and vertical surfaces should be flashed and counter-flashed; that is, pieces of tin should be bent to conform to the vertical and horizontal surfaces, and slipped under the slate or shingles so as to lap both horizontally and vertically. This is the flashing. The counter-flashings are the lapped pieces of tin which extend into the vertical surfaces, and down over the flashings proper.

All wood-work which projects in excess of one and three-eighths inch from any vertical surface, should be covered with tin. Hip and ridge coping should be covered with tin in the manner described in chapter where roofs are considered.

Down spouts should be provided to carry the water from all roofs to the ground. The presence of more than one gable in the front part of the building frequently makes more than one down spout necessary. Where the house is not too large, one five-inch spout will usually take all of the water from the roof. For a small structure a four-inch spout will serve the same purpose. Three and four inches are in common use for carrying water from the main roof where the continuous course of the gutter is interrupted by gables or dormers. The cistern down-spout should be provided with cut-off or preferably a switch spout, which connects by a drain pipe with a dry well or street gutter. Such connections should never be made with the sewer where a down spout is intended to supply a cistern. In connecting a roof with a cistern it should be borne in mind that it is not always so much the size of the cistern which insures a constant supply of water, as it is the amount of roof surface connected with the cistern.

Porches are usually provided with two or three inch down spouts according to the amount of roof to be drained.

Flat roofs are best when made with a standing seam. It admits of the expansion and contraction of the tin without injury to the joint.

Copper has been extensively used on the better class of buildings during recent years. The improvement in the quality of tin has rendered its use unnecessary excepting for down spouts and ornamental purposes. New processes in the manufacture of sheet copper, and the electroplating of other sheet metals with copper, promise to reduce the cost of that material for architectural purposes, so that it will be better and cheaper than tin. When such claims are substantiated the public will be informed thereof, through the usual channels.

Galvanized iron does not have the general architectural uses that were common to it a few years ago. For down spouts in excess of four inches, No. 26 galvanized iron should be used.

Hot-air pipes which connect the furnace pipes in basement with the second floor are usually three and three-fourths by twelve inches in size. Before they are placed, all contiguous wood-work should be lined with tin. In frame houses the pipes should be covered with iron lath. They should continue above baseboard, with register opening on second floor and below joist with collar in basement. Where pipes run in an outside wood wall, which they should do only in case of extremest emergency, the back and sides of the pipe should be lined with several thicknesses of asbestos paper.

A zinc drain should be provided from the refrigerator to the outside of brick wall. This drain is one inch in diameter, and comes up through the floor with funnel-shaped opening at the top. An ordinary six-inch tin funnel let into the tube will answer every purpose. Thus the discharge pipe from the refrigerator may be readily placed over it.

Thimbles should be provided for the plasterer when he is putting on the last coat. Flue stops should be placed therein after plastering is finished. These are for stove connections with brick flues.

## PAINTING.

Painting is not so serious a problem as it once was. We hear about people buying their own paint, the lead and everything that goes with it, and having it mixed under their personal supervision. But even this is not satisfactory. After a short time the paint begins to look chalky and dingy. When the mixing of the paint is not done under the supervision of the owner, and the result is as above stated, the painter is often accused of dishonesty.

A painter does not ordinarily have the facilities or knowledge for properly mixing colored paints. In order to get satisfactory results in painting, we may again fall back upon the integrity of an established manufacturer of proprietary goods, — that is, upon ready-mixed paints. Not all are good. Most of them are made as cheap and common as possible; but the best results can be secured from really good ready-mixed paints. Any large dealer of established reputation, who is not himself a manufacturer of a cheap paint, may ordinarily be relied upon for a correct opinion.

Preparatory to painting, all knots should be coated with shellac. All work should be painted with three coats, — one priming, and two following. One can always be sure of getting the color wanted in ready-mixed paints of the best quality. All outside frames should be primed before setting. The painter should follow the carpenter, and prime all dressed wood-work as put up. Putty work may be done after first coat, or before final color is applied. There is no advantage to be derived in painting shingles after they are put on. The paint gathers in a heavy ridge on the shingle next to the butt of the one above it in a way to let the moisture lie therein, so that it will rot at this point.

Brick-work may be painted as specified for wood-work, excepting that the first coat, or priming, should be put on very heavy.

Tin and iron work should be painted with one coat of metallic paint as soon as put up. Tin unexposed to view should receive a second coat of metallic paint before the building is completed. Tin work exposed to view should have two coats of paint on a metallic prime, same as house.

### EXTERIOR STAINING.

Shingles should be dipped in stain and then stood in a trough, so that they will drain to a barrel. Other external wood-work should have two heavy coats of stain applied with a brush. Weather-boarding is sometimes dipped into a trough filled with stain, and then set so that it will drain therein. Shingle stain is a proprietary finish, and regularly advertised in leading periodicals.

### INTERIOR STAINING.

The staining of interior finish is now rendered simple and satisfactory by the use of proprietary stains. Sometimes the stain is put on direct, without first applying filler. At other times a filler of cornstarch and oil, or a proprietary mixture, which is preferable, is used. One or two coats of prepared oil-finish follows the application of the stain. The various manufacturers of interior stains furnish wood samples which indicate the variety of this material manufactured.

### OIL FINISHING.

All wood to be oil-finished should first be filled. The antique and acid stained effects are derived by the use of different kinds of fillers, which close the pores of the wood and stain it the color desired. Proprietary fillers and oil finish may be most successfully used, for the reason that they are generally prepared by men who have put their capital into the business for the purpose of getting a return. Such people cannot put a bad article permanently on the market without feeling the result themselves. Therefore, those who are permanently successful in the manufacture of proprietary goods can generally be relied upon.

In the finishing of wood-work all under coats should be rubbed with dry hair-cloth, burlap, or fine sand-paper. On top of the filler two coats of prepared oil finish should be applied; the first one rubbed as above, and, if desired, the last left bright. A dead finish may be secured by rubbing down the last coat with fine pumice stone and water or oil.

External exposed wood-work and bath-rooms may be finished with a water-proof varnish by treating as above, excepting that the last coat should be a water-proof oil finish made by some well-known manufacturer.

### FLOOR FINISH.

All manufacturers of first-class interior finishes prepare a special floor finish. It is usually applied in two coats over a filler as described. In such cases the filler is not stained. Each coat is thoroughly rubbed. A satisfactory floor finish may be made by washing the clean wood floor with a solution of salt and water, and afterwards saturating with paraffine wax, and then rubbing.

### GLAZING.

All glass should be embedded in putty and secured with glazier's tacks and putty. American sheet glass is made in two thicknesses — single and double strength — and in four qualities. *A* or *AA* only should be used in a good house.

Plate glass costs about five or six times as much as double-strength *A* American sheet. A thumb rule for calculating the cost of plate glass, which is not strictly accurate but which gives a general idea, is to calculate on from fifty to seventy-five cents per square foot.

### CATHEDRAL GLASS.

Of cathedral glass proper there is only one quality. In ornamental and colored glass work the different kinds of glass used will not be here enumerated. Bevelled plate is becoming quite common. Generally speaking, cathedral glass may be arranged in geometrical forms in sash with wood separations or muntins. Cathedral glass proper for such purposes costs from twenty-five to thirty-five cents a square foot. Cathedral glass leaded may cost almost any amount in excess of a dollar per square foot. In selecting cathedral glass for sash with wood separations, the best and most satisfactory results may be reached by choosing the lighter tints, and not having more than one or two colors to the window.

### HARDWARE.

It is difficult if not impossible to write a general specification for the hardware which goes into a house. It cannot be done excepting by specifying particular goods, which cannot be done here. However, a few general statements in regard to hardware may not be amiss. The cheapest locks used should have brass fronts and bolts, and be of the mortise pattern. Night-locks should be provided as desired. Outside knobs of rear door and those inside the kitchen may be of bronzed iron. The price of bronzed-faced locks is not much greater than brass-faced locks. A good bronzed-iron knob has not been made up to this time. Therefore, the fixtures for the front door, if not all others, should be of real bronze.

Butts of bronzed iron have been made which are very satisfactory. Sash locks should be provided for all windows. Sliding-door hardware should be of real bronze. The locks should be what is known as "astragal" fronts, and the trimmings flush. Sliding doors should be suspended from above on hangers. Bolts of wrought-iron should be placed on all outside rear doors, and, if desired, on the inside of all chamber and bedroom doors; always on the bath-room door. Such bolts may be mortised or otherwise, as desired. Foot and top bolts may be provided for double doors and for sash. Pivots should be provided for all transoms; transom lifts as desired, also sash lifts. There should be wooden base knobs with rubber buffers at all doors. Double-spring hinges should be provided for doors leading to and from kitchen and china-closet or passage. Necessary drawer hardware should be provided, and butts, knobs, and fastenings for inside shutters.

# CHAPTER XXXIII.

PRACTICAL PLUMBING. — WOOD-WORK FOR PLUMBER. — EXCAVATING FOR PLUMBER. — WATER DISTRIBUTION. — OUTSIDE FIXTURES. — HYDRANTS. — STREET-WASHERS. — SOFT-WATER SUPPLY. — HOT-WATER SUPPLY. — SOIL PIPE. — INSIDE FIXTURES. — KITCHEN SINK. — CELLAR SINK.

IN a previous chapter plumbing was considered from a sanitary standpoint, and the conditions of safety set forth. In this chapter it remains to consider plumbing work in a more practical way; to consider it with reference to its execution, assuming that it is desired to reach the best results. This means, primarily, good work; then good work with the least expenditure of money.

The carpenter usually provides all necessary wood-work for the plumber. This means boards and runs on which pipes are to be placed, the pipe duct and other wood finish. It is best that the carpenter should do this in order that it may be well done. There should be specified in the carpenter's contract exactly what he is to do, so that he may calculate on a definite basis. All of the cutting work, where cutting is necessary, should be done by the carpenter. The plumber is not usually supplied with tools of the right kind for doing this, and is as liable to botch carpenter work as a carpenter would be to botch the plumbing work.

The plumber should do all of his own excavating. This includes trenches for pipes of all kinds to and from the house. After the pipes and drains have been placed therein, he should make fills and thoroughly tamp the earth so as to restore the surface to its original condition. This may be best done by putting in a small quantity of earth at a time, ramming it down and then pouring water on it. Even after this the drain space should be left with a slight crown, as the earth will settle a little more than it is possible to make it by artificial means. Superfluous earth should be removed from the building and lot.

Plumber's excavating is not included in the general contract. If there is any superfluous earth in connection with his work, he, and not the general contractor, should remove it. Contracting methods are explained in another section of the book.

## WATER DISTRIBUTION.

Lead should be used for all purposes where pipes are exposed to view and where they come in contact with the earth. This is common practice. Sometimes, however, brass or planished copper pipes and fittings are used where they are exposed to view. Brass makes very beautiful and satisfactory work. Iron pipe, galvanized inside and out, is occasionally used for exposed work. It does not look as well, however, as lead pipe. Galvanized iron pipe is also frequently used where not exposed to view, and where it does not come in contact with the earth. Objections will be made to this by plumbers who are used to doing lead work. In all hospitals where the best work is done iron or brass pipe is used, and lead pipe and connections are entirely dispensed with. However, the use of lead pipe where exposed to view and where in contact with the earth, and iron pipe galvanized for other places, makes most excellent and beautiful work for dwelling-houses. The connections between iron and lead pipe should be of brass.

The water works of many cities and towns are from direct-pressure mains. It is common for such pressure to be forty pounds to the square inch under ordinary conditions. A fire pressure is much greater. Therefore, all direct-pressure pipes of lead should be extra strong. Tank-pressure pipes, those which connect with a tank in the attic or above a water-closet, may be medium strong. The terms " extra strong " and " medium strong," as here used, are definite in their meaning, and apply to regular grades of pipe. The interior fixtures of an ordinary dwelling-house are supplied with lead pipe five-eighths of an inch in diameter, or iron pipe three-quarters of an inch in diameter. In the above will be found all that applies in general terms to an ordinary specification for water distribution. Special mention will be made later.

Stop-cocks should be provided sufficient entirely to disconnect and drain all pipes, fixtures, and connections. " Stop-and-waste" cocks should be provided at the bottom of all main risers where they cannot otherwise be drained. A " stop-and-waste " cock is one which shuts off the supply from its source, and drains the water from pipes above, so that it passes out to a receptacle provided for that purpose. In some instances it is allowed to run to a sink on the cellar floor, or it may be taken in a bucket.

The city water-supply for an ordinary dwelling-house is generally through five-eighths-inch extra strong lead pipe, and is provided with a stop-box so that the water can be turned off from the house at the street.

### OUTSIDE FIXTURES.

Outside fixtures which connect with the city water are a street-washer and a hydrant. The street-washer is usually placed in front, so that a hose may be attached to it for sprinkling purposes. There are many standard grades of street-washers carried in stock by all plumbers. The hydrant has about the same lower connections as the street-washer. The hose connection and opening stand well above the lot grade. It is usually placed in the back yard or stable. The outlet may have a hose coupling, and thus be used for sprinkling purposes in the back part of the lot or otherwise, as desired. Where there are no hydrants, it is common to run an iron pipe along the ground to connect the front and back yard. Thus it is not necessary to have so large a supply of hose. The pipe thus used is three-quarters of an inch in diameter. It is less expensive than rubber hose, and does not deteriorate. It should have a short hose connection in front, and hose coupling at the back.

### SOFT-WATER SUPPLY.

In many cities the water from the public pipes contains too much lime to be used for bathing or washing. In such a case it is necessary to supply cistern water for that purpose. This is done by connecting the cistern in the yard with a tank in the attic, or some place above the highest fixture. To do this a force pump is placed in the kitchen. The best kind to use are those known as double-acting, horizontal, brass-cylinder force pumps. They may be screwed to the floor, and the handle come up next to the sink or between the drain-board and the dry-board. When not in use, this handle can be next to the wall and out of the way. A motor may be used in lieu of a pump. It is placed over the kitchen sink, and has connection with city water works. When it is desired to pump water to the attic, one can turn on the city water at the cock and let it run.

Thus the city pressure is exerted through the motor to pump water to the attic, and the labor of pumping entirely done away with. The cost is about fifteen dollars more than a good pump. The suction of such a pump or motor should be one-and-one-half-inch strong lead pipe, and the supply to tank in attic one-and-one-quarter-inch lead or iron pipe where not exposed to view. Where the pump or motor is placed as indicated, it may be used to pump water directly to the kitchen sink, and it is generally best that such an arrangement be made. Of course, water may be drawn from the tank in the attic to this sink, if it is desired to so arrange it; but where this is done, it is necessary to pump all of the cold water used in the kitchen to the attic. This is unnecessary. The sink may have a direct pump connection by means of a five-eighths-inch strong lead pipe which connects with the tank supply. On the end of this lead pipe may be a brass or nickel compression cock over the sink. When it is desired to pump water into the tank this cock is closed, and the only connection is with the tank above.

The common size for tank is eight barrels capacity. It should be constructed of inch-and-three-quarters ploughed and tongued material with two three-eighths inch rods, with bolts and nuts at each end, and cleats across top and bottom in middle. The inside should be lined with four-pound sheet lead; that is, sheet lead which weighs four pounds to the foot. There should be an inch tell-tale pipe of galvanized iron which connects with the sink nearest the pump. Sometimes an overflow which runs to the roof is used, in which case a smaller tell-tale, say one-half inch in diameter, will serve. There are instances where the tank in the attic is connected with a special gutter on the roof, above the line of the tank. Then the tank is provided with a large overflow so that it may not cause trouble. However, this is a little risky. The tank is connected with the hot and cold water system and fixtures subsequently named.

The hot-water system is as simple as it is efficient. Usually a heavy-pressure galvanized-iron boiler, of from twenty-four to sixty-two gallons capacity, is located in the kitchen. It is connected with the tank by means of five-eighths-inch lead or three-quarters-inch iron pipe, and with fixtures subsequently named as being supplied with hot water in the same manner. The water is heated in the range by means of a water back or water front placed in the fire-box of the range. It is connected with the boiler by means of five-eighths-inch lead and three-quarters-inch iron pipe. One pipe from the lower part of the boiler takes the water to the back. The other carries it to the top of the boiler, the cold water naturally going to the bottom and the hot water passing to the top. The hot-water supply for fixtures is drawn from the top of the boiler. Any one may notice, by passing the hand up and down a boiler of this kind, that the top is always warmer than the bottom. Sometimes a wrought-iron pipe is used in a stove in lieu of a water back. It usually answers the same purpose, though its heating surface is not so great. It is best to use a pipe back where the boiler is not connected with soft water. The incrustation from the lime is such that the back soon becomes filled, and it is much more expensive to replace than one made of pipe. When the hot water is from the city water works, the supply is usually directly therefrom rather than from a tank in the attic. However, it is not uncommon to have a tank supply in the house where public-water supply is taken to the exclusion of all other, and it is a better system, though a little more expensive. The hot-water reservoir is usually placed on an iron stand near the stove. It should be provided with a draining connection for the purpose of drawing out all the water when desired. A vent connection from the reservoir to the tank in attic, or, in the event of no tank being used, to the roof above, is common as a guard against extra steam pressure.

## SOIL PIPE.

Before considering other inside fixtures and fittings, the soil pipe should be mentioned. It is of cast-iron, light weight, and, when it is connected with a water-closet, should be four inches in diameter on the inside, and japanned inside and out. Joints are made at the hubs, and should be leaded and well calked. Connections with this pipe should be made by means of Y's of proper size, depending on the size of the drain which connects therewith. The soil pipe should continue upward and through the roof to a point at least four feet above the nearest ridge. Below, it should continue outside of the foundation wall to connect with the drain. Where there is a sink in the cellar, the soil pipe should be below the cellar floor. Vitrified or earthenware drain pipe should never be used inside the walls of a house.

## INSIDE FIXTURES.

The kitchen sink may be considered first. They are usually of light cast-iron. Sometimes they are of pressed steel; again, they are of cast-iron with an interior porcelain finish. If a common cast-iron sink is painted, the paint soon wears off. The ideal sink, the one which is the best in every way, is of porcelain. It has the white, glazed surface of a fine dish, and is easily cleaned. Any kitchen sink should be eighteen inches wide, six inches deep, and from twenty-four to thirty-six inches in length. Thirty or thirty-six is the best. They are provided with a strainer in the bottom, and have one-and-one-half-inch light lead "S" trap connection with soil pipe or grease sink, subsequently considered. Where city water is at hand, the sink should be supplied through a five-eighths-inch brass or nickel-plated self-closing cock. Where the city water is hard, hot and cold cistern water in addition to city water should be supplied through five-eighths-inch brass or nickel-plated compression cocks. If the hot water is from the public water works, a self-closing cock should be used. All cocks should be screwed to a soldered nipple, and not "wiped" or joined directly to the lead pipe. In this way, it is not necessary to wipe a joint every time the cock gives out. A smaller sink, size as desired, may be used in the china-closet or butler's pantry. Such a sink is not in common use excepting in the more expensive houses.

The cellar sink should be sixteen by sixteen inches, ten inches deep, and should be provided with strainer, and an inch-and-a-half light lead "S" trap connection with soil pipe. If city supply only is desired, it may be had through five-eighths-inch brass self-closing cock. Where connection is made with cistern, it may be by means of one-and-one-half inch pipe and a cast-iron pitcher pump; if not this, a well, driven or otherwise, may be similarly connected by means of a pitcher or lift pump. This cellar sink is the kind that may be used in connection with the laundry previously described. Where stationary tubs are used, this sink is not necessary.

# CHAPTER XXXIV.

PLUMBING WORK CONTINUED. — BATH-TUBS. — BATH-SPRINKLERS. — FOOT-TUBS. — SAFES. — WATER-CLOSETS. — WASH-STANDS. — LAUNDRY FITTINGS. — SET TUBS. — OUTSIDE DRAINS. — GREASE SINKS. — NICKEL FITTINGS.

THE fittings of kitchen and other sinks are fully considered in Chapter V., which has to do with kitchens and pantries. It is sufficient to say, however, that the only visible wood-work is the rim and wooden legs, which support the sink proper, and the splash-boards at the side tables as described.

### BATH-TUBS.

A great deal might be said on this subject, which must be left unsaid for the want of space. The ideal bath-tub, the one which in every way is the most satisfactory, is made of porcelain, same as the sinks described. They are beautiful in appearance, easily cleaned, and altogether very satisfactory. However, they are expensive. For the tub alone the cost is about one hundred dollars more than for one of copper. They are used in houses where the matter of cost is not of great importance. Cast-iron, porcelain-lined, and cast-iron tubs, painted, are used occasionally in dwellings. They are more expensive than the copper tubs. An iron porcelain-lined tub is much less expensive than solid porcelain, and is very satisfactory. The iron and porcelain tubs do not require side or end casings of wood. They stand clear of wall and floor. As is known, tubs are of varying sizes and forms, the usual length being from four and one-half to six feet. The tubs known as the "French" pattern are commonly four and one-half feet long, and deeper and wider than the ordinary copper tub. The weight of the copper varies from nine to sixteen ounces to the foot; fourteen-ounce copper tubs are in most general use. The French pattern of tub is coming into more general use than the others in the best class of work. As stated before, it is wider and deeper, though shorter than the old six-foot tub of the common pattern. It does not require as much water to get the same depth in the shorter tub as in one that is longer. As no one cares to lie down in the bath-tub, six feet in length is not necessary; four and one-half feet is ample.

The ordinary fixtures which go with a bath-tub of moderate cost are the combination bath-cock with rubber hose and sprinkler, and a plug and chain. All the metal work is nickel-plated. A combination bath-cock connection with hot and cold water mixes the water as it passes into the tub, so that the proper temperature may be secured by the adjustment of the valves.

The most objectionable feature to the tub of general construction is the overflow which connects with the waste. It is simply a tube which has a single opening below the bath-cock to the waste pipe. This soon becomes foul. Various ingenious devices have been arranged for doing away with this kind of overflow. Arrangements are provided which connect directly with the outlet, and which may be readily removed and cleaned. These prevent the passage of water to the drain when tub is in use. By a movement of a handle in the top the passage may be opened below to allow the water to pass out. There are many devices constructed on this principle. In some instances they add only two or three dollars to the cost of the plumbing outfit, and are certainly worth the extra expense. There are arrangements where the finish is more elaborate, the details more complete, and the cost largely in excess of the figure here named. The same device applies to the various tubs, porcelain, iron, or copper. Formerly it was common to have a large sprinkler connected with hot and cold water above the tub; this is now unusual. It was impossible to use this sprinkler without wetting the head. For that reason the hose and sprinkler has largely taken its place in ordinary work. However, the sprinkler is a very good thing, though it is not put in excepting where the hose attachment is also supplied.

Another modern arrangement which has to do with the sprinkler is a surrounding rubber curtain, which is supported by a plated ring on a level with one's head when standing. This prevents the splashing of water out of the tub. It goes against the curtain, and is thus deflected into the tub. Various arrangements on this principle, looking to hot or steam baths, have been devised. They surround the person bathing, leaving only the head exposed, and discharge the warm water into the confined space surrounding the body. This is a makeshift to take the place of hot and steam baths. In some instances, one-third of the foot end of the tub is fitted with a copper-lined enclosure on three sides, with shower at top. One may stand in this space and use the shower as with the curtain. Additions are sometimes made to this arrangement, wherein the side spray or needle bath is provided. It is so called from the needle size of the streams, which are emitted from certain pipes. All of these showers are connected with regulating valves, so that any desired temperature of water may be maintained by proper adjustment. In some very elaborate bath-rooms showers are provided at the side of the room where there is a marble floor and marble wall surface. These things are arranged with a multiplicity of detail, showing the ingenuity of people who have given these matters much study, and which cannot be fully considered in this connection. Foot-tubs, with hot and cold water connections, are made of the same material that is used in bath-tubs, but are not considered in the plans furnished in this book, though they may be used at will. The bath-tub will serve the same general purpose. As stated, the bath-tubs connect with hot and cold water; they connect with soil pipe or drain by means of one-and-one-half-inch light lead waste pipe, which is trapped by means of an "S" or other trap.

### SAFES.

A safe is simply a lead pan which may be placed under the bath-tub, or other enclosed fixture, to guard against accidents from overflow or leakage. They are made of four-pound sheet lead, and are usually turned up from two to four inches all around. The lead is formed to a bevelled strip at the sides and end, the size of the pan being that of the extreme outside of the fixture. There is usually an inch waste connection to the cellar or kitchen sink. It would be highly improper to connect a safe with the drain, trapped or otherwise, as its use under any circumstances will be occasional, and any water that there might be in the trap would be certain to evaporate, and in that way the safe waste would be the means of connecting the foulness of the drain with the house. Therefore, it is right and proper that it should connect with the sink or the cellar floor. In that way, any discharge therefrom would be readily noticed. Wastes are frequently placed under bath-tubs, generally under wash-stands, when they are enclosed, but rarely or never under a modern water-closet. They are frequently dispensed with entirely.

## WATER-CLOSETS.

Fig. 7, page 68, indicates, in perspective and in section, the more common form of water-closet now in use, than which nothing better has been devised. The details of the valve connection and general form of the closet itself, and the means of flushing it, are various, but the general principle is the same. It is nothing more or less than a large bowl having an " S " trap connection with soil pipe. The bowl and trap are of white porcelain ware, in one piece. The form, as here shown, is a washout closet, and is the one in most general use. Usually a connection with public water service is provided from a tank above. Trap vent, as shown, is connected with the outer air above the roof. The seat of the closet is usually supported from the wall at the back, and rests on the body of the porcelain, on rubber buffers, which prevent the liability of breakage or noise, if it falls. Under any circumstances, water-closets should never be enclosed.

## WASH-STANDS.

It has been said that wash-stands are the most dangerous fixtures that go into a house, and for that reason the greatest care should be observed in their construction. The only material of which the bowl proper, for use in a dwelling-house, should be made is porcelain. The usual form is circular, and about fourteen inches in diameter. However, they are made in various forms. The details of their construction differ as greatly as those of the other fixtures which have been named. Bowls are made which have the same " patent " overflow arrangements as the bath-tub overflows that have been considered and described elsewhere. It is usual, however, to use a rubber plug and chain. The top and back of the wash-stand should be of marble. The top should be one and one-eighth inch thick, counter-sunk, so that the splashed water cannot run from it to the floor; the back need be only seven-eighths inch thick, and generally not more than ten inches high. Sometimes it may be less. The hot and cold water fixtures are nickel-plated; usually they are made self-closing, to prevent the waste of water. It is necessary that they should be so where city water is used. It is part of the city regulations that all connections of this kind be self-closing. Wash-stands need not be enclosed below. The marble top may be supported on iron brackets or turned wooden legs of hard wood. Traps and other drain connections can be neatly arranged so that their appearance is not in any sense objectionable in the bath-room or other place. The wash-stand should have one-and-one-half-inch light lead trapped connection with the drain or soil pipe.

Generally speaking, it is not necessary for the trap to be ventilated, unless it so happen that it is some distance from the soil pipe or drain. The soil pipe, we know, is always ventilated, and if the wash-stand is situated some distance from it, it should have a direct communication with the outer air above the roof.

Sometimes a pitcher-cock is placed on the wash-stand in the bath-room to enable the drawing of drinking water when the other connections are with the cistern, it being assumed in this instance that only the water from public water works is used for drinking purposes. The pitcher-cock is simply one with a long neck which extends above the bowl, and is directed into it, the pitcher being placed under it for the purpose of filling.

### LAUNDRY FITTINGS.

The fittings for a simple laundry apparatus, that would go into a house of very moderate cost, have been described elsewhere. In this instance we will consider only the more elaborate arrangements which have to do with set tubs. They may be of porcelain or plain cast-iron, of cast-iron porcelain-lined, or of brown glazed earthenware. The porcelain is of the same general character as that mentioned for the bath-tub and sinks, and is an expensive and very elegant material. The porcelain-lined iron tubs are in more general use, for the reason that they are less expensive than those of all porcelain. Brown earthenware tubs are coming to be favorably considered, and are in every way satisfactory. Tubs made of wood, slate, or other material, where they are in several pieces, are objectionable. Those mentioned above are one-piece tubs, and are generally set three together. The porcelain or brown earthenware tubs usually have wooden rims. Sometimes these tubs are provided with covers, though it is usual and preferable that covers be not used, and that the water be supplied from above. The hot and cold water fixtures are nickel-plated compression cocks, which connect with hot and cold water sources. Generally speaking, it is best, where set tubs are used, that an independent apparatus for heating water be provided; that is, a laundry water heater, of which there are many different kinds, and which are constructed on the same general principle as the arrangement mentioned in connection with the kitchen and other water-heating apparatus. It is entirely possible, however, to make connections with the water-heating apparatus of the kitchen.

The drain connections are of one-and-one-half-inch light lead, and are independently trapped for each tub. They lead to the main drain, connecting with sewer or vault.

## OUTSIDE DRAINS.

Drains outside of the house should be of vitrified or glazed earthenware pipe, laid below the action of frost, with proper slant. They should be well bedded and have smoothly cemented joints. The slant need be very slight, eighteen inches in eighty feet or less may be used. It is especially desirable that the joints be thoroughly cemented, and that they be smooth on the inside, so that the foul matter passing through the interior will not lodge against any projections. The surface or ends of the pipe should never be clipped or cut for connections; "Y's" or "T's" are used for all connections with other drains. Drain pipes from a dwelling-house are usually five or six inches in diameter. It is quite as important that they be not too large as that they be large enough. Where a pipe is too large, there is not enough water in the bottom to keep it clean. The illustration here given will make clear this point. A six and eight inch drain is shown with the same quantity of water in each. It is common in cases of drain connection with a vault that no trap in the drain or soil pipe itself be used. Where sewer connection is made, a vitrified trap of the same size as the drain is used; and it is provided with a trap vent connection with the outer air by means of vitrified vent and grate opening at the top.

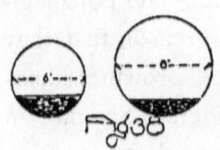

Storm-water connections may be made with the main sewer, but it is best that they be made between the house and the trap of main drain. In this way there is no danger of the sewer having connection with the down spouts in the event of the evaporation of the water in the trap of the storm-water connection. The modern plan of city sewer systems is to have independent service for storm water and house drain connections.

## GREASE SINKS.

The grease sink is lined with brick, and is usually of four or five barrels capacity. It is cemented the same as the cistern, is generally twenty or twenty-five feet away from the house, and has a four-inch vitrified drain connection with the waste from the kitchen sink or other sink in which greasy water may be deposited. The sink itself has a siphon connection with the main drain or vault, and, being provided with an iron top, the deposit of grease or other material may be removed if necessary. In some instances a sink of this kind is required to be used to collect all solid matter before the drainage connection passes from the property.

The "S" trap only has been distinctly mentioned. There are hundreds of others, all constructed upon the same general principle. Some are provided with mechanical means of closing the opening leading to the source of supply, and, in addition to this, they are provided with a seal of water depending upon some form or condition of the "S" trap. This principle is invariable in the construction of traps. No trap should be used unless provided with a trap screw of the same size as the drain itself, which will admit of its being opened when necessary. It is not uncommon that rings or other jewelry get into the waste of wash-stand or bath-tub; they may be recovered by taking out the trap screw. Again, should the trap become fouled or clogged, the matter may be removed in the same way.

## NICKEL FITTINGS.

For the kitchen sink, nickel fittings are preferable to brass, because they are more easily cleaned.

# CHAPTER XXXV.

COST OF A HOUSE. — SCHEDULES OF COSTS. — WHAT GOES INTO A HOUSE. — SCHEDULE "B." — COST DETAILS.

WHAT makes the cost of a house? Everything that has been placed on the lot when the structure is completed. Below is a form or schedule, with blanks, filled out by an architect for a gentleman for whom he made plans.

JOHN SMITH, — As I understand your wants, would estimate the cost of improvements contemplated on No. Delaware Street as follows: —

| | |
|---|---:|
| Building — 1st floor finish hard wood, 2d floor finish poplar, | $3,000 |
| Privy and Vault | $35 |
| Cistern and Connections | 50 |
| Well, Connections, and Pump | 35 |
| Walks, 40 yards at 70 cents | 28 |
| Fences — Tight board, 160 feet at 25 cents, Picket none, | 40 |
| Illuminating-Gas Pipe | 30 |
| Plumbing — Cellar sink 1, Kitchen sink 1, Bath-tub 1, W. C. 1, W. S. 1, St. Washer 1, City and Cistern Water, | 275 |
| Natural-Gas Pipe, without burners or burner fittings | 35 |
| Gas Fixtures | 50 |
| Mantels and Grates 3, Average cost $40 | 120 |
| Furnace | 250 |
| Plate Glass | 50 |
| Cathedral Glass | 25 |
| Electric Work — Door bell 2, Kitchen bell 1 | 25 |
| | 1,128 |
| Without Architect's fee | $4,128 |

Everything that goes into a house should be fully represented to the owner. Thus the costs may be fixed and the aggregate understood. If this were universally done, there would be less said about the unreliability of architects' estimates. If the architect is very careful to make known to the owner the quality of everything that he is to have, and, as well, the general quantities and costs, he is doing his full duty in this matter. Anything less than this is a neglect of duty. Furthermore, this should be made a matter of record, so that if changes are made and the cost altered, a basis for comparison may be at hand. It is the practice of the writer to use a specification which describes everything which may be a part of a brick or a frame house, and to stamp out the parts omitted. For example, in that specification there are specified brick and cemented floors for cellar. It is the custom to stamp the word " No " before the words brick floor, so that it reads " No brick floor in cellar." In other cases it may be " No lattice work in side yard," etc. Thus the owner of the house knows not only what he is to get, but what he is not to get, and the exact quality of that which is included as well as that which is omitted. He has positive and negative information with respect to his house. This form of specification has been in use three years, and has been uniformly satisfactory.

The schedule filled out for Mr. Smith is a printed form, which is handed to the owner as soon as the building cost is determined. It is in addition to the detailed specification. In the schedule the cost of the building is put down at three thousand dollars. The appurtenances are the items mentioned below the line which gives the price of the building proper, and in this instance are estimated at $1,128. The house estimate is $3,000. This makes a total cost of $4,128. The house was a well-finished building of nine rooms. The parlor and hall were finished in quartered oak, the dining and sitting rooms in quartered sycamore, the rear hall in quartered oak, the china-room in sycamore, kitchen and pantry in plain oak. It would have cost about $125 less to finish the first floor of this house in soft wood. It is not possible to give general statements as to the difference in cost of finishing between hard and soft wood. Twenty to thirty-five dollars a room is generally ample, though the difference may be greater.

The privy building was figured at twenty dollars, and the vault at a dollar a foot. The cistern and connections at fifty cents a barrel. Thus a hundred-barrel cistern costs fifty dollars. The well pump, which was located in the kitchen, was a cheap form of horizontal force-pump fastened to the floor, with the handle coming up near the kitchen table. It supplied water to the kitchen sink. It, as well as the cistern pump, was included in the plumbing contract. The walks were ordinary brick walks laid in sand. Tight-board fence was figured, as shown, at twenty-five cents a lineal foot. The illuminating-gas pipe was figured at a little less than the price given on schedule "B," but was ample. The same may be said of the plumbing work. The gas fixtures were neat brass goods that looked plain in the store surrounded with very elaborate ones, but were entirely satisfactory when in the house. The mantels and grates, as may be judged by their cost, were not very elaborate. However, they were of wood, the same style and finish as the room. There were bevelled-glass mirrors above the shelves. The hearth and facing were of unglazed tile, the grate-frame of brass, the grate itself club pattern, and altogether it was simple but pleasing. The furnace was of wrought-iron, riveted joints, with galvanized iron jacket. It would have cost about fifteen or twenty dollars more to set it in brick. This price included registers, pipes in the wall, and all connections. If the building had cost a thousand dollars more, or even two thousand, the appurtenances need not have cost more than a hundred to a hundred and fifty dollars additional. There would probably have been a little more gas pipe, a few more fixtures, and the furnace would have been somewhat more expensive; or, if the house had cost five hundred dollars less, the appurtenances would not have represented in all more than seventy-five dollars difference, providing the general requirements had been the same.

The following schedule was prepared for Mr. Brown. His was an eight-room house; smaller, less elaborate, but just as well built, as the one for Mr. Smith. He did not have quite as much plumbing, and reduced the other appurtenances somewhat. Altogether they represent $801. If his had been a fifteen-hundred-dollar house, and the same general conditions had been met, the appurtenances would not have cost any less. Likewise, if it had been a two-thousand-dollar house, they would have cost no more. Additions to size of rooms or a more elaborate finish would not have appreciably affected the cost of the appurtenances. It is well to bear this in mind when building.

WILLIAM BROWN, — As I understand your wants, would estimate the cost of improvements contemplated on No. Alabama Street as follows: —

```
Building—1st floor finish hard wood, 2d floor finish poplar,   $1,700
Privy and Vault        .     .     .     .     .     .    $40
Cistern and Connections .    .     .     .     .     .     40
No Well, Connections, and Pump    .    .     .     .
Walks, 30 yards at 70 cents   .    .     .     .     .     21
Fences — Tight board, 100 at 25 cents, Picket none   .     25
Illuminating-Gas Pipe    .    .     .     .     .    .     25
Plumbing — Cellar sink none, Kitchen sink 1, Bath-tub 1,
   W. C. 1, W. S. 1, St. Washer 1, City Water .    .    . 200
Natural-Gas Pipe, without burners or burner fittings  .    30
Gas Fixtures    .    .     .     .     .     .     .    .  35
Mantels and Grates 3, Average cost $40 .    .    .    .   120
Furnace .    .     .     .     .     .     .     .    .   240
Plate Glass    .    .     .     .     .     .     .   .    20
Cathedral Glass none    .    .     .     .     .     .
Electric Work — Door bell 1, Kitchen bell none   .   .      5
                                                         ——
                                                         801

Without Architect's fee .     .           .            $2,501
```

The two examples given show the method of filling out a cost schedule, which, by the way, is seldom presented in this form to the owner of a house by his architect. It now remains to indicate, in general terms, the basis of values as before given. It is not intended to form this book on the "every-man-his-own-architect" principle, but it is constructed on the idea that every one should know as much about the business in hand as is possible, before calling for other assistance. For this purpose certain prices are given which are a little in advance of those charged in the section of country to which they apply. This is done so that the errors, if any, may be on the side of safety. Generally speaking, there will not be any great difference in the cost of the appurtenances mentioned. It is the cost of the building proper which varies. The cost of the buildings illustrated is given, unless otherwise mentioned, on a basis of hard-wood finish for the first floor excepting kitchen, and soft wood above, all finished in oil.

Below is the schedule "B," so frequently referred to in the description of house plans.

### SCHEDULE "B."

Building. — First floor finish hard wood; second floor, soft wood.

Where estimates are given in the book on the basis of schedule "B," they include only the building, as mentioned above, and do not include the following items: —

Privy building, $20; vault, $1 per foot for each foot in depth.

Cistern and connections, $0.50 per barrel; pump, $5 to $35; well, $0.75 per lineal foot; pump and connections, $5 to $35. (Force pump included in plumbing contract.)

Walks of brick, $0.70 per square yard; cement, $1.80 per square yard.

Fences: tight-board, $0.25 per lineal foot; picket, $0.50 per lineal foot, painted three coats.

Illuminating-gas pipe, $1.50 to $2 per connection.

Plumbing — Cellar sink, plain iron . . . . set $10
Hot-water boiler and back . . . . . " 25
Kitchen sink, city and hot and cold cistern water . " 30
Force pump and tank . . . . . . " 50
Bath-tub, 14 oz. copper . . . . . . " 30
Wash-stand . . . . . . . . " 25
Water-closet " washout " . . . . . " 40
Street-washer . . . . . . . . " 12
City service, $0.35 a foot, lineal, laid.
Drain connection, $0.30 a foot, lineal, laid.
[For other piping and connections add twenty per cent of above aggregate.]
Natural-gas piping, without burners, $4 a fire.
Gas fixtures, about $1.50 per burner.
Mantels and grates, average cost, $40.
Furnace, for all pipes and connections, nine registers, $240; add $16 for each additional second-story connection; $8 for first-story connection.
Plate glass, $0.50 to $0.75 a square foot, according to size.
Cathedral glass, plain, $0.30 a foot; leaded, from $1 upward.
Electric work — door bells, each $6; kitchen bell, $6.

# CHAPTER XXXVI.

VARYING BUILDING VALUES. — COST OF APPURTENANCES. — PRICES OF LABOR AND MATERIAL ON WHICH ESTIMATES ARE BASED.

THE cost of building varies in different sections. At the end of this chapter will be found a list of prices upon which the building estimates of this book are based.

The plumbing schedule is formed so that one may see about what the different items of a completed plumbing outfit cost. Figuring sixty feet of service and seventy feet of drain, the plumbing outfit would cost, as indicated, $328. It has been furnished for less. The figures given in connection with plumbing work are not necessarily accurate. They are approximately so in detail. As no two plumbers or other mechanics will figure exactly the same on the same fixtures, or the same material and labor, it is not to be expected that an architect could form a thumb-rule schedule which would be satisfactory to plumbers and all others. In the class of work contemplated in this specification, the tendency of these figures is in the right direction. They are as nearly correct as general statements can be. It is known that a single bath-tub can be fitted up to cost more than the entire plumbing outfit here mentioned. It would afford no more conveniences to the occupant of the house, and would be no safer from a sanitary standpoint; and it probably would require more labor to care for than the one contemplated. The estimates are on the basis of a specification which would meet with the approval of the public sanitary inspectors in any of the large cities.

Where there is a material reduction in the number of fixtures and connections from the list given, the percentage for other piping and connections will have to be increased.

There are various ways of reducing the cost of the outfit. The best way is to have less of it; for instance, only city water may be used, or, possibly, only the cistern water. The completed plumbing outfit mentioned in schedule " B," with the exception of cistern-water connections, including hot and cold city water for sink, wash-stand, and bath-tub, has been put in, in plan No. 30, for $245.

The natural-gas-piping figure, like the others, is liable to vary. Piping for five fires has been put in for $20, for $15, and for $30. The burners, the burner valves and mixers, usually cost from four to five dollars a fire.

The gas-fixture schedule is priced by the burner, not by the connection. Each burner of each fixture is counted. Of course one may get a single fixture which will cost as much as the above rule would figure on a whole outfit, but that is unusual in moderate-cost houses. Some of the second-story brackets will cost from ninety cents to one dollar and a quarter apiece. This will increase the price of burner margin for the first floor, and allow more elaborate fixtures.

The mantels are priced to include grate, hearth, facings, and everything that may go there, excepting fender and blower. One may get a mantel for $25 or $30, or he may use a grate setting without a mantel, or may go as far into the hundreds as his inclination and means will lead him. Very expensive mantels in moderate-cost houses are not in good taste. A $100 or $150 mantel in a room all of the other wood-work of which did not cost over half that sum, is in exceedingly bad form. The mantel appears like a monument; everything around it is insignificant. In buying mantels from stock in mantel stores, the cheaper ones are generally the best designed from an artistic standpoint.

The furnace price is necessarily arbitrary. The owner of a house will be told that the price here given is too high and too low. A moderate-sized, two-story, eight-room house, which, counting the bath-room, would have nine connections, could be provided with a furnace of wrought-iron or steel, riveted joints, double galvanized-iron jacket, for $240. The same furnace brick-set will cost from fifteen to twenty dollars more. The owner of such a house can get a cheaper furnace, or he can get one which will be much more expensive. Oftentimes when an architect estimates the price of a furnace to the owner, the latter will respond with the statement that he has been offered a furnace complete for ninety dollars. Upon investigation it generally proves that the furnace is in some one's store ready for delivery; that it will cost extra to set it, and for all connections, fittings, registers, etc.; and that the furnace itself is of such a kind that ninety dollars is a high price for it. There is no doubt that the statement as to furnace prices will meet with general disapproval from manufacturers. Many will say that the prices given are ridiculously high, and others, ridiculously low. Other general statements as to heating apparatus may be found in a chapter given to that subject in that section of the book devoted to the Journey through the House.

The estimates given on plate and cathedral glass are about as unsatisfactory as anything can be. They merely give the owner a general idea as to what to expect.

Electric-work prices are approximately correct for localities where the facilities for doing this kind of work are at hand. Door and table bell outfits are now sold and arranged ready to be set up. The methods of their adjustment are so simple that any one who can read can put them in.

The general statement may be made that these prices are approximately correct in all the larger markets; and that in cases where the building is far removed therefrom, there must necessarily be additions for travel of workmen, and other incidental expenses in the transportation of material and labor.

The following is the list of prices of material and labor upon which the building estimates are based : —

Excavating, $0.25 a yard.
Brick in the wall, $9 per M.
Mason work, $5.50 a yard, laid up.
Cement floors, $0.70 a square yard.
Timber, joist, and scantling, less than eighteen feet long, $17 per M.
No. 1 common boards, $18 per M.
Select common pine flooring, count measure, $26 per M.
Common flooring, count measure, $22.50 per M.
First quality yellow pine flooring, face measure, $37.50 per M.
Standard yellow pine flooring, face measure, $30 per M.
No. 1 poplar flooring, face measure, $28.50 per M.
No. 2 poplar flooring, face measure, $23.50 per M.
No. 1 stock boards, $20 per M.
No. 1 poplar siding or weather-boarding, $18 per M.
No. 2, $16 per M.
No 1 pine siding, $22 per M.
No. 2, $20 per M.
Shingles, 16 inches clear butts, best, per M, $3.75.
Shingles, 16 inches extra, 10 inches clear butts, $3.25.
Pine lath, per M, $2.50.
Poplar and pine finishing lumber, $3.75 to $6 per 100 feet.
Oak or maple flooring, first class, $4 to $6 per 100 feet.
Oak finishing lumber, $4 to $6 per 100 feet.

Under certain conditions the above prices are subject to discounts.

Plastering: three-coat work, plaster-of-Paris finish, $0.25 a yard; two-coat work, plaster-of-Paris finish, $0.20; gray floated sand finish, three cents extra on above prices.

Painting, $0.06 per yard a coat.

Labor: common labor, $0.15 an hour; bricklayers and masons, $0.35 to $0.45 an hour; carpenters, $0.20 to $0.30 an hour; tinners, $0.30 an hour; painters, $0.20 to $0.30 an hour; plumber and helper, $0.50 an hour.

The above labor prices are those paid by the contractors. Rarely, however, are the maximum prices reached.

There are few subjects on which ideas vary so greatly as values. This fact may be made apparent when we call to mind that bids on a house let for $3,000 frequently range $1,000 higher than this figure.

# BUSINESS POINTS IN BUILDING.

## CHAPTER XXXVII.

LOW-COST HOUSES. — METHODS OF MAKING CONTRACTS. — ARCHITECTS' ESTIMATES. — BUILDING BY THE DAY. — THE SAFEST PLAN. — GUARDING AGAINST LIENS.

A LOW-COST, well-built house is sought by all. The cost of a house is largely a question of business management, — one of knowledge. Before considering the details of contracting for the building of a house, there are a few general points which should be mentioned. First, it never pays to make a contract to have a house built for less than it is worth. In order to get a good house, it is necessary that there be a margin of profit for the builder. Second, a good house from a constructive standpoint can only be built by competent mechanics. One may contract for the building of a house for less than it is worth with parties who are incapable of doing first-class work, and require a bond to secure the faithful execution of the contract. A contract or a bond cannot make a man do good work if he does not know how to do it. It will not save anxiety or trouble. It may indemnify against actual damages, but never against trouble and vexation; nor can it compensate for poor work done in building a home. This matter is mentioned because it is the fault of a great many people, who are inexperienced in building, that they are disposed to have work done for less than it is worth. It does not pay.

It may be remembered, however, that one builder may be able to build for less than another. One may have more energy, tact, or general ability than another. He may have better credit; may be a better buyer. The result is larger accomplishments.

In speaking of low-cost houses or cheap buildings, it is not to be understood that they are cheap or low-cost in the sense of being common or frail. I mean first-class houses at a relatively low cost; low cost in a business sense, the best for the money.

We often hear the statement made that one can tell nothing definite about the cost of a house until it is finished. One can come as near knowing what a house will cost, as he can to knowing what he wants before he begins. One can get prices on what he has in mind, if his ideas be expressed. He cannot get prices on the unknown. The expression of one's ideas of a house is through plans and specifications. The fact that architects' estimates are often too low is because the owner is not sufficiently informed in house-building to know what he wants until after the estimate is made. The owner usually expresses a price that he wishes to pay for his house before he expresses his idea. It may be well to illustrate this.

One who wishes to build goes to an architect with some sketches or prints, which he has been collecting, lays them down and says, —

"We're thinking about building a house. We want something like this. Here are four rooms and a hall downstairs, and four rooms and a bath-room above. We want to build of wood, and wish to have the house warm and substantial. Can it be built for three thousand dollars? It's all we have to put in it."

"Oh, yes," says the architect; and so it can. A good, comfortable, substantial house, from the plans indicated, can be built for three thousand dollars. The architect knows this, and says that the work can be done for that price. He is ordered to make the plans. In a day or two the owner comes into his office and says, —

"My wife and I were talking over the house last night, and concluded that we would like to have a bay window from the dining-room, — a place where we can sit in summer, and put flowers in the winter."

"All right."

"And she told me to ask where you were going to put a wash-stand downstairs. You know we will want some kind of a wash-room."

"I hadn't thought anything about that," said the architect. "Nothing was said about it. I supposed that in a house of this size the bath-room was the only place where you would put a stationary wash-stand."

"We have to have a place downstairs. We can't go upstairs every time we want to wash our hands."

Another two or three days pass. The owner visits the architect again. It is the old story. He and his wife have been studying the house question in earnest. They are educating themselves in house-building. The more they think about it, the more they want, all of which is perfectly natural and right. It is in the natural order of things. It is the way the world moves.

"We were talking about the house, and have about concluded that we will finish two front rooms upstairs in oak. What do you think it will cost?"

"If you use oak for all the wood-work, it will cost between forty and fifty dollars."

"That isn't much. We'll have it."

And so the house grows as the owners grow, a little every

day. The next day it is a little more plate glass at a cost of fifteen dollars. Again, it is bronze hardware at an extra cost of twenty dollars. Then it is bevelled-glass doors in the china-closet, plastering in the attic, a tile vestibule, a porch off from the dining-room, and so on.

The three thousand dollars is exceeded, though probably by something less than the amount represented by the growth of the owner's ideas. The architect had made a certain allowance for this development, though it was not possible for him entirely to foresee it. Of those who build, the ones who take the greatest interest in the house, those who think the most about it, are usually the ones who exceed their original calculations by the largest amount.

In building, it is important that the architect and the owner thoroughly understand each other before contracts with the builders are signed. The wants of the owner must be thoroughly understood, and carefully and accurately set forth. From the plans and specifications estimates for all parts of the work should be received, and the cost of everything known, before obligations are created. The process of making the plans and specifications, and taking the bids, is educational in its tendency. It brings to the owner's attention nearly everything that he may want. Frequently he will find that the first estimates which he gets are higher than the amount he cared to expend. This is on account of his growth. He can frequently reduce the cost without positive injury to the original scheme.

We will consider how contracts are usually made. Sometimes it is by making plans and specifications for the entire house, and then asking for bids on the building as a whole. A general contractor makes his figures on the various parts of the work, then adds them together and makes a lump bid. If he is awarded the contract under such a system, he does part of the work himself and sublets the rest. Possibly he may be a carpenter; then he sublets the brick work, plastering, tinning, painting, etc., and, if possible, he makes a profit on all of these sub-contracts. It does not always happen that he makes figures on these various divisions of the contract himself when forming his original bid. He gets sub-bids from various mechanics and adds these to his own in making up a lump bid. It is known that there is a very wide range of difference between bids which come in this way. In a house to cost three thousand dollars the bids not infrequently vary twenty-five to thirty per cent. The highest bid may be over four thousand dollars.

Another way of contracting is for the architect or owner, as the case may be, to take bids on the various details of excavating, stone work, brick work, carpenter work, painting, plastering, galvanized iron and tin, glass, plumbing, gas-fitting, etc.; in fact, to detail the work as much as possible and receive detailed bids. If the work costs too much, if the bids run too high, one can locate the excess.

At times one can get a cheaper house by pursuing this plan. Another plan of building is by the day. Usually this means to employ carpenters and a foreman, take bids on the material that the carpenters use, and to sublet the mason work, excavating, painting, plastering, tin-work, plumbing, etc. Sometimes the mason-work is also done by the day.

Each plan has its merits. The first mentioned, of letting most of the work in one contract, is the one in most general use. It is common practice in this connection to let excavating, mason work, carpenter work, plastering, tinning, painting, and hardware in one general contract; then the mantels, gas-fixtures, furnace, plumbing, electric work, and ornamental glass work are let in separate contracts. It is difficult for one to specify gas-fixtures, mantels, and similar fittings, excepting by price. There is no satisfaction in this, for the reason that the owner or his architect may be able to make quite as good or even a better bargain than the contractor. Then there is no opportunity for the builder to arrange for a relatively high price with those who furnish this class of goods. It is fair for the builder to assume that he is entitled to a certain percentage for selecting and negotiating for such articles. The owner may save this for himself by making his own purchases.

Plumbing work is frequently separated from the general contract in order that the owner may exercise his discretion as to the workmen employed to do this important work. In such circumstances it is not altogether a matter of cost. It is of the utmost importance that the best of workmen be employed.

The articles which cannot be directly specified should be secured outside the general contract. Altogether, the plan of letting most of the work in one contract, as outlined, is the best and safest for those to pursue who are not thoroughly familiar with building operations.

The plan of subletting the separate contracts to the lowest bidders is not to be recommended to those without large experience. The difficulty in locating responsibility for delays is great. There is apt to be contention, annoyance, and sometimes loss, by this confusion. The plan of building by the day is more satisfactory for experienced builders than the one just mentioned, but it has the disadvantage of not fully representing to the owner before it is finished the cost of his structure.

In nearly every city or town there are a number of good builders, not well supplied with means, who will take a contract for building a house, work on it themselves until it is finished, and then take another, never having more than one or two houses on hand. One can frequently get good work from such builders at a much less cost than from large contractors. The larger contractors employ a foreman at about the same price a day that the small contractors expect to get per day out of their entire contract. Then, in addition to that, they receive their profits of ten, fifteen, or other per cent for their time and attention. Any one building with the help of the smaller contractors must be very careful, or he will get into trouble on account of the small margin of profit.

To recur to the method first mentioned. It is well that suggestions be made as to the course to be pursued in receiving bids on work, as classified in that suggestion. In the first place, there should be accurate plans and specifications made by an architect capable of doing that kind of work. Everything should be fully represented to the owner in both a positive and negative way; that is, not only as to what is to go into his house, but as to what is not to go into it. As soon as the architect or those in charge of the work begin to take bids, the owner should be provided with a complete copy of the plans and specifications, in order that he may be fully conversant with what is to be done. It was said that everything should be represented to the owner in both a positive and negative way. Not only should it be stated to him that the first floor of the house is to be plastered, but, if such is the case, that the cellar is not to be plastered. If the cellar floor is not to be cemented, it should be stated definitely to him in that way before beginning to take bids. If fly-screens are not included in the building contract, it should be so stated. Everything should be fully represented, and a record thereof placed before the owner, so that there can be not the slightest opportunity for misunderstanding or disagreement.

Thus, if everything is presented to the owner, he will know what he is to have and what he is not to have, and his business will be done for him in a way satisfactory to all. When this is done, it is time to begin taking bids.

In doing this there should be no favoritism. The builder should be allowed to take a copy of the plans and specifications with him to his office or place of business, and keep them a day or more, in order to take off his quantities and become thoroughly conversant with everything connected with them. Then he can return the plans, and, while others are doing the same thing, he can compile his figures. Generally it takes about a day for each contractor to get through with a set of plans; that is, if five bids are received, it generally takes five or six days, assuming that only one set of plans is in use. No one should be asked to figure on a building unless the owner is willing to award him the contract, providing his bid is the lowest. Anything else is unfair. When all the bids have been received in sealed envelopes, the architect and owner may open them. After selecting the lowest, they may add to that figure the cost of everything not included in that proposition,— the furnace, mantels, gas fixtures, ornamental glass, and anything else that has not been included in the bid. This may be readily done, if the architect provide a schedule, similar to schedule " B," of everything which may go into the house.

In the matter of closing the contract, only general statements can be made. Where an architect is employed, he will give proper directions; but, as many houses are built without such assistance, it is proper to make general statements which will assist in this work. There are forms of building-contracts, or articles of agreement, which may be secured from various regular sources. It is proper to fix the time of the completion of the work, which will vary in different parts of the country according to general customs. A house to cost from fifteen hundred to four thousand dollars may be very easily finished, under favorable circumstances, in ninety to a hundred days. Such houses can be built in less time, but it is best to give the builder at least three months. He will do better work in that time than in less. For the higher figure named, or for those which approach it, it may be better to allow even a little more rather than less time. As a price for liquidated damages in event of delay in completion, the rental value of the property is the usual sum specified.

There are various plans pursued in the matter of payments. Where there is an architect or superintendent, he usually issues orders on the owner for payment of material and labor furnished by a contractor less ten or fifteen per cent. Sometimes it is stated that two-fifths of the money will be paid when the building is enclosed and under roof; one-fifth additional when building is plastered, painted on exterior, all exterior appurtenances finished, the floors laid, and the house ready for other interior wood-work; and the remaining two-fifths when all work is finished. At times this apportionment is correct, and at other times not. However, it is a very good general rule. It is a good plan to add the ten per cent discount to it when possible. Sometimes an indemnifying bond is required of the contractor in order to secure the owner the proper execution of the contract. Otherwise the ten or fifteen per cent discount is relied upon to secure that end.

The lien laws in the various States make it very important that the owner, or his agent in the matter of building, should be very careful to see that the contractor pays all his bills, or secures releases from those who have furnished material and labor on account of the building contract, before money is paid by owner.

The law is different in various States, and renders the owner liable, under varying conditions, for material and labor furnished to contractor by others as employees or sub-contractor, even though payment has been made by owner to general contractor. Where a bond is not required, it is proper for the owner or his agent to exact releases in proper form from those who have furnished material and labor to contractor. The following form is in use by the writer: —

Work located

  The undersigned, in consideration of the personal credit extended by to , Contractor, hereby consent that may pay to said contractor any sum that may be now owing to, or may hereafter become due, said contractor, on account of contract for the construction of the above works, and we hereby waive all rights to Mechanics' Liens or other claims which we have, or may have, against said property, or owner, on account of labor or material furnished by us.

  INDIANAPOLIS,  1889.

It is the custom to furnish the builder with a number of copies of the above release before it is time for him to secure an order on the owner for money. As the architect is in a position to know from whom material or labor is secured, it is possible for him to know if the list of releases is complete. If not complete, the party refusing to give a release is required to make statement as to the amount of the indebtedness for material and labor furnished on the contract. The general contractor is charged with the amount represented as being due until the matter is fully adjusted. As an additional safeguard, the contractor is at times required to fill out and make affidavit to the following: —

INDIANAPOLIS,           1889.

The undersigned, for the purpose of securing payment on account of contract with           , for the construction of a           house, known as No.      on           Street, situated on Lot      , Out-lot      , Division to City of Indianapolis, Marion County, State of Indiana, represents hereby that he has paid for all labor and material of every kind and nature had and procured therefor, excepting, however, that he is now owing the following sums to the respective parties hereinafter named for labor and materials for said building, and owes therefor no other amounts, to wit: —

In this connection it is not possible to consider all of the ramifications of the lien law. It is important to understand, however, that it is entirely possible for an owner to have to pay for part of or all of his house twice, if he is not careful in matters of this kind.

# HOW TO SECURE A HOME.

## CHAPTER XXXVIII.

MONTHLY PAYMENTS. — CALCULATIONS ON A LONG-TIME PLAN. — PURCHASE ON A RENTAL BASIS. — HOW IT MAY BE WORKED OUT.

IT is a pleasant thought that every one can own a home of his own. With only a moderate salary, and little or nothing ahead, a thought of this kind may appear more pleasant than real. It may be affirmed, however, that, with few exceptions, any one who can pay rent may own his home. This will require certain sacrifices and at first great economy, but in the end the result justifies the means. There is no reason why any one should pay rent. Building associations are instrumental in securing more homes for people on a long-time plan than any other scheme. In the large towns, however, houses are sold on various kinds of instalment plans. By way of illustration, the writer calls to mind a five-room house, pleasantly situated, which was built about three years ago. This house is being paid for in instalments of $15 a month. An arrangement of this kind is good for all concerned. It is an easy way for one to get a home. It is a good use of money, from a business standpoint, for the one who has the money to invest. A little demonstration will make this plain. The lot on which the house was situated was valued at $400. The house, with walks, well, cistern, and outbuildings, cost $900. Here is a total investment of $1,300. The purchaser paid $300 in cash. There remained $1,000 unpaid. The interest on $1,000 for a year at six per cent is $60; but as the volume of interest is reduced as the payments are made, the actual interest for the full period averages about one-half of $60, or $30, per year. To make this point clear, I will state it in another way. The principal is being reduced as the monthly payments are made. As the payments advance, the amount of interest necessarily decreases, as there is not so much principal on which to pay interest. As a matter of fact, one pays six per cent interest on just one-half of $1,000 for the full period, or, what amounts to the same thing, the average interest on the full period is three per cent. Thus, one is paying an average interest of $30 per year; and, as he pays $15 a month, this would be $180 a year for principal and interest, $150 of which would apply to the principal. Thus it is that in six years and eight months the one paying $15 a month will own the house and lot. I know of other cases where less each month is paid and a longer time is taken. It would take $10.83[1] per month to pay for a house of this kind in ten years, with a cash payment of $300.

It may be said that nobody but a philanthropist would sell property in this way. In the case of which I speak, the philanthropist is the manager of the property of a life-insurance company which owns quite a large amount of unimproved real estate in a Western city, and had a surplus capital on which it desired to realize. It is a good thing for the company. By this means it is enabled to dispose of its real estate, and to use its money profitably.

This is not strictly architectural, but it may result in showing some one how to get a home, or others how to make use of idle capital in a safe and profitable way. It is better for one who has money to invest to sell houses in this way than it is to rent them. He gets profit on the sale, and interest on his money, which latter is all he expects under other circumstances, and disposes of the houses before they need repairs. This is the view which the capitalist takes of the situation. By looking into it a little further, he may see that he will not be troubled by insurance, a vacant house, or repairs. The cash payment is sufficient to protect the expense of foreclosing the mortgage and the rental of the house during the time of the redemption. In some instances the property is leased on the payment of a small cash bonus, with the stipulation that when one-third, one-fourth, or other agreed portion of selling price is paid in, that a deed will be given; further payment being secured by mortgage.

Building associations are not common in all sections of the country. Those who are ambitious to build, and are not provided with facilities which a building association offers, may ask what to do. The answer is short: form an association. This can be done in a small community. Two hundred shares paid in, say, by fifty people, would represent a hundred dollars a week. Any one who wishes to do this can provide himself with text-books and other information on the subject, which are now published in different parts of the country. Any bookseller with a good catalogue can give the necessary information.

It is sometimes assumed by those unfamiliar with building-association methods, that they only provide means for building small, low-cost houses. This is an error. It is not at all unusual that complete houses, costing from three to five thousand dollars, are built by men of large means, who secure their money from a building association. One has, say, forty or fifty thousand dollars profitably occupied in a regular business; he may not care to disturb this money except to buy a lot with which to establish a basis of credit with the building association. The price of the lot may vary from one-fourth to one-half the total investment. One wishes to borrow three thousand dollars from an association on the plan which is subsequently fully described. He would have to take out fifteen shares on a payment of fifty cents a share a week. This would represent seven dollars and a half weekly, or about thirty dollars a month. On the plan where the interest and premium are charged in addition to the regular weekly dues, a little over fifty dollars a month would be required to keep up the building-association charges. This would be less than house rent. These calculations are made assuming that the premium is not more than ten cents and the interest six per cent.

## CHAPTER XXXIX.

BUILDING ASSOCIATIONS. — WHY DIVIDENDS ARE LARGE AND INTEREST LOW. — BUILDING ASSOCIATIONS AND SAVINGS BANKS. — ASSOCIATION SECURITIES. — BUILDING-ASSOCIATION METHODS. — DIFFERENT PLANS. — BORROWING FROM A BUILDING ASSOCIATION. — A BUILDING-ASSOCIATION REPORT.

BUILDING-ASSOCIATION methods become more popular as they are better understood. Savings banks are unnecessary in communities where building associations are common. The savings bank will give place to the building association, for the reason that the latter affords greater security and more profit to the depositors at the same time that it affords greater conveniences to the borrowers. It is often asked by those not fully acquainted with building-association methods, " How is it that the association pays such large dividends, and the borrower such a small rate of interest? The profit is made by the loaning of money; and, consequently, the borrower must pay a high price for his money, or the association does not make large dividends."

This appears to be a logical argument. However, it is not true that the borrower pays a high price for his money. The dividends declared are made from the borrowers, by the rapid compounding of interest and other sources of profit. Money paid in as interest is immediately re-invested as a loan, and thus pays interest the next week. The interest on this is at once put to use, and so on. It is compounded. The premium paid for money is another source of profit. This comes from the borrower, and represents a part of the cost of the money to him; but, unless the premium is excessive, the earnings on his stock counterbalance the amount paid as premium, so that in the end a borrower does not pay in excess of the regular rate for his money at the same time that the stockholder is more largely benefited.

A building association has only a tithe of the expenses of a bank. The cost of doing business is very small. An association has a very great advantage over a bank in its earning capacity in that it does not have to carry a surplus. All of its money is invested at all times. Frequently it is receiving interest upon money that is not a part of its assets. This happens when an application for a loan has been accepted, a building is under way, and the money not all paid out.

The percentage of loss in a building association is necessarily smaller than in the best-conducted bank. Its securities are all first mortgages on productive real estate, and loans are made to members only, and under the condition that the immediate repayment of the loan be commenced. The security begins to improve at once, by the repayment of a part of the principal each week. It is usual for each member of a family to become interested in the immediate repayment of a loan. The payment of building-association dues is constantly in mind; as they become due from week to week, they cannot be overlooked. The fact that the debt is growing less, and, as well, the incentive to avoid small fines in case of failure to make payment, contribute to the value of the security. A loan on an ordinary basis, secured from a savings bank, insurance or trust company for a long period, is not thought of in this way. The usual thought in such a case is to pay the debt in a large sum at a time in the future. The time of the repayment of an association loan is always present. The security afforded to building associations is much better than to savings banks and loan companies, even where the margin above the amount of loan is less because of this difference in plan of repayment. Again, the margin of security from the first is always sufficient to protect a mortgage and the payment of all foreclosure costs and charges. Furthermore, the rentals in case of foreclosure are, or should be, sufficient to pay all dues and other fixed charges. This will prevent loss, and in the end pay for the property.

Another element of safety in building associations is the small risk of loss from the duplicity of the officers. This risk is unusually light, for the reason that in a well-managed building association there is little in sight to lose. The money is usually all invested. Any small amount in the hands of the officers is there for only a short time. There are demands in all well-managed building associations for all the money in hand. While this is true, it is always required that the officers who handle the association money give bond for a much larger sum than it is possible for them ever to have in charge. This makes the loss, if any, readily collectible.

It may be well to illustrate building-association methods, and thus call attention intelligently to the points of superiority which one plan may have over another.

The idea which first gave rise to associations is that of enabling persons belonging to a class whose earnings are small, to place themselves in a position where the process of gradual accumulation is, in a certain sense, compulsory. The method of operation is simple enough when it is understood. Say that a number of stockholders agree to form an association with a thousand shares, each share to represent $200. This would make a full capital stock of $200,000 when all paid in. The various individuals forming the association subscribe for as many shares as they feel competent to pay upon, it being agreed that for each share of stock subscribed, fifty cents per week shall be paid until the sum-total of the payments shall aggregate $200; at the end of which time a division shall be made according to the original subscription and subsequent payment. It is clear that if all are prompt in their payments, the treasury will be ready for distribution at the end of four hundred weeks. The period of four hundred weeks will, however, be shortened if all the money paid in is at once invested at interest upon safe securities, with the addition of interests compounded weekly, as is the case with these associations. For instance, it may appear that at the end of three hundred and twelve weeks, with a payment of fifty cents a week, and the accrued earnings that are credited to the shares, they are worth $200, the amount fixed for the value of the stock when it is paid up. At such a time the depositing members withdraw their funds, and those who are borrowers pay off their obligations to the association with stock, and the mortgages are released.

Money in building associations is generally sold to the highest bidder; that is, those who want to borrow bid a premium for the money. For instance, a sale of money is advertised. Bids are then received on the money to be loaned, and it is given to the highest bidder after the security has been approved. Suppose one wishes to borrow a thousand dollars. If each paid-up share is to represent two hundred dollars, five shares must be taken out to represent the payment of principal on a thousand-dollar loan. It may appear that the premium bid was ten cents on each share. This means that the borrower must pay ten cents premium each week, on each share, during the course of the loan, or until the principal is paid out. Thus he would pay fifty cents a week as principal, and ten cents a week as premium, and the interest on two hundred dollars at six per cent, which would be twenty-four cents a week. Thus he would pay eighty-four cents a week on each share; or on five shares, four dollars and twenty cents a week. This would pay out in about five years, depending upon the average rate of premium, the cost of doing business, and other conditions which may be readily understood. When the principal paid in, together with the accrued earnings, represents two hundred dollars, the obligation to the building association is released.

There are various plans of starting and arranging building and savings associations, which differ one from another only in matters of detail. The price of the share may be two, three, or four hundred dollars, or any other sum. The amounts paid in a week vary from ten cents to any larger sum. In the past, most associations have been started on the series plan, which is defined as follows by Henry S. Rosenthal of Cincinnati in his "Manual for Building Associations:" —

"In an association, organized on the terminating plan, all the stock is issued as of one date. A terminating association is organized on the presumption that all the stock will be subscribed for at the open meetings. This, however, is seldom done. The consequence is, that shares sold after the first meetings must be sold at such prices as to make them equal in value to those already issued. To do this a sum must be charged equal to the amount already paid in in instalments by the subscribers to the original shares. If the regular dues on shares should be one dollar per week, a person subscribing for a share after the association has been running ten weeks must pay ten dollars for the share. In like manner, if the association has been running for a longer period, he must pay an additional dollar for each additional week. Moreover, if he does not subscribe until after the profits have been declared, he must pay such an additional amount on his share as will correspond to the earnings of the original shares up to that time. The same rule holds through the entire existence of the association, each year making it more difficult to enter. After an association, organized on this plan, has run for a time, it is impossible for many persons, who would gladly become members, to raise a sufficient sum of money to pay up the back instalments, the initiation fees, the accrued profits, and other incidental expenses. In its practical workings, therefore, an association organized on this plan is not well adapted to meet the conditions of that particular class of persons who most need such an organization, and are most likely to be benefited by it.

"In a terminating association all the shares are, of course, at all times of equal value. Whenever the total amounts of the dues paid in and of accumulated profits equal the par value of all the shares, the association terminates and its affairs must be wound up. Each stockholder who has not borrowed his money in advance receives the full value of his shares. To those who have secured their money in advance, their mortgages, cancelled and receipted in full, are returned.

"PERMANENT ASSOCIATION.

"Building associations were established originally on the terminating plan. It is obvious that working on this plan they cannot, in some respects, reach their greatest degree of popularity and usefulness. On this account there has been a gradual departure from this plan. The first departure from the terminating plan consisted in an arrangement for issuing the stock in series instead of all from the same date. Associations were chartered for a certain number of years, as before, and with a specified amount of capital stock. But instead of selling all the stock as of the same date, it was divided into series: one series being sold as of the date of the beginning of the first year, the second series as of the date of the beginning of the second year, and so on until all the shares were sold. The issuing of a new series does not necessarily occur annually, but at such periods as are made necessary or desirable by the business of the association. The serial issue may be monthly, quarterly, semi-annually, or otherwise, as the directors may determine. By the time the last series is issued and the stock is exhausted, the first one or two or more series of shares, if the business of the association has been prosperous, have usually reached their full value, and are paid back and cancelled. Associations conducted on this plan usually have the right to issue new stock to take the place of that which is cancelled from time to time, and thus their perpetuity is insured. A successful association working on this plan can usually secure the issue of a new charter, and can thus continue its existence. But there are manifest disadvantages and risks under which an association operating on this plan must labor.

"Another plan of operation has been inaugurated which has proved very popular, and which is being generally adopted by the associations in the different States. Associations are granted perpetual charters, the amount of the capital stock being fixed at a certain sum. They are allowed to begin operations as soon as a certain amount of stock is subscribed. After the association is in operation, new subscribers are allowed to enter at any time on an equality with the original subscribers, the stock of each member dating from the time of his entry. Thus the business of the association runs along from year to year, until finally all of the stock is subscribed. After a time the shares first issued begin to reach their full value. As they thus mature, the owners draw out their money,—if they have not borrowed it in advance,—and their shares are cancelled, and their membership ceases. If they have borrowed their money in advance, their bonds and mortgages are returned to them receipted in full. If a member, whose stock has thus matured, has not borrowed his money in advance, and does not wish to draw it out, a certificate of paid-up stock is issued to him, and he leaves his money in the association as a matter of investment. An association operating on this plan may, after a time, when its original stock has all been subscribed through application to the incorporating authorities, secure the right to increase its stock. If, in the course of time, this increased stock becomes exhausted, another increase may be secured in a like manner, and so on indefinitely."

Herewith is given an extract from the yearly report of a successful savings and loan association on the perpetual plan. It will illustrate more fully the method and results of this method than could a less formal description. It may be explained in this connection that in this society the payments are uniform for depositing and borrowing members; that is, instead of having the premium and interest added to the weekly dues, the amount of premium and interest is charged against the weekly payment of fifty cents. Ten cents is the limit of premium, the officers and stockholders believing that to be as much as any one should pay.

### OBJECT.

THE PLYMOUTH SAVINGS AND LOAN ASSOCIATION, No. 2, is organized with two main objects in view: —

FIRST. — To furnish a convenient, safe, and profitable method of investing the savings of working people.

Members can come in and go out at will.

Subscriptions can commence at any time without having to pay back dues or wait for new series.

Withdrawing members obtain their money without loss (fines excepted), and are paid as promptly as the finances of the Association will admit, without having to wait ninety days. In the history of the Association there have been no delays.

SECOND. — To furnish persons who wish to borrow for any purpose the means for doing so at a reasonable rate of interest. In other words, it is an association composed of borrowers and lenders, and established for their mutual convenience. It gathers together the savings of the people, which, scattered and in small sums, could not be invested to advantage, and loans the money thus obtained on first mortgage security, and in sums to suit, to those who wish to build, to pay off mortgages, or for other purposes.

All members of the Association are, therefore, divided into two classes: —

*First.* — Those who desire to use the society as a means of saving or investing money. These are called *depositing members.*

*Second.* — Those who wish to make use of the organization as a means of borrowing money. These are called *borrowing members.*

### MANAGEMENT.

THE PLYMOUTH SAVINGS AND LOAN ASSOCIATION is a strictly co-operative or mutual organization. All the shareholders are *pro rata* owners of all the assets of the society. Every member is a partner in the enterprise in proportion to the amount paid in by him. He is entitled to his share of all the earnings of the Association. and he must also stand his share of the losses, if there be any.

The By-laws contain the rules and regulations under which money is received and loaned, or otherwise disposed of, and the business of the society is carried on by a Board of Directors, elected annually by the members.

## SHARES AND SHAREHOLDERS.

The amount of interest which each member has in the Association is indicated by the number of his shares.

Shares are $200 each, and no member can hold more than twenty-five shares. The weekly payment required is fifty cents on each share of stock.

When a member joins the Association he indicates the amount of weekly payment he desires to make by the number of shares for which he subscribes. He may, however, if he wishes, pay more than his shares call for, and such over-payments will receive dividends the same as the regular weekly instalments.

Each member is supposed to keep up his payments until what he has paid in, together with the dividends declared thereon, shall amount to the face value of his shares, at which time he must cease payments, and either take his money out, or, if the society be willing, allow it to remain and draw dividends.

## DIVIDENDS.

On the 1st of January and July of each year the net earnings of the Association are divided *pro rata* among all the members, and the amount due each member is credited on his pass-book.

Persons joining the association between January and July must continue payments until the following January before the dividend will be credited, and those joining between July and January must likewise pay until the following July; and if the money be withdrawn before that time, the dividend will be forfeited.

The right to dividend also ceases from the date of the notice to withdraw the stock.

When dividends are credited on the pass-books they are just like money paid, and are themselves entitled to draw dividends the same as cash payments. Thus it will be seen that all dividends compound semi-annually.

The following table will show how long it takes to pay up a share to face value by paying the regular dues only, supposing the society to earn six per cent dividends per annum.[1] It also shows the value of each share at the close of each year:—

| | | |
|---|---:|---:|
| First year .... Dues ...... | $26 00 | |
| " ...... Dividends ..... | 78 | $26 78 |
| Value at close of first year ......... | | $26 78 |
| Second year ..... Dues ...... | $26 00 | |
| " ...... Dividends ..... | 2 41 | 28 41 |
| Value at close of second year ........ | | $55 19 |
| Third year ...... Dues ...... | $26 00 | |
| " ...... Dividends ..... | 4 53 | 30 53 |
| Value at close of third year ........ | | $85 72 |
| Fourth year ...... Dues ...... | $26 00 | |
| " ...... Dividends ..... | 6 10 | 32 10 |
| Value at close of fourth year ........ | | $117 82 |
| Fifth year ...... Dues ...... | $26 00 | |
| " ...... Dividends ..... | 8 34 | 34 34 |
| Value at close of fifth year ........ | | $152 16 |
| Sixth year ...... Dues ...... | $26 00 | |
| " ...... Dividends ..... | 10 41 | 36 41 |
| Value at close of sixth year ........ | | $188 60 |
| Seventh year (16 weeks) . Dues ...... | $8 00 | |
| " . Dividends ..... | 3 40 | 11 40 |
| | | $200 00 |
| Time, 6 years and 16 weeks. | | |
| Total dues paid ............. | | $164 00 |
| Total dividends ............. | | 36 00 |
| | | $200 00 |

## METHOD OF LOANING MONEY.

The society loans money only to members. For each $200 share held by a member he may borrow $200, secured by first mortgage on real estate, interest on which is twenty-four cents per week.

The right to precedence in borrowing is sold at auction at stated times at the office of the Association (notice of which is given beforehand) to the member who bids or agrees to pay the highest weekly premium in addition to

---

[1] The present rate of dividend is nine per cent, with an added surplus.

the twenty-four cents per week interest. Ten cents per week is the average rate at which money was sold during the year 1887, and is now selling.

Members not desiring or not able to attend the sale of money in person may have some one else bid for them, or they may leave a written bid with the Secretary, on blanks prepared for that purpose, who will make it for them at the sale.

The society also loans to depositing members in sums equal to ninety per cent of the dues paid in. Security is had by the member pledging his stock for the payment of the loan and interest due (if any) on notes prepared for that purpose. Interest on such loans has for the present been placed at the rate of eight per cent per annum.

## PAYMENTS.

The depositing and borrowing members alike pay fifty cents per week per share. There are no additions for expenses, interest, premiums, or fines. These are charged up at the close of each dividend period, or at the closing up of an account.

Each borrower is required to pay at least fifty cents per week on each $200 of loan made to him, which is credited as follows:—

First the premium and interest are taken out, the interest being twenty-four cents. When the premium bid is ten cents, both together would amount to thirty-four cents. Then the balance, which in this case would be sixteen cents, is credited as a payment on the share on which the loan is taken. These payments are continued until the amount credited on the shares, together with the dividends thereon, will equal the amount loaned. For instance, suppose the loan to be $200, and the premium bid to be ten cents per week,—

| | |
|---|---|
| The payment each week would be | 50 cents |
| The premium each week would be | 10 cents |
| The interest each week would be | 24 cents |
| | ———34 cents |
| The credit on the share each week would be | 16 cents |

These credits of sixteen cents per week begin to draw dividends on the succeeding dividend period, which are compounded semi-annually, and the weekly payments' must be continued until the weekly credits of sixteen cents and the dividends thereon amount to $200.

Members are at liberty to pay every two weeks or monthly, and as much beyond the required weekly payment as they may desire to. The overpayments are credited like any regular payment and share in the dividends.

This enables borrowers to pay their loans off as fast as their circumstances will admit. This method is very helpful, as the interest and premium will be stopped on as many full shares as are paid off, and the cost of a loan is materially reduced thereby.

The minimum payment only is fixed. The borrower may at any time pay the whole balance due on the loan and have it cancelled at once.

It is always good policy for a borrower to pay more than the weekly dues if he can, in order that in case of sickness, loss of work, or other unforeseen hindrance, he may be paid ahead, and hence suspend payment for a time without being fined or in danger of losing his property.

By the following table it is shown that with the premium at twenty-four cents on each $200, and that the society is able to earn six per cent per annum dividends (both of which are being done now[1]), and the required weekly dues only being paid, a loan will be paid up in fifteen years and six months. This time, as already mentioned, can be shortened at the will and ability of the borrower, and may be paid off at any time without any penalty whatever. This is a great advantage, and the society can do this only because of the great demand for loans, and the money does not have to lie idle if a loan is paid off, but is immediately loaned again. Here is a loan which you may take fifteen years to pay if you wish, or you may pay it off at any time.

### TABLE.
#### SHOWING COURSE OF LOAN OF $1,000.

Premium 50 cents per week.
Interest $1.20 per week.
Six per cent dividends compounded semi-annually.

FIRST YEAR:

| | | |
|---|---:|---:|
| Loan . . . . . . . . . . . . . . . . . | | $1,000 00 |
| Payments for year . . . . . . . . . . | | $130 00 |
| Interest and premium . . . . . . . . . | $88 40 | |
| Less dividends . . . . . . . . . . . | 62 | |
| Net cost of loan . . . . . . . . . | | 87 78 |
| Principal reduced . . . . . . . . . | | 42 22 |

[1] Since this report was made the earnings have been nine per cent, with an added surplus.

SECOND YEAR:
Balance due at end of first year . . . . . .                         $957 78
Payments for year . . . . . . . . . . .            130 00
Premium and interest . . . . . . . . . .   88 40
Less dividends . . . . . . . . . . . .    3 18

    Net cost of loan . . . . . . . . .    85 22

    Principal reduced . . . . . . . . .                                  44 78
THIRD YEAR:
Balance due at end of second year . . . .                          $913 00
Payments for year . . . . . . . . . . .            130 00
Interest and premium . . . . . . . . .    88 40
Less dividends . . . . . . . . . . . .    5 91

    Net cost of loan . . . . . . . . .    82 49

    Principal reduced . . . . . . . . .                                  47 51
FOURTH YEAR:
Balance due at end of third year . . . . .                         $865 49
Payments for year . . . . . . . . . . .            130 00
Interest and premium . . . . . . . . .    88 40
Less dividends . . . . . . . . . . . .    8 79

    Net cost of loan . . . . . . . . .    79 61

    Principal reduced . . . . . . . . .                                  50 39
FIFTH YEAR:
Balance due at end of fourth year . . . . .                        $815 10
Payments for year . . . . . . . . . . .            130 00
Interest and premium . . . . . . . . .    88 40
Less dividends . . . . . . . . . . . .   11 88

    Net cost of loan . . . . . . . . .    76 52

    Principal reduced . . . . . . . . .                                  53 48
SIXTH YEAR:
Balance due at end of fifth year . . . . .                         $761 62
Payments for year . . . . . . . . . . .            130 00
Interest and premium . . . . . . . . .    88 40
Less dividends . . . . . . . . . . . .   15 12

    Net cost of loan . . . . . . . . .    73 28

    Principal reduced . . . . . . . . .                                  56 72

SEVENTH YEAR:
Balance due at end of sixth year . . . . . . $704 90
Payments for year . . . . . . . . . . . 130 00
Interest and premium . . . . . . . . . 88 40
Less dividends . . . . . . . . . . . . 18 60

Net cost of loan . . . . . . . . . 69 80

Principal reduced . . . . . . . . . 60 20
EIGHTH YEAR:
Balance due at end of seventh year . . . . $644 70
Payments for year . . . . . . . . . . . 130 00
Interest and premium . . . . . . . . . 88 40
Less dividends . . . . . . . . . . . . 22 26

Net cost of loan 66 14

Principal reduced . . . . . . . . . 63 86*
NINTH YEAR:
Balance due at end of eighth year . . . . . $580 84
Payments for year . . . . . . . . . . . 130 00
Interest and premium . . . . . . . . . 88 40
Less dividends . . . . . . . . . . . . 26 13

Net cost of loan . . . . . . . . . 62 27

Principal reduced . . . . . . . . . 67 73
TENTH YEAR:
Balance due at end of ninth year . . . . . $513 11
Payments for year . . . . . . . . . . . 130 00
Interest and premium . . . . . . . . . 88 40
Less dividends . . . . . . . . . . . . 30 27

Net cost of loan . . . . . . . . . 58 13

Principal reduced . . . . . . . . . 71 87
ELEVENTH YEAR:
Balance due at end of tenth year . . . . . $441 24
Payments for year . . . . . . . . . . . 130 00
Interest and premium . . . . . . . . . 88 40
Less dividends . . . . . . . . . . . . 34 65

Net cost of loan . . . . . . . . . 53 75

Principal reduced . . . . . . . . . 76 25
TWELFTH YEAR:
Balance due at end of eleventh year . . . . $364 99
Payments for year . . . . . . . . . . . 130 00
Interest and premium . . . . . . . . . 88 40
Less dividends . . . . . . . . . . . . 39 30

Net cost of loan . . . . . . . . . 49 10

Principal reduced . . . . . . . . . 80 90

## HOW TO SECURE A HOME. 309

**THIRTEENTH YEAR:**
Balance due at end of twelfth year . . . . . $284 09
Payments for year . . . . . . . . . . 130 00
Interest and premium . . . . . . . . . 88 40
Less dividends . . . . . . . . . . . 44 22

Net cost of loan . . . . . . . . . 44 18

Principal reduced . . . . . . . . . 85 82

**FOURTEENTH YEAR:**
Balance due at end of thirteenth year . . . $198 27
Payments for year . . . . . . . . . . 130 00
Interest and premium . . . . . . . . . 88 40
Less dividends . . . . . . . . . . . 49 41

Net cost of loan . . . . . . . . . 38 99

Principal reduced . . . . . . . . . 91 01

**FIFTEENTH YEAR:**
Balance due at end of fourteenth year . . . $107 26
Payments for year . . . . . . . . . . 130 00
Interest and premium . . . . . . . . . 88 40
Less dividends . . . . . . . . . . . 54 99

Net cost of loan . . . . . . . . . 33 41

Principal reduced . . . . . . . . . 96 59

**SIX WEEKS:**
Balance due at end of fifteenth year . . . . $10 67
Payments for six weeks . . . . . . . . 15 00
Interest and premium . . . . . . . . . 10 20
Less dividends . . . . . . . . . . . 5 87

Net cost of loan . . . . . . . . . 4 33

Principal reduced . . . . . . . . . 10 67

Time, fifteen years and six weeks.

Total amount of payments . . . . . . . . . . . . $1,965 00
Total interest and premium . . . . . . . . . . . 1,336 20
Total dividends . . . . . . . . . . . . . . . . 371 20
Net cost of loan . . . . . . . . . . . . . . . 965 00

With the reasonable prospect in view that the Association will be able to pay larger dividends at some future time, it will be easy to understand that the cost and the time of payment of a loan will thereby be correspondingly reduced.

## MORTGAGES.

All loans must be secured by first mortgage on real estate in Marion County, Ind. An appraising committee, consisting of three members of the Association, appraise the value of all real estate offered as security for loans and report to the board. No loan can be made until the security has been approved by the Board of Directors.

This Association is now paying four per cent semi-annual dividends, and adding largely to its surplus.

A new feature in building-association work has recently been put into practice. The association will buy for cash a house and lot, or buy a lot and build a house thereon, and sell at a fair price to the member whose application is accepted. Where the house and lot are bought at a cash price, it is usual to charge a ten per cent bonus when selling it on time to a member. The purchaser then completes the transaction by securing the purchase money to the association, the same as in case of a loan on any other property, except that instead of a deed from the association he will receive a lease, with an agreement to sell and convey to him the premises as soon as one-third of the purchase money shall have been paid in regular dues on his stock. His stock will be assigned as collateral security, and the payments will be credited as rent until the deed is made. Then the purchaser will execute his mortgage for the unpaid balance due on the property on the terms of his original bid for the money. It is usual to require a cash payment equal to the amount of the bonus; that is, ten per cent of the purchase price. This is a valuable feature in building-association methods. It adds to the profits of the association. This plan is adaptable to private enterprise, and is liberal in its terms to the purchaser.

In most associations organized on the perpetual plan, as previously described, the demand for funds is greater than can be supplied from depositing members. This has given rise to the "paid-up stock" feature of building associations. Under this plan one may invest money in any sum according to the terms of the charter and secure from the association a certificate of paid-up stock which participates in the regular dividends of the company. In this way, funds in larger amounts may be secured than come from the ordinary payments by regular weekly dues. It is not unusual for individuals to purchase paid-up stock to the amount of several thousand dollars. This is a great help to an association which is short of funds, as it serves to increase its membership by addition of borrowers. There is no better place to invest trust funds than in the paid-up stock of well-managed building associations. Primarily, for the reason that each stockholder is pledged in the amount of his stock to pay principal and six per cent interest on all withdrawals; hence, the funds may be withdrawn at any time, and six per cent interest thereon demanded. Furthermore, building-association stock is not taxable in most States.

Individual and moneyed corporations are coming to consider the matter of loans, and means leading to their repayment, on the building-association plan. This will be brought about largely by the low price of money throughout the country at this time. Savings banks, mortgage companies, and life-insurance organizations are finding it difficult to loan their funds at a price that will pay their fixed obligations; hence, they are seeking means which will lead to a more profitable investment of their funds. The building-association plan of loaning money is one solution of the problem. The low price of money is one of the elements which within the next few years will enable nearly every one who so desires to secure a home through the building association, or some plan which has its outgrowth therefrom.

## CHAPTER XL.

PURCHASE OF A LOT. — THE BEST THE CHEAPEST. — A GOOD LOT AS A BASIS OF SECURITY. — THE BASIS OF VALUE IS THE RENTAL.

THERE are many things to consider in connection with the building of a house other than those which are constructive. One may lay aside that which has to do with appearances, convenience, stability, and all that is architectural, and yet have food for thought in connection with the making of a home. For instance, the lot. No one can afford to build on one that is absolutely cheap, or one that is cheap because it is not well located or favorably thought of by the large number of people. A lot that is absolutely cheap is not often worth even what is paid for it. One of small means can least of all afford to put his money in a questionable piece of property. A lot may be relatively cheap, and be a good investment. For instance, there is a street lined with comfortable houses. On this street live people of more or less wealth and unquestioned ambition. Three or four squares beyond the last house of this street the lots may be relatively cheap. The sum asked for them is not great, for the reason that few care to go out so far. Still, by adopting a little of the pioneer spirit, one can make a purchase of these lots and be reasonably certain of being rewarded for his foresight. It is much better to buy such a lot, and live for a year or two without immediate neighbors, than to buy one which is absolutely cheap because the surroundings are positively unfavorable.

A man of small means least of all can afford to buy a lot that cannot readily be sold for all it cost. We often hear people say, in regard to lots that are surrounded unfavorably, "What is the difference? It suits us; we can be as happy and comfortable there as any place. If we like it, why should any one else complain?" No one else will complain. It may occur that the owner of this absolutely cheap property may wish to sell. He may become embarrassed in his business, or one of many things may happen to cripple him financially. If he can sell at all, it is at a sacrifice. If a mortgage is foreclosed, there is no reasonable chance of redemption. If the lot is well located, and he becomes financially embarrassed, he can sell for full value and thus relieve himself. If there is danger of foreclosure, a sale can be readily effected, and thus all danger of loss be averted. The idea in buying a lot is to get one which can be readily sold. This is an important matter.

In carrying out this principle, one of moderate means will often buy a lot of higher cost than is apparently justifiable. However, this may be the best thing for him to do. It may be good business. If he wishes to borrow money with which to build, he has a better basis for credit. If he puts his house on a good lot, there is opportunity of selling it because of its favorable location, and thus the danger of embarrassment is averted. One can afford to borrow money to build on a good lot, for the reason that there is little danger of losing either the lot or the money. The house and the lot, if it rates well in the public mind, can be easily sold. The lot should not be selected or the house built, if its sale is not entirely possible. There are towns as well as localities in which no one of moderate means can afford to buy or build. Yet such locations are often selected because they are cheap, and living is cheap. The fact of this cheapness is against it. The property is cheap because it is worth little or nothing. It is cheap because no one can get out what he puts into it. This may apply to a lot in a particular town, a particular part of a town, or to property in general in a county or a State. Thus it is that no one of moderate means can afford to buy absolutely cheap property.

A young man once went to an architect to advise with him in regard to the selection of a lot. He said, —

"There are two lots on a certain street that I can get for $1,200 each. That is a little more than I want to pay, as even then I would have to borrow more money than I wish in order to build my house. One of the best lots I know anything about is on another street, but I can hardly think of that, for they ask $1,500 for it."

"I know the lot," said the architect, "and the $1,500 lot is the one to buy. The $1,200 lots are of questionable value. The surrounding conditions are such that their value is not liable to increase. The $1,500 lot is in the swim; two squares below, lots cannot be bought for $2,400; in fact, they are not in the market. They are owned by people who desire to hold them. In two years you will be reasonably certain to realize at least twice the difference between the values of the $1,500 and the $1,200 lots. In one case, the value of the lot is not liable to increase; it may decrease. In the other instance, there is reasonable certainty of a large increase within a short time. It is on the edge of high values."

"But I shall have to borrow so much money with which to build, if I take the high-priced lot."

"What of it? Say your house is going to cost you $3,000. You say you have $2,800 in cash. In one instance you would have to borrow $1,400, and in the other $1,700. You are running much less risk in borrowing $1,700 than you are in borrowing $1,400. If you had to sell, there is a reasonable certainty that you could always make a profit on your $4,500 investment, and a very questionable probability as to the $4,200 investment."

There are those who do some very remarkable things for the sake of keeping out of debt, which, in the end, develops into more loss than would be possible in the case of debt. For instance, one will buy a lot for $1,500, and put a $1,500 house on it. In time the value of the lot increases; at the same time the value of the house decreases. The lot in itself would be worth more if the house were off it. It is a cheap house on a good lot. Thus it is that such property is often sold and the improvements counted as nothing. Again, exactly the other thing may happen. An expensive house may be built on a cheap lot. When finished the house is worth much less than it cost because it is not well located. One cannot expect to get full value for the lot without moving the house, and altogether the situation is disagreeable. How much better it would be, from a business standpoint, not to build at all, use the money some other way, or borrow enough money to have the house and lot properly located. In one case there is positive loss; in the other, a reasonable certainty of profit.

Another thing for a man of moderate means to bear in mind in building a house is, that the investments as to the house and lot should be such that in case of rental the return derived would pay a fair interest on the investment, and leave a sufficient margin for taxes and repairs. As long as this condition exists, there need be no fear of loss through foreclosure. The sale of the property may become necessary through embarrassment in business, loss of situation, or illness; but in such a case the property can either be sold without loss, or it can be rented at a figure that will pay all fixed charges, which fact in itself establishes a value above its cost price. If these principles are all carried out, there is little chance of loss.

# INDEX.

"A" DOOR, 226.
Air supply to heating apparatus, 75-79.
American architecture, 26-28.
American architectural development, 104-105.
Architects' estimates, 278-281.
Architect, the, and the housewife, 9-27.
Architectural design, 101-105.
Areas, 206.
Ash-pits, 206.
Attic, 62.
Attic bedrooms, 63, 138.
Automatic heat regulators, 81.

BACK PLASTERING, 237.
Base, 228, 229.
Basement, 56.
Bath-tub, 73, 74, 230, 255-258.
Bath-tub wood-work, 230, 231.
Bedrooms, 60-63.
Bedrooms in attic, 63.
Bedroom closets, 61.
Bedroom, first floor, 164.
Bedrooms, grates in, 62.
Bedroom for servants, 62.
Bond in brick-work, 201, 202.
Brick, hollow walls of, 203.
Brick of wood, 204.
Brick joints, 199.
Brick pavement, 212.
Brick piers, 200.
Brick, selection of color, 202.
Brick veneer, 203.
Brick-wall foundations, 200-204.
Brick-work, 199-206, 209-212.
Brick-work bond, 201, 202.
Broom closets, 61.
Broom-rack, 232.
"B" schedule, 268.
Building associations and savings banks, 296, 297.
Building association, a new feature in, 310.
Building association, object, 302.

Building associations, permanent plan, 300, 301.
Building-association profits, 295.
Building-association report, 302-310.
Building associations, safety of, 296, 297.
Building association, terminating plan, 299, 300.
Building-association methods, 293-311.
Building by the day, 281.
Building contract, 284-287.
Building material, cost of, 273.
Business points in building, 275-287.

CAPACITY OF CISTERN, 210.
Carpenter work, 213-233.
Casings outside, 218.
Cathedral glass, 245.
Cedar closet, 232.
Cellar, 51-53, 133.
Cellar brick-work, 203, 204.
Cellar closet, 52, 53.
Cellar doors, 226, 227.
Cellar laundry, 54-58.
Cellar plan, 142.
Cellar sink, 254.
Cellar-sink wood-work, 230.
Cellar-way, outside, 206.
Cement pavement, 212.
Chamber decoration, 99.
Chimneys, 204-206.
Chimney-breasts, 205, 206.
Chimney tops, 204.
China-closet fittings, 46.
China-room, 44-46, 232.
Cistern, 210, 211.
Cistern filter, 211.
Cistern-water supply, 71.
Clock shelf, 232.
Closets, bedroom, 61, 138.
Closets, broom, 61.
Closet fittings, 231, 232.
Closet of cedar, 232.

317

## INDEX.

Coal-bins in cellar, 51, 52.
Colored bricks, 202, 203.
Colored plastering, 237.
Color of mortar, 202.
Combination stairs, 59, 60, 137-141.
Combination pantry, 45, 132.
Competition in building, 281-283.
Conservatory, 99.
Contracting methods, 277-287.
Copper, 240, 241.
Cost of appurtenances, 271, 272.
Cost of building material, 273, 274.
Cost of one-story houses, 163.
Cost schedules, 264, 267-269.
Cost of a house, 264-274.
Cut stone work, 208, 209.

DAMP COURSE, 200.
" D " door, 227.
Deck roof, 216.
Depth of foundation, 200.
Dining-room, 37, 38, 96-99.
Dish-warming, arrangement for, 84.
Dish-washing, 11, 42.
Doors and frames, 225-227.
Dough-board, 46, 47.
Double joists, 215.
Down spouts, 240.
Draining, 198, 199.
Drain board, 43, 230.
Drain connections, 261.
Drain from refrigerator, 241.
Drain outside, 71.
Drain ventilation, 71.
Dressed shingles, 218.
Drop siding, 217.
Dry-box, 48, 232.

" E " DOOR, 227.
Eastlake, Charles, 104.
Estimates of architects, 278-281.
Evaporation in traps, 67-68.
Evolution of a house-plan, 109-117.
Excavating, 198.
Excavating for plumber, 247, 248.

FIFTY CONVENIENT HOUSES, PLANS OF, 107.
Fig. " A," frontispiece. Fig. " B," 106.
Fig. 2, 41.
Fig. 3, 43.
Fig. 4, 45.
Fig. 5, 46.

Fig. 6, 67.
Fig. 7, 68.
Fig. 8, 116.
Fig. 9, 116.
Fig. 10, photographic view (page 116).
Fig. 11, 117.
Fig. 12, 124.
Fig. 13, 133.
Fig. 14, 147.
Fig. 15, 149.
Fig. 16, 151.
Fig. 17, photographic view (page 152).
Fig. 18, 154.
Fig. 19, 154.
Fig. 20, 160.
Fig. 21, 168.
Fig. 22, 169.
Fig. 23, 181.
Fig. 24, photographic view (page 182).
Fig. 25, 186.
Fig. 26, photographic view (page 190).
Fig. 27, 191.
Fig. 28, 191.
Fig. 29, 193.
Fig. 30, 199.
Fig. 31, 205.
Fig. 32, 206.
Fig. 33, 215.
Fig. 34, 217.
Fig. 35, 226.
Fig. 36, 227.
Fig. 37, 227.
Fig. 38, 262.
Filters for cisterns, 211.
Finish of floor, 244.
Finishing in oil, 243, 244.
Fireplaces in bedrooms, 62.
Fixtures in plumbing enumerated, 66.
Flashings, 239.
Flat roofs, 240.
Floors, 222, 223.
Floor of kitchen, 49.
Floor finish, 244.
Flour-bin, 47, 233, 234.
Flues, 203.
Fly screens, 228.
Foundation depth, 200.
Foundations, stone, 207, 208.
Force-pump, 249.
Framing, 213-219.
Framing lumber, sizes of, 213, 214.
Fresco tinting, 92.

## INDEX.

Freezing of plumbing, 70, 71.
Fuel in cellar, 51, 52.
Furnace, defined, 76.
Furnace and hot-water combination, 83, 84.
Furnace-room in cellar, 52.

GALVANIZED IRON, 241.
Gas-piping, 237, 238.
German siding, 217.
Glazing, 244, 245.
Grates in bedrooms, 62.
Grease sink, 72, 73, 263.
Gutters, 239.

HALL, 33–35.
Hall, reception, 35, 36.
Hardware, 245, 246.
Hard-wood floors, 223.
Heating apparatus, how to get a good, 83, 85.
Heating and ventilation, 75–85.
Heating by hot water, 80, 83.
Heating by steam, 80.
Heating by stoves, 80.
Heating, ideal conditions, 76.
Heating plants, cost of, 81, 82, 83.
Heat regulators, automatic, 81.
Height of stories, 214.
Hip coping, 240.
Hip finish, 217.
Hollow walls of brick, 203.
Hot-air flues in brick walls, 203.
Hot-air pipes of tin, 241.
Hot-water boiler, 71.
Hot water and furnace combination, 83, 84.
Hot-water heating, 80.
Hot-water plumbing, 70.
Hot-water system, 252.
House decoration, 86–100.
House drain, 71.
House ventilation, 75, 79.
Housekeeper, the, and the architect, 11–15, 26–28.
Housekeeping operations, 16–20.
How to secure a home, 289–316.
Humidity of air, 77, 81.
Hydrant, 249.

INSIDE CASINGS, 228.
Inside shutters, 229, 230.
Inside finish, table of, 224.
Inside wood-work, 222–235.

JOINTS, RODDED, 199.
Joists, 214, 215.
Journey, a, through the house, 29–105.

KITCHENS, 39–50.
Kitchen fittings, 42, 43.
Kitchen floor, 49.
Kitchen plans, 41, 45.
Kitchen pantry, 45–48.
Kitchen plastering, 50.
Kitchen safe, 48.
Kitchen sink, 43, 253, 254.
Kitchen tables, 43, 230.
Kitchen utensils, 48.
Kitchen ventilation, 49.
Kitchen wainscoting, 49.

LANDINGS FOR STAIRS, 60.
Lattice porch, 220.
Laundry, 54–58.
Laundry fittings, 260, 261.
Laundry, low-cost, 55–58.
Laundry stove, 56.
Laundry tubs, 57.
Library, 95, 96.
Lien laws, 285, 286.
Lighting bedrooms, 61, 62.
Lintels in brick-work, 204.
Locating the house, 197.
Lot, purchase of, 312, 316.
Low-cost laundry, 55–58.
Lumber for framing, 213.

MANTEL COSTS, 271.
Mason work, 199–209.
Medicine-chest, 232.
Modern architects and the housekeeper, 26–28.
Modern conveniences, 21–25.
Moisture in heated air, 77–81.
Monthly payments, 291–293.
Mortar, color of, 202.
Mortgages, 310, 311.
Motor, 251.

NATURAL-GAS PIPING, 238.
Nickel fittings, 263.

OIL FINISH, 243, 244.
Old colonial houses, 26, 27.
One-story houses, 157–163.
Ornamental brick, 203.

Outside cellar-way, 206.
Outside finish, 217-221.
Outside shutters, 219, 220.
Outside steps, 220, 221.

PAINTING, 242, 243.
Paint, ready mixed, 242.
Painting of shingles, 216.
Pantry boxes, 234.
Pantry, combination, 45, 132.
Pantry fittings, 46.
Pantry shelves, 47.
Pantry specification, 233.
Pantry utensils, 48.
Parlor, 35-37, 93-95.
Pavement of brick, 212.
Pavement of cement, 212.
Permanent plan, building associations, 300, 301.
Picture mouldings, 231.
Piers of brick, 200.
Pipe boards, 230.
Pipe duct, 70, 230.
Plastering, 236.
Plastering, back, 237.
Plastering, gray, 236.
Plastering in kitchen, 50.
Plate-glass, 245.
Plans of fifty convenient houses, 107.
Plan No. 1, cost $1,700, 110.
Plan No. 2, cost $1,550, 111.
Plan No. 3, cost $1,550, 112.
Plan No. 4, cost $1,800, 113.
Plan No. 5, cost $1,900, 114.
Plan No. 6, cost $2,600, 115.
Plan No. 7, cost $2,900, 121.
Plan No. 8, cost $2,200, 129.
Plan No. 9, cost $2,500, 132.
Plan No. 10, cost $2,600, 136.
Plan No. 11, cost $2,000, 141, 142.
Plan No. 12, cost $2,600, 144.
Plan No. 13, cost $1,600, 146.
Plan No. 14, cost $1,500, 148.
Plan No. 15, cost $2,550, 150.
Plan No. 16, cost $2,800, 153.
Plan No. 17, cost $2,200, 154.
Plan No. 18, cost $1,600, 155.
Plan No. 19, cost $1,400, 158.
Plan No. 20, cost $1,200, 158.
Plan No. 21, cost $1,700, 161.
Plan No. 22, cost $800, 161.
Plan No. 23, cost $1,600, 162.

Plan No. 24, cost $1,100, 162.
Plan No. 25, cost $1,400, 163.
Plan No. 26, cost $2,000, 163.
Plan No. 27, cost $3,000, 165.
Plan No. 28, cost $2,800, 165.
Plan No. 29, cost $2,600, 166.
Plan No. 30, cost $3,000, 167.
Plan No. 31, cost $2,400, 169.
Plan No. 32, cost $4,000, 172.
Plan No. 33, cost $2,800, 173.
Plan No. 34, cost $2,500, 174.
Plan No. 35, cost $2,250, 175.
Plan No. 36, cost $2,000, 175.
Plan No. 37, cost $2,100, 176.
Plan No. 38, cost $2,000, 177.
Plan No. 39, cost $3,500, 178.
Plan No. 40, cost $3,100, 179.
Plan No. 41, cost $3,400, 179.
Plan No. 42, cost $2,800, 180.
Plan No. 43, cost $2,200, 183.
Plan No. 44, cost $5,000, 184.
Plan No. 45, cost $2,100, 184.
Plan No. 46, cost $3,400, 185.
Plan No. 47, cost $10,000, 187.
Plan No. 48, cost $3,400, 189.
Plan No. 49, cost $3,400, 190.
Plan No. 50, cost $10,000, 192.
Plumbing, 64-74.
Plumbing costs, 268-270.
Plumbing fixtures, 65.
Plumbing, practical, 247-263.
Porcelain water-closets, 69.
Porches, 31, 220.
Practical house-building, 195-274.
Preface, 3, 4.
Prevention of freezing in plumbing, 70, 71.
Privy vault, 209, 210.
Purchase of a lot, 312-316.
Purchase on a rental basis, 291-293.


RADIATION, DIRECT, 80, 81.
Radiation, indirect, 80, 81.
Ready mixed paint, 242.
Rear stairway, 60.
Reception-hall, 35, 36.
Reception-hall decoration, 88, 89.
Reception-hall mantel, 89.
Refrigerator, 47.
Refrigerator drain, 48, 241.
Ridge coping, 240.
Ridge finish, 216, 217.

## INDEX.

Rodded joints, 199.
Roof, 216, 217.

SAFETY IN PLUMBING, 64.
Safes, 258.
Sash weights, 219.
Savings banks and building associations, 296, 297.
Schedule "B," 268.
Sealed proposals, 284.
Second floor, the, 59–63.
Servant's bedroom, 62.
Service pipes, 249.
Sewer and vault connection, 65.
Sewer connection, 72, 261, 262.
Sewer gas, 66, 67, 72.
Sheet glass, 245.
Shower-bath, 257.
Shingles, 216, 217, 218.
Shingles, painting of, 216.
Shingles, stained, 218.
Shingle walls, 217.
Shutters, outside, 219, 220.
Shutters, inside, 229, 230.
Siding, drop, 217.
Siding, German, 217.
Side-hall plans, 164–166.
Sink in cellar, 254.
Sink in kitchen, 43, 230, 254.
Sitting-room, 35, 36, 91.
Sizes for framing lumber, 213, 214.
Sliding doors, 225.
Soap-box, 48, 49, 232.
Soft-water supply, 250.
Soil pipe, 66, 67, 253.
Splash board, 230, 231.
Splash board in bath-room, 231.
Spouts, 240.
Staining, exterior, 243.
Staining, interior, 243.
Stained shingles, 218.
Stairs, 234, 235.
Stairs, combination, 59, 60.
Stairways, 59, 60.
Stairway, combination, 137, 140, 141.
Stairway, rear, 60.
Steam heating, 80.
Stone foundations, 207, 208.
Stone sills, 208.
Stone steps, 208, 209.
Stop beads, 227.
Stop cocks, 249.
Storm water connections, 262.
Stories, height of, 214.

"S" trap, 66, 67, 263.
Street washer, 249.
Stove heating, 80.
Stud walls, 215, 216.

TABLES IN KITCHEN, 230.
Table of inside finish, 224.
Tank wood-work, 231.
Terminating plan in building associations, 299, 300.
Terra cotta, 209.
Tin hot-air pipes, 241.
Tin-work, 239–241.
Transoms, 226.
Traps, 66, 67, 263.
Traps fail to act, 76.
Trap screws, 263.
Trimmer arch, 205, 206.
Trimmers, 214.

VALLEYS, 239.
Vault and sewer connection, 65.
Veneered doors, 225, 226.
Veneer of brick, 203.
Ventilation and heating, 75–85.
Ventilation, drain, 71.
Ventilation, house, 75, 79.
Ventilation of kitchen, 49.
Vestibule, 31–33.
Vestibule decoration, 87, 88.

WAINSCOTING, 229.
Wainscoting in kitchen, 49.
Walls of shingles, 217.
Wash-stand, 72, 259, 260.
Wash-stand wood-work, 231.
Waste pipe, 66, 67.
Water-closets, 68, 69, 70, 259.
Water-closets, porcelain, 69.
Water-closet, washout, 68, 69.
Water-closet wood-work, 231.
Water distribution, 248.
Water for builder, 197.
Water for laundry, 56, 57.
Water motor, 251.
Water tank in attic, 71.
Water seal, 67, 68.
Windows, 218, 219.
Wooden brick, 204.
Wood carving, 90.
Wood-work for bath-room, 231.
Wood for inside finish, 225.
Wood-work for plumber, 230, 231.
Wood-work for water-closet, 231.

*"THIS BEAUTIFUL BOOK."*
— *Standard Union.*

# BEAUTIFUL HOUSES.
## BY LOUIS H. GIBSON, ARCHITECT.
AUTHOR OF "CONVENIENT HOUSES."

WITH OVER 250 ILLUSTRATIONS. 8VO. CLOTH. $3.00.

SINCE the publication of his "Convenient Houses" Mr. Gibson has been abroad, where he made a careful study of the national architecture of many countries. Mr. Gibson is remarkable for the skill with which he manages to utilize ordinary waste spaces, to place every possible convenience in the housekeeper's hands; in short, to apply common-sense in an uncommon manner. No one interested in building a new house, or altering over an old one, could fail to obtain valuable hints from his books. The volume is sumptuously illustrated, and will be a delight to all connoisseurs, both of architecture and of book-making.

### Contents of the Book.

**HOUSE-BUILDING AN ART.** Ugly houses, uneducated architects, cost never measures the artistic development of art in building, the primitive house, first principles, the Greek temple and the Indian hut, the old Roman and the Old Colonial, Romanesque architecture, Gothic architecture, decline of the Gothic, the Renaissance, modern architecture of Europe, characteristics of modern American architecture, etc.

**THE WORLD'S HOMES.** French domestic architecture, twelfth century building, floor plans of domestic structures, picturesque stair towers, half-timber architecture of the twelfth century, our use of French examples, Breton customs, furniture, French châteaux, English domestic architecture, domestic buildings of the sixteenth and seventeenth centuries, picturesque details, from the Gothic to the Renaissance, modern architecture of Germany, Swiss architecture, Old Colonial architecture, a classic development, characteristic New England architecture, luxurious character of the Old Colonial in the South, etc.

**SOME HOUSE PLANS.** Relation of the exterior to the location, the dormers, the inside finish, mantels, a centre-hall plan, frame building, a little room for cloaks and wraps, decorative forms, interior photographs, external details, Greek mouldings, a wide central hall open at each end, large rooms, a picturesque stairway, color schemes in decoration, description of floor plan, a fine location, a river front, picturesque stair-hall, a smoking-room under the balcony, etc.

**MATERIALS AND DETAILS.** Shingle-houses, the proper surroundings, the stains of time, artificial stain, examples, slate walls, fireplaces and mantels, character in mantels, tile facings, onyx and brick, doors, the defensive, hospitality, material, foreign examples, domestic doors, stairs, foreign examples, broad landings, Old Colonial stairways, iron railings, furniture, architects' designs, sideboards, bookcases, seats, lounges, screens, grilles, walls and ceilings, etc.

**THE ARCHITECT.** The architect and the housewife, business and the arts, costs, proper understanding of the client's wishes, plenty of time to make plans.

### Press Notices.

**New York Sun.**
" A handsome book, copiously illustrated, giving foreign examples in domestic architecture, a collection of American house plans, and including a consideration of materials and details for the benefit of the artistic house-builder."

**Chicago Evening Post.**
" A most timely publication, and will find admirers among amateur builders as well as trained architects."

**Boston Advertiser.**
" Mr. Gibson's book is something more than an enunciation of theories. Under the headings ' Some House Plans' and ' Materials and Details,' there is a practical working out of the architect's general idea. This part of the work is most valuably suggestive, and the intending house-builder will find it greatly to his interest to consult Mr. Gibson's books. The present volume is one in which marked utility is combined with great beauty."

**Detroit Free Press.**
" It would hardly seem possible that a work on house-building could be such pleasant reading as is this handsome volume."

**Congregationalist.**
" His former book met a real need. His present work is full of wise and practical suggestions as to securing beauty without sacrificing convenience or running into extravagance. All about to build or reconstruct a house will find it helpful."

**Indianapolis News.**
" This work is a credit to Mr. Gibson and to his profession. It is a reflection of deep knowledge of architecture, and of experience in the practice of the profession. The illustrations are abundant and excellent, and the whole is a beautiful piece of book-making. An appropriate cover is designed by David Gibson."

**Literary World.**
" The author is an architect of knowledge, ideas, and tastes. . . . To any family projecting a home of their own this volume will bring a multitude of helps."

**Bookseller, Newsdealer and Stationer.**
" One of the handsomest and at the same time most practical books ever published by the Crowells."

*For Sale by all Booksellers, or sent postpaid by the Publishers on receipt of price.*

## T. Y. CROWELL & CO., New York and Boston.

www.ingramcontent.com/pod-product-compliance
Lightning Source LLC
Chambersburg PA
CBHW021150230426
**43667CB00006B/328**